D1124230

WITHDRAWN
UTSA LIBRARIES

ARMED WITH EXPERTISE

A volume in the series
American Institutions and Society
Edited by Brian Balogh and Jonathan Zimmerman

ARMED WITH EXPERTISE

The Militarization of American Social
Research during the Cold War

Joy Rohde

CORNELL UNIVERSITY PRESS   **ITHACA AND LONDON**

Published in association with the University of Virginia's Miller Center of
Public Affairs

University of Texas
at San Antonio

Copyright © 2013 by Cornell University

All rights reserved. Except for brief quotations in a review, this book, or parts
thereof, must not be reproduced in any form without permission in writing from
the publisher. For information, address Cornell University Press, Sage House,
512 East State Street, Ithaca, New York 14850.

First published 2013 by Cornell University Press

Printed in the United States of America

Library of Congress Cataloging-in-Publication Data

Rohde, Joy, 1977– author.
   Armed with expertise : the militarization of American social research during
the Cold War / Joy Rohde.
      pages cm. — (American institutions and society)
   "Published in association with the University of Virginia's Miller Center of
Public Affairs."
   Includes bibliographical references and index.
   ISBN 978-0-8014-4967-3 (cloth : alk. paper)
   1. Social sciences—Research—United States—History—20th century.
2. Sociology, Military—Research—United States—History—20th century.
3. Social sciences and state—United States—History—20th century. 4. Cold
War—Social aspects—United States. I. Title.
   H62.5.U5R64   2013
   300.72'073—dc23   2013010654

Cornell University Press strives to use environmentally responsible suppliers and
materials to the fullest extent possible in the publishing of its books. Such materials
include vegetable-based, low-VOC inks and acid-free papers that are recycled,
totally chlorine-free, or partly composed of nonwood fibers. For further
information, visit our website at www.cornellpress.cornell.edu.

Cloth printing   10 9 8 7 6 5 4 3 2 1

Library
University of Texas
at San Antonio

To my mother

Contents

Acknowledgments

Writing history often feels like a solitary enterprise, but this project bears the imprint of a number of archivists, scholars, friends, and institutions. The research for this book rested primarily on unprocessed records of the Department of the Army. I haunted the National Archives at College Park for months in search of every scrap of information I could find that was even remotely relevant to my story. Even though Richard Boylan probably thought I was looking for needles in every haystack I saw, he was instrumental in that search. Susan McElrath of American University and Janice Goldblum at the National Academy of Sciences were models of knowledge, efficiency, and hospitality. At Trinity University, Maria McWilliams heroically tracked down dozens of obscure research reports—including a number that I thought I would never have the opportunity to see.

Special thanks are due to Michael Sherry, whose critical insights pushed me at a crucial stage to engage with the ambiguities of militarization and the continuities linking the Cold War to the War on Terror. I also thank Ellen Herman for encouraging me to consider the relationship between national security expertise and the explosion of partisan think tanks. Brian Balogh has supported this project since its inception and helped me envision this story as a book. So did Susan Lindee, who has been a constant source of intellectual inspiration and moral support for over a decade. I am deeply indebted to David Sehat, who read most of this manuscript more than once, and who provided more than a few pep talks over the last few years.

John Carson, David Engerman, Sarah Igo, Henrika Kuklick, Shobita Parthasarathy, and Mark Solovey also gave generously of their time, reading parts of this book in its painful early stages. I also thank my colleagues at Trinity University, who have provided encouragement and advice.

I could not have written this book without the unrelenting support of my partner in life and learning, Perrin Selcer. Perrin read various iterations of this text more times than he probably cares to remember. Equally important, he kept our daughters in good spirits when mommy seemed to prefer her computer to their Cootie Bugs. I am grateful, too, to Bruce and Sandra Rohde, who encouraged my academic pursuits over the years.

My work was supported by fellowships from the American Academy of Arts and Sciences, the Science, Technology, and Public Policy Program at the

University of Michigan's Ford School of Public Policy, the Miller Center of Public Affairs, and Trinity University.

A version of chapter 2 appeared as "Gray Matters: Social Scientists, Military Patronage, and Democracy in the Cold War" in the *Journal of American History* 96 (June 2009): 99–122. Sections of chapters 1 and 4 appeared in *Cold War Social Science: Knowledge Production, Liberal Democracy, and Human Nature*, edited by Mark Solovey and Hamilton Cravens (New York: Palgrave MacMillan, 2012). I thank the publishers for permission to include that material here.

My greatest debt is to my mother, Anne Skinner, who has always supported my love of books and who did more than I ever could have asked to ensure that I was able to write one of my own.

HEARTS, MINDS, AND MILITARIZATION

In 2007, a handful of American social scientists arrived in Iraq and Afghanistan. They were armed with conventional military weapons, but more significantly, they possessed an arsenal of cultural knowledge. Embedded in army brigades, their job was to bridge the military's culture gap. They provided commanders with information about the battlefield's "human terrain"—military parlance for the beliefs, values, grievances, and social structures of the populations living in war zones. These civilian social scientists were part of the Human Terrain System (HTS), the army's new, controversial counterinsurgency weapon. HTS was designed to make the Iraq and Afghanistan wars less violent and the American military effort more successful. With social scientists behind the front lines in the War on Terror, the American military might at last discover, in the words of the HTS training manual, "the reasons why the population is doing what it is doing and thereby [provide] non-lethal options to the commander and his staff."[1]

In the short term, HTS's designers anticipated that the system would improve the military's understanding of the complex local environments in which counterinsurgent forces fought. But HTS was not intended to be a mere wartime project. Its architects argued that over the long term it could "anthropologize" the military. If soldiers could see the world through the eyes of the people affected by U.S. military actions, they might come to rely less on combat and more on social, economic, and political development. The Human Terrain System, its advocates hoped, would make the War on Terror less warlike; it would demilitarize the military, creating "a kinder, gentler counter-insurgency."[2]

1

But HTS quickly attracted criticism from social scientists who argued that it encouraged an inappropriate, even unethical, collaboration between researchers and the military, used scholarship as a cover for gathering military intelligence, and repackaged violence as humanitarianism. After all, critics pointed out, HTS scientists often wore military uniforms and carried weapons. Lacking transportation of their own, they gathered their data while accompanying soldiers on patrol. And their duties included identifying important local leaders and dissidents—information that the military could use for lethal targeting.[3]

HTS's critics not only indicted the system for militarizing social science. They also argued that it was part of a quasi-governmental network of private defense contractors and corporations that, since 9/11, reaped billions of dollars in profits. HTS's creators and the majority of its staff hailed from the world of private defense contracting. Anthropologist Montgomery McFate, a veteran of RAND and the Office of Naval Research, helped design the program while working at the Institute for Defense Analyses, a nonprofit civilian contract research institute that has worked exclusively for the government since the Defense Department created it in 1956.[4] According to one count, as many as thirty-five other defense firms were engaged in research and development efforts related to the War on Terror's human terrain. Global defense giant BAE Systems held a five-year, $380 million contract with the army to recruit HTS team members.[5] The army hired the multibillion-dollar defense consulting agency Booz Allen Hamilton to train new Human Terrain System researchers. And the massive defense research and contracting firms MITRE and CACI held multimillion-dollar contracts for developing the software that would manage the growing HTS database.[6] Until 2009, all the social scientists deployed in Iraq and Afghanistan, as well the HTS program director, were external contractors. Even a congressionally mandated review of the HTS system was performed by a private contractor.[7]

To its critics, HTS's ties to the private sector validated their suspicion that, by relying heavily on contractors for research and services, the Pentagon was creating a privatized warfare state where national security strategy—and war fighting itself—was being outsourced to profit-seeking institutions run by militarized experts. In the decade after the 9/11 attacks, Pentagon contracts for weapons, military services, and intellectual expertise more than doubled. In the past, private firms had offered support services to deployed military personnel. But in the age of the War on Terror, firms increasingly provided services directly linked to warfare. Private contractors assisted with strategic and combat planning, gathered and assessed intelligence, and even interrogated POWs.[8]

It seemed to critics that the Pentagon was destroying the democracy it was supposed to protect. By outsourcing vital intellectual expertise and paying a premium for it, the government seemed to be eroding its own intellectual capacity, crippling the public sector. Furthermore, both the public and the government seemed to lack the oversight capabilities necessary to manage the contract state. Because private corporations were exempt from the Freedom of Information Act, the extent and nature of the military's relationship with contractors was opaque to Congress, the courts, and the public. Critics from academia, law, and public policy argued that contracting undermined the democratic norms of transparency and accountability, while allowing the private sector to shape national security policy. Most dangerously, they charged, by ceding so much responsibility to contractors, the Pentagon was creating a powerful private sector that might become invested in perpetuating war for its own profit.[9]

Yet neither the contract state, nor the experts that populated it, nor even the criticisms directed at it were new to the War on Terror. Decades earlier, national security concerns drew the United States and its social scientists into areas long peripheral to military and diplomatic policy. Those efforts, and their unexpected consequences, are the subject of this book. The original targets of American counterinsurgency programs were communist guerrillas, not Islamist terrorists. As new nations emerged from decaying empires—thirty-seven former colonies declared independence by the end of the 1950s—Soviet political and ideological expansion appeared almost as threatening to the United States as the specter of nuclear war. In the minds of American policymakers, military men, and many social scientists, the political instability and economic deprivation that haunted the developing nations were powerful incubators for communist revolution. As one counterinsurgency expert argued, to win the ideological battle, "the first essential is knowledge—knowledge about the enemy himself."[10] In the Cold War, as never before, the attitudes, beliefs, and frustrations of the inhabitants of the geopolitical periphery mattered in Washington. And, as never before, the military required scholarly research and advice to understand, manage, and influence the men and women of the developing world.

With the future of the free world in the balance, the Pentagon and social scientists joined forces to open a new front in the Cold War. As researchers set out to win the hearts and minds of the third world, social science, like so much else in the Cold War, became tangled up with the interests of American national security. Like the hard sciences before it, social research became implicated in militarization, the process historian Laura McEnaney describes as "the gradual encroachment of military ideas, values, and structures into the civilian domain."[11] Americans—scholars and soldiers included—embraced militarization with ambivalence. They were devoted to protecting American national security against what they perceived as an unscrupulous, often invisible, and aggressively expansionist enemy. But they were fearful of creating what Harold Lasswell famously termed the garrison state—a centralized, secretive, dictatorial behemoth that dominated political, intellectual, and even private life in the name of national security.[12] Americans faced a quandary: in the Cold War, militarization might be necessary to protect democracy, but it also threatened to destroy it. And so they struggled to reap the benefits of militarization while mitigating its negative consequences.

They did so, in part, by turning to civilian experts. The fusion of social science and national security reached its acme in the Special Operations Research Office (SORO), a multidisciplinary research institute created by the army in 1956. SORO was the brainchild of the Office of the Chief of Psychological Warfare, the section of the army responsible for all aspects of psychological, political, and guerrilla warfare. The military designed SORO to be a hybrid institution that would seamlessly meld social scientific expertise with the operational concerns of army officers. While most of the Pentagon's Cold War research focused on the physical matériel of war, SORO's work centered on ideas and doctrine. Seeking to manage global politics and usher in gradual, stable change toward an American-led world order, SORO's researchers produced classified area studies handbooks that pithily described the inhabitants, military forces, and national psychologies of communist-threatened countries. They marshaled empirical evidence to test popular theories that disaffected intellectuals and poor peasants might be to blame for violent revolution. They probed the organization of communist underground movements in Greece, Vietnam, and Guatemala. And they used cutting-edge social psychology to design new psychological warfare and propaganda programs for dozens of nations.[13] Decades before Human Terrain System experts promised to humanize the military with their cultural knowledge, SORO's researchers promised the same. They dedicated themselves to helping the Cold War military pursue a new, less militaristic mission: "the establishment of a community of stable nations, where political change occurs peacefully."[14] SORO embodied the faith, common in the early years of the Cold War, that intellectuals could scientifically guide geopolitics. It also reflected the hope that experts could form a bulwark against militarization; victory in the Cold War could come from technical expertise, not military engagement, thus proving the ultimately pacific nature of the United States.[15]

Although created by the army, SORO was a legally private institute staffed and managed by American University in Washington, D.C. In fact, it was only one of a number of quasi-independent Pentagon-funded research institutes born during the early Cold War. The practice of contracting with academic institutions for scientific research had developed in World War II, when civilian scientists and engineers working on contract with the federal government delivered the technologies—atomic bombs, radar, and solid state electronics— that helped the Allies win the war. As the Cold War replaced the world war, the Pentagon extended its funding. In the decade after the armistice, the military funded more research than any other federal agency.[16] A significant amount of military research took place on university campuses, in university labs, and in Pentagon-created, nominally independent research institutes. Social science attracted the Pentagon's support later than the physical sciences, and it followed their model. The military's social experts worked in settings ranging from academic institutes that relied only partially on government contracts, such as the Massachusetts Institute of Technology (MIT) Center for International Studies, to think tanks such as RAND that, like SORO, were created by the military but were legally autonomous. They also worked in an expanding sector of for-profit research agencies such as Human Sciences Research Incorporated and Psychological Research Associates.[17] According to one count, twenty-one private research institutes concerned with the political problems of the Cold War conflict were created between 1950 and 1960 alone. By 1967, the capital city boasted over three hundred private research and development institutes, many which employed social scientists.[18]

In the 1950s, contract research institutes seemed a promising means of containing the potentially dangerous consequences of Cold War militarization. Because these institutes were organizationally separate from the military, their designers and staffs hoped they could protect their scholarship from becoming too heavily marked by the imprint of the national security state. They even had the potential, it seemed, to demilitarize the military, diffusing the Cold War conflict by focusing on the human side of the battle for democracy. Even further, policymakers hoped that private experts working on contract could provide the Pentagon with much-needed knowledge without adding to the size and power of the state itself. Contracting was not only a response to militarization; it was shaped by the long-standing American wariness of the state. By privatizing research, Americans sought to bring expertise to bear on national security without fostering an expert-directed, centrally planned state.[19] Contracting seemed to protect American democracy.

Yet, fifteen years later, those same experts and their research institutes increasingly appeared to be a stark embodiment of the perils of militarization and technocracy: secrecy, corruption, centralization of state power, waste, and coercion. President Dwight D. Eisenhower had warned as much in his oft quoted, largely unheeded farewell address of early 1961. By the late 1960s, as Americans attempted to come to terms with the costly brutality of the Vietnam War, his admonitions about the military-industrial complex and its "scientific-technological elite" gained traction.[20] Critics charged that the military and its experts had created a "warfare state" where scholars and scientists thrived by producing militaristic, often classified knowledge, that undemocratically shaped federal policy and wasted untold millions. Once hailed as protectors of democracy, experts now appeared a profound threat to it.[21]

These critiques would have significant but unexpected consequences. Critics sought to tame the militarization of knowledge by dismantling SORO and other nodes in the military-industrial-academic complex. But even more important, they hoped to tame the militarization of American government institutions and policy. Instead, and through no fault of their own, their actions would leave the government even more dependent on the institutions of the warfare state that would survive the end of the Cold War and thrive in the War on Terror.

By tracing the optimistic rise, anguished fall, and unexpected rebirth of Pentagon-sponsored social research, this book examines the ways that Americans embraced, challenged, and adapted to political and intellectual militarization. For those who believed that the government's social research was a neutral, reliable foundation for decision making, and that expertise mitigated militarization, science was a crucial component of democratic statecraft. But for those who believed that power and politics were embedded in military-funded social knowledge, SORO's social scientists were little more than reactionary defenders of the status quo—militarism, exploitation, and international hubris. Yet militarized knowledge and institutions proved to be remarkably flexible. Some academic social researchers, convinced that their expertise was militaristic and antidemocratic, withdrew from national security research and returned to the ivory tower in the early 1970s. But militarized expertise lived on in a growing number of nonacademic nonprofit and for-profit research and consulting agencies.

The conflict over Cold War social research was at its core a battle over both the role of experts in American democracy and the acceptable limits of militarization. The Pentagon's social researchers in the 1950s and 1960s claimed to represent the best interests of their nation and the developing world at a time when both expertise and militarization were under debate. This was no mere academic dispute. It touched the heart of questions about democracy in an era of immense anxiety about national security. And so the attack on military-funded social research moved beyond the confines of disciplinary communities into Congress, the White House, and American embassies around the world.

These contests played out in venues public and private, civilian and military, academic and popular. But they reverberated most loudly in hybrid institutions like SORO. SORO was perched within an ill-defined gray area between academia and the national security state. The gray area was the front line in the intellectual and political battles over the militarization of national security expertise. Research in the gray area never conformed to the scientific ideal of pure, objective inquiry directed at the discovery of universal truths. The requirements of national security influenced the direction of study, challenging researchers to protect their intellectual autonomy from what many scholars considered to be the polluting effects of external influence. Security classification collided with scholarly openness. Patronage and political urgency clashed with scientific detachment. Because SORO's research dealt directly with political matters—from the causes of social revolution to the mechanisms of persuasion and social control—its objectivity was all the more suspect to academics and the public. In the gray area, researchers struggled to reconcile their scholarly commitment to the production of disinterested knowledge with their professional accountability to the military, their own ambivalence about militarization, and their dedication to both American democratic values and containment. It was in the hazy gray area, not in the more rarefied air of elite academia, that the problems of expertise, democracy, and national security became acute. The denizens of the gray area were not elite intellectuals. Unlike better-known social scientists of the era who commented on the relationship between scholarship and the national security state from the safety of universities, they grappled with it daily in word and deed. To understand the complex problems of militarization, expertise, and democracy, this book looks to the men and women who sought to resolve them.

The protagonists of my narrative are men and women who have been the focus of hostility and rebuke. It is easy to censure the people who performed contract research into foreign areas for the national security state. Their work often lent scholarly legitimacy to ill-conceived U.S. military interventions abroad that resulted in staggering losses of life. This book is not a defense of or an apology for the intellectuals who participated in SORO and similar projects. But it does take seriously their understanding of the Cold War threat and the ways in which they believed their expertise might alleviate it. Cold War social scientists were actors who sat in the middle of a vexing network of scholarship and state power during what they perceived to be a profoundly perilous historical moment. Their views illuminate persistent tensions in the application of expertise to a democratic state that itself owes its size and shape, in large part, to national security anxieties. My goal in understanding the perspectives of the men and women who served the national security state is not to defend their political, ethical, or intellectual choices. Rather, the beliefs and careers of

SORO's researchers underscore the changing contours of epistemological values and ethical commitments in American scholarship, and the changing convictions about the relationship between expert knowledge and democracy in the Cold War. To peel back the fables by which we have understood this period is to encounter a set of problems that remain central to American governance and intellectual life. The history of SORO is a story of the evolving contest over the relationship between democracy, national security, and expertise in recent U.S. history.

CREATING THE GRAY AREA

Scholars, Soldiers, and National Security

In 1946, sociologist Philip M. Hauser confronted his fellow social scientists: Were they ready, he asked, "for the supreme challenge of providing enough knowledge about human institutions and human relationships in time to prevent the suicide of the human race?" World War II had ended, but dire threats remained: social dislocation and physical destruction threatened Europe's future; inequality and anti-imperialist unrest loomed in Asia and Africa; and a growing ideological chasm divided the Americans and the Soviets. Although the physical sciences produced miraculous results in the last war, their triumphs only intensified the destructiveness of military conflict. It was time, Hauser argued, for experts in human relations—those who could tackle the fundamental causes of war—to engineer a lasting peace.[1]

As the euphoria of victory gave way to the stark reality of Cold War, social scientists laid claim to the management of international conflict. Whether hot or cold, they argued, war was at its most basic a form of communication. Armed encounters, Princeton psychologist and Pentagon adviser Charles Bray argued, arose "as an extension of the conflicts of societies of men which have different political, social, and personal values and goals." "The proper concern of the Department of Defense with the atom, with space, with missiles and airplanes and submarines," he elaborated, "is only to persuade other men, in other parts of the world, that they cannot, without reason, impose their wills upon us." Johns Hopkins University's Paul Linebarger concurred; in war, "you are fighting against *men*. Your purpose in fighting is to make them change their minds."[2]

Many military officials and civilian policymakers found these arguments compelling. Even some physicists concurred. Luis Alvarez, veteran of the Manhattan Project, explained to Pentagon officials that if World War I had been the chemists' war, and World War II the physicists' war, then "World War III . . . might well have to be considered the social scientists' war."[3] And indeed, over the course of the 1950s and 1960s, the Pentagon mobilized experts on human behavior, persuasion, culture, and psychology to create an arsenal of social knowledge designed to contain communism and, they hoped, avert future wars.

The world war that Alvarez forecasted never came to pass, but the Cold War nevertheless became a social scientists' war. After Chiang Kai-shek's defeat in 1949, American military strategists seeking the philosophy and techniques that had propelled the communists to victory turned to Mao Tse-tung's writings. They took to heart his argument that revolutionary warfare was above all political. As military historian Andrew J. Birtle explains, a number of American military experts "believed Mao had created a whole new form of warfare . . . for which all previous experience was irrelevant." According to Marine Corps lieutenant colonel T. N. Greene, Mao's work indicated that future wars would be fought "not only in the sharp black and white of formal combat, but in a gray, fuzzy obscurity where politics affect tactics and economics influence strategy." In such a war, "the soldier must fuse with the statesman, the private turn politician."[4]

Social scientists hoped to provide the foundations for a successful counterinsurgency doctrine. But the synthesis of civilian and military expertise was uneasy. As social scientists mobilized to protect American national security from the communist threat, their efforts thrust them onto the front lines of militarization. It was an experience as heady as it was perilous. Military patronage provided social scientists with access to scarce financial resources, presented new and exciting intellectual problems, and promised power and prestige. It seemed that disciplinary values and national values complemented each other. But mobilization also posed significant challenges. It threatened scholars' intellectual autonomy and fundamentally challenged long-standing national values. Americans viewed themselves as a peaceable people, forced into conflict only by the actions of an unprincipled enemy. By reorienting civilian institutions and scholarly interests toward national security concerns, the Cold War threatened to undermine that cherished identity. If Americans willingly directed their intellectual, political, and economic resources toward warfare, they might themselves become belligerent.[5] As social scientists mobilized from the late 1940s to the early 1960s, they pursued intellectual projects and created institutions that reflected these competing convictions.

Cold War militarization was tied to two further problems, each potentially devastating to Americans' national identity, which would also forcefully shape social scientists' Cold War efforts. Despite the nation's long history of inter-vention and empire, many Americans were deeply ambivalent about the global reach of their power; they tended to think of themselves, at worst, as reluctant imperialists. Furthermore, they worried that national security concerns might centralize political power at home. Pitted in a life-and-death battle against a statist, imperial behemoth, many Americans believed that they must not fall victim to the very state centralization and global expansionism they sought to fight.[6]

Cold War social science was forged in the crucible of these anxieties. As they mobilized, scholars and their patrons sought intellectual tools that would extend the nation's global role while maintaining the conviction that American power stood for freedom, liberty, and self-determination. They often pursued these goals unconsciously, and the results of their efforts would be complex and contradictory. They sought institutional arrangements that would keep re-searchers at arms' length from the state, but they struggled for a decade to strike a balance between military and civilian, public and private. By the end of the 1950s, government-funded social scientists would work on military problems from private, university-managed research institutes. Military experts would expound counterinsurgency methods as peaceful techniques. With militari-zation hidden behind social-scientific rhetoric and creative institutional con-figurations, scholars and soldiers would try to recast the spread of American military power as democratic reform and the militarization of social knowledge as an antidote to Cold War militarism.

Wars' Lessons

The conviction that social science could render global affairs legible and man-ageable was not new to the Cold War. When the nation entered World War II, social scientists mobilized. They amassed information about enemy morale and analyzed propaganda for the Office of Strategic Services, the Office of War In-formation, and the Library of Congress; they designed psychological warfare campaigns against the Germans for the Psychological Warfare Division of the Supreme Headquarters Allied Expeditionary Force; they studied manpower mobilization for the armed services; and they managed the home front, super-vising Japanese American internees for the War Relocation Authority. As Ellen Herman argues in her masterly study of American psychology, World War II taught social scientists to equate "social responsibility with government ser-vice, democracy and tolerance with psychology, and enlightened planning with behavioral expertise."[7]

The line between the martial and the civil, notoriously blurred at the height of the Cold War, had already grown hazy by the early 1940s. In fact, it had been blurrier for social scientists than for physical scientists. While social researchers generally worked in uniform or from within civilian wartime agencies during World War II, physical scientists and engineers conducted their research at arms' length from the government. Instead of drafting civilian scientists into wartime labs—which would increase the reach of the national security state while militarizing scientific careers—the wartime Office of Scientific Research and Development (OSRD) offered government-funded research contracts to researchers who remained within their university laboratories. Between 1940 and 1944, over 60 percent of war research was carried out on contract in university- and industry-based labs. American scientists credited the OSRD with developing a system that mobilized the sciences for war, yet insulated universities and the private sector from military control, intellectual rigidity, and other wartime disruptions. The system also appeared to mitigate one of the potentially pernicious consequences of wartime mobilization. Its creator, Vannevar Bush, was a staunch opponent of government growth; the OSRD created a decentralized system that harnessed private institutions and specialized expertise to the war effort without unduly extending the federal government's reach. And it delivered the goods that won the war.[8]

In engineering and the physical sciences, the federal government maintained this model after the war, keeping scientists and engineers invested in military questions during peacetime by negotiating contracts for innovative research. Social scientists, on the other hand, found themselves demobilized after the armistice. Margaret Mead wrote that social scientists "took their marbles and went home."[9] But some did not want to give up the game. In Washington, social scientists found challenging research questions, welcome visibility and influence, and much-needed funding. As peace devolved inexorably toward Cold War, social scientists like Bray and Linebarger continued to argue for their disciplines' relevance to global affairs.

The military, however, was more ambivalent in the late 1940s. It made some room for research, but its efforts were decentralized and, in the opinion of many social scientists, dangerously inadequate. Programs in tried-and-true fields like military psychology and man-machine systems continued. But in the areas that social scientists' argued were most crucial to the Cold War—propaganda, psychological and political warfare, area studies, and nation-building efforts— their arguments for inclusion went largely unheeded. Between 1946 and 1950, when funding for all non-psychological research was cut, the Office of Naval Research provided the only significant source of money—approximately $2 million annually—for social science research related to problems of American national security. Other efforts enjoyed more longevity, but not more influence. The air force think tank RAND, established after World War II to advise the air force on strategy, established a social science division in Washington in 1948. But its researchers toiled in obscurity and geographic isolation until the division was welcomed to RAND's Santa Monica headquarters in 1956. Even then, RAND's most important contributions to the Cold War effort, such as deterrence theory, came out of other divisions. Social scientists found little sympathy for their efforts from the civilian side of government, where congressional misgivings about the utility of social science and the politics of its often liberal experts constrained research funding. Congress voted to exclude the social sciences from the planned National Science Foundation in 1946—three years before it managed to pass legislation creating the organization.[10]

The Korean War—and the military's abysmal propaganda showing in it—provided social scientists with fodder for the argument that they could help improve American national security. Although army chief of staff Dwight Eisenhower had instructed the army to maintain its psychological warfare capacity in the late 1940s, the military, believing that such an activity was manipulative, dishonest, and not "real soldiering," had allowed it to atrophy. But the Korean experience indicated to some military officials that propaganda and psychological warfare might be crucial to preserving democracy.[11] Becoming convinced that "war was a struggle for national and international psyches," the military turned once more to social scientists for help.[12] Researchers from the army's Operations Research Office (ORO) interviewed North Korean POWs to evaluate the effectiveness of the army's multibillion-dollar propaganda leafleting campaign. Their conclusions were damning. One assessment found that the military's psychological warfare and propaganda programs "ranged from the unplanned, . . . the unorthodox, and all the way to the inept."[13] ORO officials lamented their institution's lack of behavioral expertise; created to perform operations research, its staff was composed primarily of physicists, mathematicians, and engineers. They recommended that the army make an effort to recruit "properly qualified social psychologists" to devise techniques to destabilize communist regimes in peacetime as well as during hot war.[14]

Social Science and Special Warfare in the 1950s

The army took this advice to heart. By the mid-1950s, it was apparent that American psychological, cultural, and political shortcomings in Korea were only one manifestation of the military's lack of preparation for the era's conflicts. As the Cold War drew the United States into regions once peripheral to national security and intellectual interests—Iran in 1953 and the islands of Quemoy and Matsu in 1955 to name only two instances—some national security officials concluded that the attitudes, beliefs, and perceptions of foreign peoples might be as important to the Cold War confrontation as missile silos and regional alliances. The army's ground forces would bear the brunt of Cold War special operations, an amorphous category of military activity that included psychological and political warfare, guerrilla operations, and counterinsurgency, each of which was often conducted in cooperation with indigenous allies. To mobilize its new, unfamiliar partners and intimidate its seemingly exotic enemies, the army turned to social scientists and area studies experts for help. The Office of the Chief of Psychological Warfare (OCPW) led the charge. Created in 1951 to jump-start psychological operations in the Korean War, OCPW was a unique, autonomous army office that reported directly to the chief of staff. Despite its name, the office was responsible for all aspects of special warfare. Recognizing the military's deficit in social science and area knowledge after the Korean War, OCPW began looking for "eminent civilian specialists" from elite universities to write fifty-five "special warfare area handbooks"—compilations of area studies information on strategically important countries, from the Soviet satellites to the new nations threatened by communism.[15]

The army tempered its suspicions of psychological and special warfare by the early 1950s, but overcoming scholars' disciplinary qualms about national security work proved more challenging. Despite the rhetoric of social science boosters like Bray and Linebarger, many academic social scientists and university administrations were wary of working too closely with the military. As one anthropologist explained, "The academic world lives on free and open interchange of hypotheses and findings," an activity that government work, particularly work relevant to psychological warfare and special operations, might preclude. Administrators expressed concern that close government ties might endanger universities' ability to advance knowledge regardless of its utility. It was one thing to tailor scholarship to operational needs in a time of war, but doing so during peacetime might permanently subvert free inquiry.[16]

Scholars needed to look no farther than Harvard University's Russian Research Center to substantiate their concerns. In the late 1940s and early 1950s, its staff sought to produce knowledge useful to national security agencies. Funded by the air force, Sovietologists endeavored to create a "conceptual model" of Soviet society—a functionalist description of its social, economic, and political structures—which could be used to shape American foreign and military policy. As historian David Engerman explains, scholars at the center initially "envisioned their job as equal parts scholarship and government service." They believed they could meld their intellectual interests to strategic work, advancing social science while providing the military with predictions about the consequences of the "simultaneous atom-bombing of twenty major cities," for example. They soon found otherwise. Security and secrecy posed one barrier. Believing that sound intellectual work required an open environment, Harvard University banned classified research contracts. But research with operational implications could not be published openly, so the Russian Research Center was forced to negotiate a second, classified contract to skirt Harvard's rules. And while the project's staff viewed themselves as disinterested social scientists, they had to undergo the cumbersome process of gaining security clearances before they could access their research subjects, who included Russian refugees living in West German displaced-persons camps.[17]

The conflicts between intellectual and military goals hampered the center's work. As the air force pressed for useful results, such as lists of hard and soft targets that could destabilize the enemy, social scientists feared they were being treated as intelligence gatherers rather than scholars. The center concluded its air force work in 1954 with both parties chastened by the experience. Its outgoing director, Clyde Kluckhohn, encouraged his replacement to focus on "the development of scholars and scholarship." A 1954 survey of Harvard social science faculty confirmed that the Sovietologists' experience was not an isolated case. Many Harvard social scientists who had worked with the federal government reported that their sponsors often interfered with study design, methodology, and results. Others explained that they avoided government work for fear it would come with too many strings attached.[18]

Experiences like these indicated that it would take creative institutional efforts to fuse the scholarly and the martial. Rather than contract with a university for research, as the air force had done, the army's psychological operations staff turned instead to a quasi-academic institution that had a long history of military service: the Human Relations Area Files. HRAF was an outgrowth of Yale's Cross-Cultural Survey, founded by anthropologist George Murdock in 1937 to collect and systematize information about "primitive" cultures around the world. The outbreak of World War II proved a boon to Murdock's outfit. Hoping that the Yale effort could assist the military in its operations in the Pacific, the navy assumed a significant portion of its financial burden during the war. Murdock's researchers—some of whom served in uniform as members of the Naval Reserve—worked with naval intelligence officers to produce materials designed to help American military governments manage nations liberated from Japanese control. After the war, the armed forces, the CIA, and private philanthropies each contributed to expand the HRAF survey into a massive, systematic classification system of cultures around the globe. By 1954, it had grown into a consortium of sixteen academic institutions, many with excellent reputations in the social sciences and area studies.[19]

HRAF's institutional structure seemed well suited to OCPW's needs. In place of direct contracts between the army and individual scholars—a prospect that many area studies researchers found problematic if not downright distasteful— the army negotiated a $3 million contract with HRAF in 1954 for the special warfare handbooks. HRAF then subcontracted individual books to scholars in its consortium. The military and Clellan Ford, the president of HRAF, believed that this system would overcome academics' reluctance to work with the army by establishing indirect liaisons; the subcontracting system could mobilize social scientists without threatening their sense of academic independence or presenting them with the menacing specter of professional and intellectual militarization.[20]

A year into the contract, HRAF officials argued that the system was a resounding success. In a letter to army officials, its contract manager enthused, "I cannot state too emphatically that in every case I've encountered there is a general reluctance at every stage" among academics to take on army contracts for special warfare handbooks. However, "once I make it quite clear that the subcontract is with HRAF and not directly with the Army, they are more likely to consider a subcontract. HRAF's position as a buffer between the academic and the government worlds is, in my opinion, a major contribution toward getting the academic specialists to work on government problems."[21]

In reality, the situation was not quite so rosy. The handbook program merged scholarly and military goals incompletely at best. Between each party's narrow field of interest in area studies lay a chasm. The bounty that HRAF anticipated accruing from the army contract (in addition to its annual $50,000 overhead fee) was largely academic. Ford and his colleagues thought that handbook contracts offered area studies scholars the opportunity to evaluate the state of knowledge in their fields, take stock of "the free world's research resources," and translate esoteric foreign texts "hitherto barred from most Americans." Ford also reported that HRAF planned to use the subcontracts to fund graduate students, thus "increasing our reservoir of persons with some intimate and critical area knowledge."[22] The army's psychological warfare office, however, had no interest in advancing area studies. Rather, psychological warfare officials sought to understand "the intellectual and emotional character of strategically important peoples," knowledge that would help "field commanders to communicate with target groups in a way that will influence target group thoughts and actions."[23]

The army's intentions were not obscure. The contracts were, after all, for volumes officially titled *Special Warfare Area Handbook*; they were unmistakably military products. The army did not seek generalized compilations of area studies knowledge. Even though each handbook included sections on the history, geography, ethnic groups, and political structure of a nation, OCPW officials insisted that all information be carefully tailored to special warfare considerations. To this end, it issued a template to which each handbook was to conform. A chapter on public information, for example, should describe which media—whether newspapers, radio, or word-of-mouth communication—most effectively reached target audiences in each nation. Likewise, a chapter on "Attitudes and Reactions of the People" assessed each nation's level of modernization and included lists of symbols that inhabitants found particularly meaningful. And a chapter on "Subversive Potentialities" assessed the probability and possible sources of internal unrest and revolution.[24]

That the army's special warfare officials thought elite area studies scholars were the best reservoirs of information about psychological warfare and communist insurrection—and that HRAF officials could construe writing special warfare handbooks as scholarship—indicates how unclear the boundary between civilian and military matters was in the early Cold War. But the army's special warfare officers soon modified their relationship to scholarly experts. In 1958, the special warfare office allowed its contract with HRAF to expire. It handed the task of producing special warfare area handbooks over to a new institution. Its name, the Washington Area Human Relations Area Files branch, was cumbersome, but its organization was elegantly streamlined. The army had created the Washington branch in 1955 to conduct the classified research necessary to produce the final section of the handbooks, which described the military organization and strength of the nation under question. Its staff was housed on American University's campus in Washington, D.C., in proximity to the State Department, the Pentagon, and intelligence agencies, whose files the army's security-cleared researchers combed for the most up-to-date information. The Washington office was as successful as HRAF was disappointing. To ensure that handbooks conformed to army needs but also reflected social scientific expertise, writers worked in teams of five: three social scientists, one retired military specialist with a background in psychological or special warfare, and one professional writer whose job it was to convert social scientists' prose into "less technical social science jargon" accessible to "the educated layman." These teams churned out classified addenda to the handbooks, producing many ahead of schedule; by contrast, as of 1957, university researchers working on subcontract with HRAF had yet to deliver a product on time.[25] When the HRAF contract expired, the Washington branch took on the task of writing entire handbooks.

The Washington branch bore the imprint of the military far more visibly than did the HRAF system. This, in fact, contributed to its success. The army found the lesson of the HRAF experience unambiguous. By subcontracting, it had enticed academics into its orbit, but the results failed to fulfill military requirements. Buffers were counterproductive; "eminent civilian specialists" were too hard to militarize. It was more efficient and productive to create one's own research institution, one designed to commingle social science with military expertise. The calibration of balance between military and academic culture and influence was crucial. The army did not place the handbook program on a university campus cynically. They believed that in order to be useful to soldiers and military planners, handbooks had to be hybrid products, part social-scientific and part military. And the arrangement seemed to work. By the early 1960s, military officials regularly pronounced the special warfare handbooks the "bread and butter" of the army's social science program. American University officials were pleased as well. As the university's president, Hurst R. Anderson, wrote to the head of the handbook unit, "Everywhere I go I find the Area Handbooks recognized and well regarded, and am glad to see the University's name on them."[26]

The Gray Area's Anti-Statist Roots

The *Special Warfare Area Handbook* series was guided by the conviction that knowledge about the attitudes, beliefs, and perceptions of people on the geopolitical periphery was crucial to winning the Cold War, or at least to containing communism. But military officials and social scientists worried that area studies knowledge was too feeble a compass to navigate the overwhelming complexity of Cold War geopolitics in an era of rapid decolonization. The handbooks alone could be overwhelming, revealing a dizzying variety of peoples, cultures, and political systems Americans might encounter abroad. Global events punctuated that complexity. The handbook program got under way as representatives from twenty-nine unaligned Asian and African nations gathered at the Asian-African conference in Bandung, Indonesia, to chart their futures. While conference participants sought a course independent from American and Soviet hegemony, Americans interpreted the conference as a sign that 1.5 billion people might be drifting leftward. With so many hearts and minds up for grabs, psychologist and longtime military adviser Leonard Doob argued, the government required something less unwieldy than a catalog of the "likes and dislikes, attitudes, emotional and intellectual characteristics" of peoples from various nations, tribes, and ethnicities. Rather, he argued, the military needed to invest in behavioral science, which would reveal the "basic concepts involved . . . any place in the world because everywhere there are human beings."[27] Why get bogged down in knowing and influencing individual nations if one could know and influence humans the world round?

Anthropologist Catherine Lutz has argued that the armed forces drove the militarization of American relations with the third world during the Cold War. But Doob's comments indicate that the behavioral scientific project was also an engine of militarization. Many civilian behavioral scientists actively—although not necessarily consciously—pursued the militarization of American foreign relations, for it resonated with their professional and intellectual interests. Influential social scientists in the early Cold War believed that they were nearing the discovery of a theory of human behavior that was applicable across time and space. Drawing on universal principles, they would eventually be able to explain any human activity, whether the behavior in question took place at a polling station in New York City or in a guerrilla conflict in rural Indonesia. This conviction was well suited to national security concerns. Doob argued that researchers armed with the laws of communication could help psy warriors successfully persuade foreign populations to embrace American values—perhaps without firing a shot. Likewise, social scientists claimed that they could help the military manage the third world's transition to capitalist modernity by untangling the complex relationships between political stability, economic development, and psychological satisfaction that drove modernization. And, they argued, they could vanquish communist-directed insurgencies by revealing the social and political dynamics of "internal warfare"—the popular social-scientific term for revolution. If the state could support the quest for universal social laws, perhaps behavioral science could win the Cold War by suggesting scientifically derived strategic principles applicable to the national security state's Cold War efforts around the world.[28]

Few members of the armed forces were convinced that Cold War victory lay principally in social research about special operations and unconventional warfare. But they had other motivations, including the instinct for self-preservation, that led them to embrace both behavioral science and unconventional warfare. By the mid-1950s, the army brass worried that President Eisenhower's New Look policies, which privileged nuclear weapons and downsized conventional forces, threatened the service's future. The president argued that the policy would contain the escalating costs of American national security. Invoking Harold Lasswell, he warned that if the army's size increased further, "we might just as well stop any further talk about preserving a sound U.S. economy and proceed to transform ourselves forthwith into a garrison state." Compared to conventional forces, nuclear stockpiles were thought to be cheap, but Eisenhower's policies, which slashed the number of army divisions from twenty-one to fourteen, threatened to reduce the army's relevance and status.[29]

Eisenhower had offered the New Look to contain military spending. His critics, on the other hand, argued that because the policy was strategically unbalanced, it threatened to make war more likely and more destructive. While pursuing tactical nuclear capabilities, army heroes like Matthew Ridgway and Maxwell Taylor also argued that, rather than nuclear confrontations between the superpowers, future conflicts might be limited wars—low-level, nonnuclear engagements that could arise anywhere in the world but would most likely surface in the third world. Such wars, they insisted, would require ground forces equipped with enhanced special warfare capabilities, including the kinds of tools social science offered. This approach allowed them to contain the threat of militarization, but it was an approach different from Eisenhower's. By keeping conflicts limited, they argued, they could extinguish postcolonial "brushfires" before they led to full-scale war.[30]

SORO emerged out of these competing visions, each of which was designed to contain militarization. Although army officials were not so naïve as to take behavioral scientists' promises at face value, they were lured by the explanatory potential of social knowledge. Hoping that prescriptions for action might emerge from social knowledge, the army's OCPW opened the Special Operations Research Office (SORO) in 1956 and charged it with supporting and clarifying the service's psychological and unconventional warfare mission. The army instructed SORO's staff—a motley of political scientists, social psychologists, sociologists, anthropologists, and area studies experts—to conduct research that provided "commanders and staff agencies . . . with scientific bases for decision and action." In past conflicts, the military could rely on experience to formulate doctrine and strategy. But if all previous American military experience was irrelevant to the age of revolutionary warfare, perhaps experts in social change could help the army formulate that crucial body of knowledge. SORO's researchers took to calling themselves Sorons, with a heavy dose of good humored self-deprecation, motivated by their sense of the enormity of the task they faced. The free world, after all, might rest in the balance.[31]

The research office started small. By 1957, its staff numbered a meager twenty-one researchers, and its budget totaled only $225,000. But it grew steadily in the early 1960s under a president who shared army officials' faith in the potential of special warfare. After winning the election in part by blaming the Republicans for creating what was in fact a fictional missile gap, John F. Kennedy turned his attention to the military's counterinsurgency gap. Kennedy's advisers worried that the Soviet Union had "many years of experience with the techniques of subversion and insurgency," and Nikita Khrushchev's 1961 declaration that he would provide unswerving support for so-called "wars of national liberation" seemed to confirm their fears; the Soviets, they warned, possessed "a comprehensive, tested doctrine for conquest from within."[32] To meet the communist challenge, the president doubled the army's Special Forces numbers, elevated their status in the army, and increased the military's counterinsurgency budget by hundreds of millions of dollars. At the same time, Kennedy's national security team expanded the list of trouble spots from three—Laos, South Vietnam, and Thailand—to nearly a dozen, including Burma, Iran, the Cameroons, Guatemala, and Venezuela. SORO benefited. By 1966, it boasted over one hundred researchers and a budget well over $2 million. Its research reports became a staple of counterinsurgency training at the Special Forces' headquarters at Fort Bragg, North Carolina.[33]

The army intended the research office to be a hybrid institution, one that melded behavioral scientific expertise with operational practicality. SORO embodied the conviction shared fervently among a number of social scientists and soldiers that the Cold War necessitated seamless cooperation—not only between civilian and military experts, but also between public and private institutions. The army accordingly sought to establish a middle ground between academic social science, which the HRAF experience had taught was often too scholarly to be of immediate use, and programmed research performed by in-house scientists, which often lacked the flexibility, intellectual creativity, and highly trained research personnel that winning hearts and minds required. Accordingly, the psychological warfare office designed SORO as a Federal Contract Research Center. FCRCs grew out of World War II weapons and operations research projects; MIT's Rad Lab, which mobilized academic scientists to work on government-funded national security projects like the development of radar, was an early inspiration. Developed to fulfill the state's urgent need for original, high-quality research, FCRCs were fully funded by the government, but institutionally private and staffed by civilian scientists. Some FCRCs, like the air force's RAND Corporation, operated as autonomous private institutes. Others, including SORO, were managed by universities. Although legally autonomous, SORO was located on the grounds of American University, which operated the facility under an exclusive contract with the army.[34]

Pentagon officials touted FCRCs as the ideal solution to the peculiar challenges of mission agency research. They were thought to be superior to university research contracts, which often failed to produce results of sufficient operational relevance, and to in-house research laboratories. Because FCRC researchers were not technically employees of their sponsoring agency, they were thought to be more objective than in-house researchers who, by virtue of their close relationship to their sponsoring agency, might rubber-stamp ineffective policies and plans. According to this logic, SORO's researchers would have no qualms about challenging the army's outdated approaches to the technically complex challenge of special warfare. And the army's doctrine desperately needed updating. Army officials waxed eloquent about the importance of special warfare to winning hearts and minds in the third world, but their doctrine was still steeped in the experience of World War II, in which special warfare was synonymous with supporting Eastern European partisan movements.[35]

Despite their ability to question their sponsoring agencies' approaches, FCRC staff were also thought to be more likely than university-based researchers to provide operationally relevant products. Because FCRC employees worked solely for their sponsoring agency, they were intimately familiar with and invested in its mission. SORO, for example, had no purpose unless it embraced the logic of battling for hearts and minds. And FCRCs boasted further benefits over universities. Because they were problem oriented and interdisciplinary, they were freed of the disciplinary inflexibilities of traditional academic departments. They also offered longevity. Unlike short-term contract research projects, which assembled temporary teams of experts, FCRCs maintained a permanent pool of expertise geared toward the operational requirements of their sponsors.[36]

To SORO's creators, FCRCs seemed well equipped to nurture the remarkably hybrid expertise that winning hearts and minds would require. Federal Contract Research Centers were known by the late 1950s as havens for retired military men; many of them, including SORO for a time, were directed by retired officers. Furthermore, retired psychological warfare and intelligence experts were regular fixtures on SORO's staff. Between 1956 and 1969, the research office was home to fifteen retired career military officers whose ranks ranged from lieutenant colonel to brigadier general. They came to the research office with hands-on experience in psychological operations, guerrilla warfare, and other aspects of "politico-military affairs." Their expertise and careers indicate the social scientific status accorded to those with appropriate military experience in the 1950s and early 1960s. Lieutenant Colonel Hartley Dame joined SORO in 1964 after serving twenty-five years in the army. Although he had no training in the social sciences, his extensive experience warranted his hiring as a senior research scientist. Dame spoke seven languages, had served with the American forces in Berlin after World War II, was a member of the elite Diplomatic Corps, and had been a military attaché to the American embassy in Turkey. He was awarded the Legion of Merit for building and administering the Koje-do prisoner-of-war camp during the Korean War. SORO suited him. Over the course of six years, he coauthored at least eight research reports on politics and culture—not in Europe or Asia, despite his long experience there—but in Latin America. Dame also pursued a master's degree at American University in political science while working at SORO.[37]

Dame and his fellow officers worked side by side with trained civilian social scientists, many of whom had military or intelligence experience. Nearly half of SORO's civilian staff had spent time in the military or worked for national security agencies during World War II or the Korean War. They brought their experience with special warfare to the research office. Asianist and Harvard PhD Norman Jacobs had been stationed in the Philippines with an army intelligence unit during World War II. After the war, he served as an economist for the American occupation forces in Tokyo. At SORO, he specialized in cross-cultural communications with Chinese communists. His colleague political scientist William E. Daugherty spent the first half of World War II analyzing Asian propaganda programs for the Department of Justice before enlisting in the marines as a psychological warfare and intelligence officer, specializing in Japan.[38] For these men, working in the gray area provided a natural opportunity to meld their national security experience and scholarly interests.

SORO was one site in a rapidly expanding landscape of federally funded research. By 1962, the federal government ran sixty-six FCRCs, forty-three of which were funded by the Pentagon. A sizable social science community thrived in these institutions. Much of the government's investment in social research—particularly research related to Cold War strategy—took place in the Defense Department's quasi-civilian FCRCs. By the end of the 1950s, each of the armed services had its own social science research organization. The army, not typically considered a research innovator, maintained two social science FCRCs alongside SORO. The Operations Research Office, renamed the Research Analysis Corporation in 1961, was founded in 1948 in collaboration with the Johns Hopkins University. Its staff assessed field operations, psychological warfare, and bombing tactics during the Korean War. Those efforts earned 113 of its researchers the United Nation's Korean Service Medal. After the war, ORO researchers busied themselves with strategic studies of military aid programs and other operations research projects. The army's Human Resources Research Office (HumRRO), created in 1951 with the cooperation of George Washington University, employed military psychologists who conducted studies of human performance, leadership, motivation, and man-machine systems.[39]

These research sites were central nodes in the growing scholarly and bureaucratic gray area—an informal network of institutions poised productively, yet also uncomfortably, between academia and the state. The gray area was a physical, institutional space where scholars worked on military problems, and even with military officials. It was also a cultural and intellectual space where military and scholarly worldviews, conventions, and ideas met, clashed, and merged. This landscape encompassed FCRCs like SORO, RAND, and the Institute for Defense

Analyses, founded in 1956 to perform strategic analysis for the Joint Chiefs of Staff and the Pentagon. It also included private, nonprofit research institutions like the Hudson Institute, established in 1961 by former RAND nuclear strategist Herman Kahn. And it encompassed for-profit research corporations like Ithiel de Sola Pool's Simulmatics Corporation, which took advantage of the national security state's largesse to send Pool's graduate students to Vietnam, where they completed their doctoral work while investigating counterinsurgency techniques for the Pentagon.[40]

As the incubator of the military-industrial-academic complex, the gray area brought the promises and perils of Cold War militarization into high relief. As Michael S. Sherry explains, Americans were willing to meld military and civilian institutions and values because they believed that "in an age of instant and total warfare, the vigilant nation must be constantly prepared." This conviction animated Sorons and their colleagues at RAND, Hudson, and Simulmatics. But their projects came with political and psychic costs, for they were part of the broader Cold War mobilization many Americans worried could expand the size and power of the state itself. If protecting national security required growing the state, a phenomenon that seemed unavoidable in the anxious climate of the 1950s and early 1960s, then a secure America could become a statist America. Many Americans—Sorons included—worried that the pursuit of national security might counterintuitively threaten the very democracy the national security state sought to protect, by allowing government intrusion into intellectual life and private institutions.[41]

Contracting seemed to offer protection against statism. As political scientist Aaron Friedberg argues, federal legislation encouraged the practice in the 1950s and 1960s. Convinced that private research institutions were more efficient, more innovative, and more in line with American political and economic values than publicly managed ones, Congress imposed salary caps on government scientists, limited the number of civil service positions, and slowed federal facility construction, all in an effort to encourage the state to invest in the private sector. Policymakers' fears of the negative consequences of militarization encouraged the gray area's growth. Over the course of the 1950s and 1960s, research contracting spread dramatically as investment in atomic research, space science, and social knowledge intensified. The number of federal contract research centers tripled between 1951 and 1967; funding for them skyrocketed, from $122 million to $1.16 billion.[42] Most federal officials endorsed this development. As one 1962 assessment concluded, contracting with the private sector offered "the largest opportunity for initiative and the competition of ideas" while stimulating "the long-term strength of the Nation's scientific resources."[43] Contracting seemed to foster a private, decentralized research sector that circumvented the dangers of state growth and created institutions that were attuned, but not beholden, to the needs of American national security.

Although the notion that FCRCs were private was illusory, it shaped Sorons' professional identities. They did not consider themselves military employees. Their university environment made their mission seem more scholarly than martial. Although all of SORO's operating funds, including researchers' salaries, came from the army, when Sorons published their research in academic journals or attended conferences they identified themselves as employees of American University. SORO attracted social scientists eager to apply their expertise to problems of national security but disinclined to join in-house military research laboratories, where the pay was less and prestige was lower. SORO's researchers were, in fact, better paid than AU's tenured faculty. A senior staff scientist, for example, reaped approximately $23,000, compared to the less than $13,000 earned by the average full-time tenured faculty member.[44] While federal funding for social science generally lagged far behind that for the physical sciences, SORO offered social scientists the opportunity to pursue research for rather generous pay.

SORO arose amid a tangled web. National security seemed to dictate military vigilance and preparedness; but preparedness also threatened to turn the nation into a garrison state. Caught in this contradiction, SORO's architects designed the research office in a way that they hoped would protect democracy at home while providing the military the knowledge to project it abroad. For civilians and military officials alike, research contracting appeared to insulate scholarship from undue military interference. Sorons and their champions anticipated that tremendous intellectual, economic, and national benefits could flow from scholars' arms-length alliance with the military.

Civilian Engines of Military Control

Social scientists and their military patrons were not the only groups who fostered the militarization of American social science. University administrations and Congress also strengthened the close relationship between the military and scholars. At American University, administrators actively encouraged SORO's militarization. More ironically, Congress, which had sought to contain the growth of the national security state by encouraging the creation of public-private research partnerships, would bear significant responsibility for the heavy hand the military exercised over its social researchers. Unlike American University, it would do so rather unwittingly. But the result was the same. Civilian institutions did much to allow and encourage the military to exercise tight control over its social researchers.

By accepting SORO onto its campus in 1956, American University joined the ranks of dozens of middling institutions that used national security funds in an effort to catapult themselves into the intellectual elite. Defense funding was a particularly attractive commodity for AU, which by the early 1950s was far from competitive with its peer institutions; it had twice lost its accreditation and was suffering from tight budgets and a deteriorating physical plant. The university took SORO on with zeal; unlike short-term research contracts, FCRCs offered a potentially permanent source of lucrative overhead payments. In its early years, SORO earned the university $54,000 annually; by 1967, that number topped a quarter of a million dollars. In exchange, the university provided office space for researchers, but gave the army nearly free rein over its daily operations and research. The arrangement benefited the army by enabling it to attract social scientists unwilling to work for in-house military research facilities. The university benefited as well. AU was far from a powerhouse in social research before taking SORO on; until 1950, it had no psychology department and no reputation to speak of in any of the social sciences. By 1966, owing principally to SORO's presence, it ranked among the top ten universities contributing to federally funded social research.[45]

American University's militarization did not begin with SORO, nor with the Washington branch which preceded it and was absorbed into the research office. The campus boasted a long history of service to American national security. During World War I, the university loaned its ninety acres to the War Department, transforming the ivory tower into Camp Leach. Its small student population was ousted from its classrooms—students attended classes in their professors' homes—as the War Department installed barracks and trained over one hundred thousand troops. The centerpiece of Camp Leach was its contribution to the chemists' war: at the American University Experiment Station, a staff of over two thousand researchers developed and tested mustard gas and ricin. AU continued its tradition of service during World War II, loaning its grounds once more to the military. Students were again displaced as the campus converted itself to wartime efforts, including housing navy WAVES.[46] While American University did not contribute to the physicists' war in any meaningful intellectual capacity, SORO gave it the opportunity to make a difference to the social scientists' war, and to reap the institutional, intellectual, and financial benefits of militarization.

Yet American University officials were somewhat ambivalent about the pursuit of national security. Instead, they framed their institution's participation in the processes of militarization as a commitment to intellectual internationalism. American University's president Hurst Anderson embraced SORO as part of his broader educational vision. A self-proclaimed devotee of "international learning" owing to his family's longtime dedication to Christian mission efforts—Anderson was a Methodist bishop—he fervently believed that education could foster international peace. He defined worthwhile intellectual work as that which prepared men "to live and work in the complex world of many cultures and national aspirations." In the context of the Cold War, such a conviction translated seamlessly into militarized social research, but the rhetoric of internationalism masked the elision. A few months after SORO was opened, Anderson's institution took further steps to pursue his vision by inaugurating the School of International Service. Just as SORO was intended to give soldiers some of the qualities of statesmen, the School of International Service was designed to cultivate a new breed of policymaker and diplomat who combined expertise in international affairs with area studies. While SORO toiled by design in relative obscurity, the School of International Studies earned the endorsement of none other than President Eisenhower, who remarked at the school's inauguration ceremony that "the waging of peace demands the best we have."[47]

Anderson's educational philosophy was suited to the nation's hybrid Cold War mission in more ways than one. He abhorred knowledge pursued for its own sake. In his self-published memoirs, he devoted more than a passing comment to complaining about faculty who placed their scholarly interests, which he called "personal intellectual hobbies," above their pedagogical and public responsibilities. No one could accuse Sorons of toiling in pure research. He also had the right politics for a man at the helm of a militarizing university during the Cold War. He openly boasted that he had no qualms about firing suspected communists who made their way onto AU's faculty. Nor did he worry that an alliance with the army might corrupt his university's intellectual or educational mission.[48] While university administrators occasionally complained in private that the army treated SORO as if it were "merely a Pentagon office located elsewhere," publicly Anderson framed SORO as one of his institution's central efforts to mobilize education for global peace.[49]

Congress, by contrast, was as suspicious of social research as American University was enthusiastic. Social scientists, particularly those working on the sensitive subjects of communism and revolution, had few allies on Capitol Hill in the 1950s and early 1960s. Instead, viewing social research as wasteful and useless, legislators subjected it to repeated ridicule. In 1953, the air force's Human Resources Research Institute—the sponsor of Harvard's study of the Soviet social system—came under sustained attack when a congressional subcommittee labeled it an example of the air force's profligate research spending. The State Department, which claimed to be engaged in a similar research study, joined in the attack. Within a year, the Human Resources Research Institute was forced to close its doors, even though the Harvard study yielded over three dozen military reports and scholarly publications describing the social and psychological strengths and weaknesses of the Soviet Union.[50] This process was repeated almost annually as congressmen recited lists of government-sponsored social research studies and determined on the grounds of their titles alone that they were wasteful. Names like "Area Analysis of Afghanistan with Illustrations" and "Communism in India" led one committee to conclude that "much of the information to be compiled is already available."[51]

Because the military relied on congressional appropriations to fund its research programs, it began implementing techniques to avoid Capitol Hill's scrutiny. Psychologist and psychological warfare expert Leonard Cottrell insisted that the problem was so bad that the nation's enemies might well exploit it. He joked, "I wonder if the Russians have noted in their psychological warfare handbooks that a proper use of words like 'congressional investigation' can almost certainly unnerve and immobilize certain parts of our military structure." Russian propaganda notwithstanding, congressional attacks on military-funded social research programs had consequences at SORO, even informing the institution's name. In early 1956, after two months of careful thought, the psychological warfare office announced that it had decided to name the new agency the "Psychological and Guerrilla Warfare Research Office," or PSYGRO for short. But three days after American University and the army executed the PSYGRO contract, the army announced that the name would have to be changed. According to NATO and army rules, security concerns precluded military officials from mentioning guerrilla warfare. For the trained psychological warrior, however, there was a more important reason for renaming the fledgling institution. One official pointed out in a classified memo that the research agency might also be subjected to ridicule should anyone "twist the name" to associate PSYGRO with Vigoro, a common fertilizer. Even a psyops novice could recognize the problem with another suggested name, the Bureau of Special Operations, or BOSO. Although who might take advantage of the research office's name was left unstated—after all, it was anyone's guess if the Russians or Congress would discover it first—the committee settled on the more benign SORO.[52]

On its face, SORO's name was of minor consequence, but it was in fact one part of a larger effort on the part of the military and social scientists to avoid public scrutiny. Congressional distrust of social science also led the military to encourage its researchers to embrace secrecy. Experts on Soviet and Asian politics and culture were seen in Washington not as useful reservoirs of national security information, but as security risks, for their research required that they read subversive literature and interact with current and former communists. That suspicion was a source of unwelcome scrutiny. In 1953, a congressional investigation into foundation-supported social science singled out studies conducted at Harvard's Russian Research Center as security risks. Members of Congress insisted that research into communism should not receive research funding—whether private or public—unless all researchers were carefully screened. SORO's army handlers took this entreaty to heart. Every Soron, from the lowliest administrative assistant to the most senior researcher, underwent full security screenings by the Defense Department and the FBI—at the very least, employees had to have "secret" clearance—and signed a statement asserting that they were not affiliated with any institution on the U.S. attorney general's extensive roster of ostensibly communist and front organizations. The same held true for researchers at RAND, ORO, and other institutes. Owing in part to congressional fears, social scientists in the gray area learned the habits of secrecy. They became accustomed to checking out their research materials from document-control offices, storing their work in special safes, and reading and publishing carefully guarded classified reports.[53] Congressional scrutiny had the unintended consequence of enhancing the culture of secrecy in the military-industrial-academic complex.

Not all congressional actions that fostered militarization were unintentional. Elected officials also had the habit of attacking social research for being insufficiently militaristic. In 1958, an outraged Senator Richard Russell called on Congress to ban the public funding of "defeatist" social research. The target of the Georgia Democrat's wrath was *Strategic Surrender*, a study conducted by RAND's Paul Kecskemeti that explored post–World War II cases of military surrender. Russell objected that the study was designed to discover "when and how or in what circumstances the Government of the United States should surrender this country and its people" to the communists. Although a senator who had read the Kecskemeti study informed Russell that nowhere did the text recommend American surrender, Russell and his supporters insisted that such research only "weaken[ed] the determination and will of the American people to make the sacrifices" that nuclear war required.[54] Social science, Russell seemed to imply, was not becoming dangerously militarized by its association with the military. Rather, it was weakening American national security. Minnesota Republican Edward Thye concurred, reporting that he was "as shocked as anyone could be" when he learned of the project, "because this Nation is not contemplating surrendering to anyone. We never have." Republican Senator Styles Bridges suggested that the amendment require that every researcher who studied surrender be fired, as well as any bureaucrat in the Defense and State Departments who allowed such research to proceed. He charged that communists were behind the study; whoever allowed *Strategic Surrender* to go forward, he raged, was employing "the typical Communist technique of working from within [the American government] in order to brainwash our people, pave the way for appeasement, soften us up, and then destroy us." Russell's amendment banning "defeatist" research passed easily, although Bridges's suggestions were not included.[55]

The congressional stance toward military-funded social research was nothing if not ambivalent. When congressional officials endorsed research contracting, they seemed to share Americans' broader concerns that the Cold War might create a garrison state at home. But many elected officials in the 1950s and early 1960s were more concerned about communist subversion and other threats to American national security than they were about the threat of Washington's militarization. Regardless, the climate of suspicion legitimated the military's careful control of its social research programs at the same time that Congress tried to contain the growth of the national security state. Cognizant that "a military social science research program will receive long-term support only if it emphasizes the conduct of research and refrains from journalistic comments on world affairs," SORO's military supervisors insisted that researchers avoid becoming embroiled "in debates on social philosophy or engaged in political commentary."[56]

The prospect of congressional scrutiny justified the army's heavy-handed control over SORO's research planning. Its "work program," which was generated annually, was the result of extensive negotiations between SORO, its patrons, and other interested parties in the Defense Department. Each fall, SORO's army supervisors carried out what they called a "dragnet." They sent short descriptions of SORO's proposed research projects throughout the service. The various commands ranked their interest in each task, and if they felt that the proposals did not meet their needs adequately, they proposed their own studies. Armed with this feedback, SORO's staff redesigned and refined their work program. In an activity that resembled an advertising pitch, SORO's leadership then spent an hour attempting to convince their patrons of the relevance and viability of their plans. Army officials then met without Sorons to finalize SORO's research projects. In its early years, the army even suggested the appropriate methodological approach, which military officials called the "method of attack," for each study. The whole process ended nine months after it began, when SORO's patrons notified their researchers which projects the army would fund. Only then could research begin. Ongoing projects were subject to the same process and could be suspended at any time.[57]

The army endorsed this time-consuming, top-down method as instrumental to keeping researchers responsive to military needs. But Sorons and the military found it difficult to identify the point at which SORO's work was sufficiently, but not too, operationally relevant. In 1960, researchers proposed "Task Target," a study designed to identify social psychological tools that would make it easier for the army to communicate with foreign anticommunist guerrilla forces receiving military support from the United States. Sorons viewed the project as an investigation of cross-cultural communication in Cold War environments, but the army deemed it "not militarily useful." The project was canceled in 1961. Yet the army also rejected studies on the grounds that they were too militaristic. In June 1957, SORO forwarded a final plan for "Task SUPO" to the psychological warfare office. Shorthand for Determination of Subversive Potential of Specific Social Groups in the Enemy Territory, SUPO promised to identify Soviet social groups that might be opposed to the Soviet government, uncover their political, cultural, and psychological needs, and design programs to encourage them to destabilize the regime. For social scientists, the study was a classic application of theories of persuasion and communication to the communist threat. But while the army pronounced the project "sound in concept," it concluded that the study strayed too far into the realm of "operational" work. Psychological warfare officials rejected it.[58]

The gray area was shot through with the institutional and bureaucratic consequences of American ambivalence about militarization. American University embraced national security problems, allowing military needs to influence its institutional configuration and its educational mission. But it did so largely under the aegis of intellectual internationalism. Congress was even more conflicted. Yet it did more than AU to encourage the militarization of research and the culture of secrecy in the gray area. Congressional scrutiny—whether designed to weed out communist subversives or rein in defense spending—encouraged SORO's managers to be hypervigilant.

Hiding Empire

Yet Sorons did not frequently lament the militarization of their research or their careers. Their professional, intellectual, and personal interests were frequently well served by their alliance with the national security state. Even though they were subject to what could become intrusive military oversight, they viewed themselves as restraining militarization; their knowledge, they argued, could render the military a more pacifistic organization. Social science could turn war into peace. By constructing these narratives of civilianization, social scientists hid the negative consequences of the American embrace of national security, even from themselves. They also helped construct the prevalent American Cold War narrative. By shielding the expansion of American power behind the language of scientific expertise, social scientists helped ease themselves and their fellow Americans into their Cold War role. They helped protect Americans' exceptionalist sense of their nation's identity and mission.

Cold War social scientists believed that their research was intellectually innovative. As MIT modernization theorist Lucian Pye explained to an audience of scholars and military officials, the problems of counterinsurgency were fundamentally indistinguishable from exciting questions of modern social and political development. He explained to those in uniform, "the range of problems which you now identify as counterinsurgency" were all subsumed underneath one crucial social scientific problem: "how to build the most complex of all social institutions . . . : the modern nation-state." Likewise, Princeton's Harry Eckstein explained, because violent revolution was at its most basic a form of social and political change, scholarly studies of national upheaval yielded insights central to the rapidly growing fields of political, social, and economic development.[59] By this line of reasoning, SORO's work—investigations of the causes of internal revolution, the mechanisms of persuasion, and the structures of communist guerrilla cells, to name only a few—could be crucial to the larger behavioral scientific goal of determining the universal laws of human and social behavior. The research office, by this logic, was on the vanguard of scholarship.

In this context, the Pentagon's requirement that researchers make use of military and intelligence files, and the onerous system of security clearances and classification that went with it, was not a dangerous signal that national security concerns seeped into scholarship and subverted academic freedom. Rather, it was an opportunity. The researchers' work afforded them access to sources unavailable to academic social scientists. Most of SORO's research projects required them to mine classified government intelligence files and military records for information. Their work often remained classified as a result, keeping researchers from gaining public credit for their toil. But for many, that was a fair trade-off for access to the most up-to-date sources on international politics in the Cold War. Indeed, even some university scholars took on private government contracts precisely for these benefits. One Harvard social scientist reported that his access to classified materials benefited his research: "I find that I get intelligence work of the highest order in the reports we have [from the government]. . . . I participate in the preparation of all kinds of reports there [in the government office], and I have access to materials that I otherwise wouldn't get." Another cited his work for the government as "indispensable to a man working in my field."[60] Secrecy could be a boon to scholarship.

The government's researchers understood themselves as the beneficiaries of rich, untapped sources and sites of knowledge that improved their research. Irwin Altman, a psychologist and head of psychological warfare research at SORO, argued that most academic research in psychology suffered from a major methodological shortcoming: it was typically performed on college students in laboratory environments. As such it was oversimplified, sanitized, and almost irrelevant. SORO, on the other hand, offered access to real-world subjects; it brought researchers face to face with the men and women living on the front lines of the global Cold War. Psychologist Ray Hackman, a seasoned veteran of Pentagon-funded research—he had worked with the Office of Naval Research, ORO, the Systems Development Corporation, and the private, for-profit Psychological Research Associates over the course of the 1950s—concurred. In the pages of *Scientific Monthly*, he disparaged university researchers as cowards and extolled his colleagues as brave risk takers. So-called "pure" research, he argued, was in fact research of little consequence. Scholars of real-world problems, by contrast, tackled important and exciting scientific challenges, unpacking the complicated causal forces at work in multivariate social systems.[61]

For Sorons, the Cold War rendered the tired distinctions between pure and applied science as obsolete as those of war and peace or martial and civilian. SORO's mission reflected a faith that the subjects of social research and military operations were closely connected, perhaps even indistinguishable. Research could benefit academic social science, the military, and the free world. While some of SORO's research resulted in modest area studies reports with titles like "An Ethnographic Summary of the Ethiopian Provinces of Harar and Sidamo," and others led to annotated bibliographies of counterinsurgency scholarship, researchers aspired to produce social systems models and generalizable theories of social change that would enhance both military strategy and social scientific knowledge. Even projects that sounded heavily militarized were thought to generate new insights about and methodological approaches to social scientific problems. For example, SORO designed Project Propaganda Infiltration, or Propin for short, to develop counterpropaganda techniques. But Propin researchers argued that this effort also yielded breakthroughs in knowledge about the relationship between communication and attitude change among nonliterate populations. Propin researchers grounded their research in Elihu Katz's and Paul Lazarsfeld's "two-step flow" theory of communications, which stipulated that rather than flowing directly from the media to the audience, information was mediated by opinion leaders and other "key communicators." The Propin research team, aided by indigenous social scientists and graduate students in Thailand, administered communications questionnaires that sought to identify key communicators, their favored media, and the audiences with whom they communicated. While the military publication resulting from the study indicated which audiences and media psy warriors could target to greatest effect, Sorons argued in the academic literature that the study was a methodological breakthrough that demonstrated that rigorous sampling and mass interviewing could be brought to bear on research in the developing world.[62]

Thus projects with far-reaching military implications could yield insights relevant to scholarship. Project Revolt, initiated in 1960, was designed to help the army anticipate and prevent communist revolutions around the globe. If successful, it could give the army a blueprint for stabilizing friendly nations in the third world, circumventing violence while containing communism. Predicting violent social change required Sorons to identify the underlying social, political, economic, and psychological factors that sparked revolution. To this end, they compiled historical case studies of revolutions to test a variety of popular theories, including the hypotheses that marginalized, economically powerful intellectuals played key roles in instigating revolutions, and that a growing middle class militated against revolution. They also investigated the kinds of countermeasures—from military aid to martial law—that counterinsurgency forces could deploy to contain violence. In the pages of the peer-reviewed journal *Rural Sociology*, Soron Ritchie P. Lowry explained the seamless intellectual relationship between his field and government-funded counterinsurgency research. SORO's work, he argued, was little different from academic social research, for it was ultimately "concerned with the larger academic questions of processes and techniques of social control and social change," the bread and butter of midcentury behavioral science. His work, he explained, satisfied equally his desire to advance knowledge and improve human welfare: "The opportunity afforded by the Army's current interest in special warfare," he elaborated, "goes far beyond the possibility to contribute to contemporary American foreign policy. Results could accrue which would influence the development of social knowledge and theory for years to come."[63]

Lowry downplayed the foreign policy implications of his work, but he and his peers believed that their research would avert violence and, perhaps more important, remake the military as an engine of peace and development. Social scientists prided themselves on producing information that could contain, and even prevent, conflict. As SORO's William Lybrand explained to an audience of military officials and social scientists in 1962, "rather than destructive, our aims are constructive—to create internal conditions and encourage political, social, and economic systems which remove hunger, disease, poverty, oppression and other sources of discontent." Armed with social scientific knowledge, "our military establishment is a direct, positive instrument for human progress." Lybrand was not blazing new ground with his claims, of course. He echoed the values of President Kennedy, who argued to West Point soldiers that same year that their Cold War mission was not to kill, but to "help those who have the will to help themselves."[64] Sorons, like most Americans in the early years of the Cold War, acclimated themselves to the spread of American power by arguing that they acted with the best of intentions. They took on secret military work with a sense of scientific and national duty, and the nation took on its expanding empire with benevolent reluctance.

Even further, social scientists implied that their contributions to American foreign policy enhanced democratic values at home. In his pioneering 1957 volume *Limited War*, Robert E. Osgood justified the intellectual pursuit of limited war by arguing that "the liberal and humane spirit needs an environment conducive to compromise and moderation." The political and social milieu likely to follow nuclear holocaust was certainly not conducive to democracy.[65] Social scientists who studied insurgency did not threaten American democracy by enhancing the militarization of scholarship and foreign policy; they strengthened it. Militarization, according to this logic, actually fulfilled the promise of American democracy.

Social scientists even argued that their military work helped bring Americans back in touch with their revolutionary origins. As the Smithsonian's Advisory Group on Psychology and the Social Sciences explained in 1957, "some of the demands of the future—such as the involvement of large segments of the citizenry in direct defense activities—recall the roots of our democracy that produced the frontiersman, the minuteman, and the vigilante."[66] Of course, each of those sought to battle and conquer its enemies, but the advisory group implied that many of them operated in the name of liberty, progress, and manifest destiny. Militarization and global interventionism revitalized American national identity.

This sentiment, however, was uncommon. On the rare occasions that Americans addressed militarization directly, they revealed their anxieties about its implications for democracy. In January 1961, President Eisenhower issued a grave warning to the nation. Since World War II, he said, Americans had directed an astonishing quantity of economic, intellectual, and human resources to national defense. He conceded that such an effort was a necessary response to Soviet antagonism. Yet he admonished Americans to "guard against the acquisition of unwarranted influence, whether sought or unsought, by the military-industrial complex." Its "total influence," he intoned, was "economic, political, even spiritual . . . felt in every city, every Statehouse, every office of the Federal government." It was also felt in science. The threat here was twofold. The president warned scholars to guard against the danger that contracts become "a substitute for intellectual curiosity." But equally treacherous, he cautioned, was the "opposite danger that public policy could itself become the captive of a scientific-technological elite."[67]

That the first president to warn against the militarization of American politics and science was also the one who did much to encourage it speaks volumes about Americans' ambivalence about militarization in the 1950s and early 1960s. By the time Eisenhower issued his warning, large swaths of American social research were unquestionably militarized. The roots of this process were diverse; the military, social scientists, university administrations, and even elected officials both wittingly and unwittingly encouraged Americans to envision military problems as scientific subjects. With revolutionary war recast as a social, economic, and political problem, it moved easily into the purview of civilian strategists working in the gray area. But the flip side of "civilianization" was militarization. The boundaries between war and peace were so blurred by the early 1960s that army psychological warfare manuals defined peace as "simply a period of less violent war in which nonmilitary means are predominantly used to achieve certain political objectives."[68]

Yet, by rendering national security questions the subjects of science, researchers and their patrons hid the fact of military influence over scholarship and policy—even from themselves. Research contracting seemed, at the time, to insulate academic inquiry from undue military influence. It also seemed to guard against statism. And while Eisenhower warned that the denizens of the military-industrial complex might endanger American democracy, social scientists argued the opposite. Counterinsurgency doctrine, designed cooperatively by social scientists and military experts, would help keep wars limited and could perhaps avoid conflict altogether. Their work, it seemed, enhanced American democratic values. For reasons that the next chapter explains, the particular ways social scientists framed the nature and function of Cold War democracy would do much to draw their attention away from their complicity in the processes of militarization.

A DEMOCRACY OF EXPERTS

Knowledge and Politics in the
Military-Industrial-Academic Complex

Eisenhower's 1961 farewell address introduced a new term into the American lexicon, but his fear that the national security state's experts might endanger democracy was not new. In fact, it was one that social scientists had anticipated. Harold Lasswell's "garrison state" and C. Wright Mill's "power elite"— a symbiotic triumvirate of political, military, and corporate leaders—both reflected a concern that the nation's obsession with security might endanger American democracy by allowing "specialists on violence" to assume control of political decisions.[1] These men's warnings gained some popular attention in the 1950s and early 1960s but inspired little action. Even so, social scientists working in the gray area could not escape the implications their expertise held for democratic politics. A number of them chose to confront the tensions between esoteric expertise and democratic governance head-on.

In fact, social-scientific engagement with the problematic relationship between expertise and democracy preceded the rise of militarization. Long before the gray area's creation, generations of social scientists had sought to elevate politics to the level of science. But that aspiration presented social scientists with vexing epistemological and ethical challenges. Since the late nineteenth century, social scientists who sought to use their knowledge to reform society faced a pressing question: what was the expert's proper role in a democracy? The basis of modern scientific authority lies in the ostensibly objective and disinterested character of its empirical claims. Scientific knowledge is politically powerful in part because it seems to exclude the arbitrary and subjective. If scientists could provide universally valid, impersonal, nonideological conclusions about society and politics, they could transform questions of power and politics into the subjects of rational, value-neutral inquiry. Social science might be a powerful tool for decision making in democracies. But many Americans, scholars and citizens alike, long suspected that social research might not be disinterested. Applying social science to political questions not only threatened to bring scholarship into the subjective realms of moral argument and individual values. It raised fundamental questions about public accountability and popular participation in debates about social and political goals. Social scientists' mission presented them with a quandary: Could they provide knowledge and apply it to social and political problems without undermining democracy?[2]

These issues were raised in high relief in the institutions of the gray area, where anxieties about national security threatened to contaminate knowledge, challenging researchers' scientific and political authority. In the context of a battle waged for democracy, the stakes were high. The stark contrast between liberal democracy and totalitarianism underpinned the Cold War. According to this binary scheme, communist polities were morally absolutist, driven by the ideologically motivated dictates of ruling elites who forced their values and beliefs on their subjects. By contrast, American democracy had to be pluralist, nonideological, and morally relativist. Neither elites nor experts could rightfully impose their values on the public. But if social science were biased—if it merely masked political ideology or subjective political values—it might offer no better basis for public action than did the dictates of communist leaders. If social-scientific expertise were normative, it might also be antidemocratic. And so social scientists confronted a challenge in the Cold War that transcended the problem of militarization: since social knowledge was crucial to the informed, efficient management of modern political and foreign affairs—a position that few disputed in the era of containment—how could it be properly produced and applied? State patronage was problematic not merely because it imperiled objectivity; even goal-directed studies could produce reliable and trustworthy facts. As the historian Robert Proctor writes, "Neutrality and objectivity are not the same thing. Neutrality refers to whether a science takes a stand; objectivity, to whether a science merits certain claims to reliability." The dilemma facing Cold War social scientists was the proper place of values in research. In the name of democracy, experts had to ensure that their scholarship did not mask and surreptitiously promote subjective values. They must not conflate the *is* of scientific fact with the *ought* of moral and political belief.[3]

The social scientists who inhabited the gray area between the ivory tower and the national security state responded to these problems with a surprising spectrum of epistemological and ethical positions. All shared a belief in the importance of social-scientific knowledge to governance. This chapter examines the positions of three Sorons. Their epistemological and ethical self-fashioning reveals that the question of the proper relationship between knowledge and policy was subject to debate—a debate that reveals that social scientists contested the meaning of American democracy itself.

When SORO was attacked in 1960 for legitimating a cynically manipulative foreign policy, political scientist Earl H. DeLong rose to its defense. Of the three positions outlined here, his is most recognizable as that of the quintessential Cold War social scientist. DeLong defended SORO's scientific integrity by insisting on a stark separation of the roles of scholar and policymaker, value-neutral knowledge producer and value-directed knowledge user. Social scientists best served the state by restricting themselves to advising policymakers on matters of fact. For DeLong, the expert was a service intellectual who provided rational, objective knowledge that allowed policymakers to transcend the mess of interests, values, and power that often seemed to accompany participatory democracy. For service intellectuals, democracy worked best when guided by experts and political elites.

DeLong's approach was far from hegemonic among social scientists working in the gray area. Asian area studies expert Jeanne S. Mintz built her career on the argument that the social scientist best served the national security state by producing rigorous, empirical social knowledge that was directed only toward ends the researcher deemed ethical. Mintz rejected DeLong's rigid cleavage of knowledge and action, arguing that social scientists were responsible for the ultimate ends to which their work might be applied. Yet she maintained DeLong's position that scholars best served human freedom by providing their expertise to government officials, not by trying to shape policy goals. For Mintz, experts were scientific advocates for elite-guided democracy. Values and goals dictated the scholar's choice of work. Once those ends had been chosen, the means to them could be deduced scientifically.

Dismissing outright DeLong's cleavage of means and ends and Mintz's ideal of a circumscribed scientific advocacy, the sociologist Robert Boguslaw rejected any boundary between science and action. For Boguslaw, scientific knowledge was inherently political, and when it was treated as value neutral, as DeLong recommended, or as explicitly supportive of government, as Mintz recommended, it threatened public participation in democratic decision making. Boguslaw sought social-scientific engagement that could disrupt antidemocratic models of expertise by providing objective but self-consciously value-laden knowledge to the public to help citizens make informed decisions about the means and ends of U.S. policy. For Boguslaw, the expert was a scientific crusader for participatory democracy, or, as he termed it, a scholar of "radical social action."[4]

Boguslaw, Mintz, and DeLong were not intellectual elites. They represent the rank and file of Cold War social research—the proliferating community of men and women who served the national security state, each with relatively clear consciences and often a messianic sense of mission. Because they were focused on the long-standing epistemological challenges of objectivity and neutrality, they were each slow to recognize militarization as a threat to democracy. Although their solutions to the problem of expertise and democracy differed, each validated and extended the militarization of American politics and foreign policy, sometimes by design and sometimes by implication. To understand the complex, intertwined problems of expertise, militarization, and democracy, we must look to the men and women who sought to reconcile them.

Social Science in the Gray Area

As Mark C. Smith has observed, "American social science has always suffered from an ambivalence found in its very name." It is scientific: amoral, factual, and technical. But it can be normative, for its origins lie in moral commitments to social welfare, reform, and progress. As Franklin Sanborn explained in the late nineteenth century, "To learn patiently what is—to promote diligently what should be—that is the double duty of all the social sciences."[5] The merger of social science and social policy was never easy. Social scientists hotly debated its intellectual and moral implications throughout the first half of the twentieth century. At one extreme, Chicago sociologist William Ogburn decried any "interpretation, popularization, and emotionalism" in social research, calling instead for a rigorously statistical social science directed only toward advancing knowledge. At the other extreme, scholars like Charles Beard condemned that approach, arguing that it produced research that was "myopic," "sterile," and resulted in an emphasis on technique that yielded only "meticulous banality." More common was a position like that of Charles Merriam, the don of American political science, who urged his colleagues to carefully insulate inquiry from application. Social scientists must distinguish, he insisted, "between scientific fact finding on the one hand and the determination and execution of policies on the other."[6]

Social scientists working in the gray area between scholarship and the national security state inherited this unresolved problem. The growing contract state owed its very existence to the belief that experts could find rational, unbiased solutions to urgent social and political problems. As historian Richard V. Damms explains, Americans in the 1940s and 1950s, including Eisenhower himself, possessed an enormous "faith in the ability of selfless scientific experts to provide objective analyses of pressing national problems free of any narrow political or service viewpoint."[7] In the physical sciences, the trust in expertise seemed particularly sound, and it led to the creation of a number of advisory committees, like the President's Scientific Advisory Committee and the Defense Science Board, that turned to physical scientists for advice on national security policy.

The faith in expertise also justified the Pentagon's growing research and development budgets in the social sciences. There, the relationship between knowledge and action was more complicated. Although the content of their work and the sources of their financial support positioned them close to the Pentagon, social scientists working in the gray area did not often express concern that federal patronage circumscribed their intellectual freedom or compromised their objectivity. Even at SORO, where autonomy to choose research problems was limited, scholars seldom complained publicly about constraints on their inquiry. Nor did they worry that their work was tainted by politics. In the climate of the early Cold War, anticommunism, containment, and the protection and extension of democracy were rarely identified as partisan positions that betrayed subjective values.[8] Most social scientists, whether or not they worked on contract with the national security state, did not consider patronage acutely problematic until the second half of the 1960s.

Rather, they confronted their work for the national security state within the framework of long-standing anxiety about the appropriate relationship between scholarship and political action. Researchers working on contract with SORO were driven by the hope that social knowledge could serve as an instrument for rational decision making. If behavioral science proved itself—if researchers could discover the laws of social behavior—then policymaking would become the straightforward application of truth to politics and policy. But many social scientists expressed concern that the political relevance of their work might threaten its neutrality on matters of value. Cold War research projects, like the social reform projects of decades previous, drew scholars into obvious contact with the ends their work might serve. MIT economist Max F. Millikan spoke for many of his colleagues when he explained that the social researcher working on policy issues "is plagued by the fear that this will plunge him back into the confusion between norms and observed reality from which he has been struggling so hard for decades to free himself."[9] That problem was not specific to militarized research, but contract research thrust it into high relief. In the gray area between academia and the Pentagon, researchers continued their struggle to produce politically neutral, applicable knowledge—facts that, when applied, would not endanger the democracy they had been enlisted to protect.

Earl DeLong and "the *Use* Which Should Be Judged"

In 1960, Sorons openly confronted that challenge when McGill University's Wilfred Cantwell Smith approached American University's president about a research study he regarded as deeply troubling. SORO's staff had invited Smith to serve as an expert consultant for a study called Project Prosyms Pakistan. SORO created Prosyms—shorthand for "propaganda symbols"—in 1957 to help the army plan its psychological warfare programs in nations threatened by communism. Prosyms researchers provided the military with handbooks filled with propaganda messages that would help soldiers "persuade, rather than force, the enemy or enemy-dominated peoples to support the national objectives of the United States" in the event of a communist-initiated war. By 1960, SORO had produced handbooks for ten countries in Asia and the Middle East. As many as four hundred pages long, they described the nations' diverse inhabitants, their political and social susceptibilities to psychological operations, and the cultural symbols—visual and linguistic—that were most politically powerful. Smith had a store of knowledge upon which Prosyms Pakistan could be built. The founding director of McGill's Institute of Islamic Studies, he was an expert on comparative religion in South Asia.[10] Appalled by Prosyms' application of social science to Cold War politics, he constructed a detailed attack on the project and on SORO.

Smith questioned American University's willingness to "subordinate (sell?) itself to the private interests of a powerful but limited group in society." Prosyms, he insisted, was not science. Rather, it was a "project for elaborating methods for effectively manipulating people in another country" for U.S. benefit. Smith argued that Prosyms was a brazen exercise of expertise for social control. That a university would support such an endeavor was, he charged, "a serious contradiction of the principles of the academic tradition itself: the disinterested pursuit of knowledge, the making available of the fruits of knowledge to all mankind, and the objective, universalist quality of the academic life." SORO's research, Smith argued, threatened the integrity of social science, the freedom of Pakistani citizens and American scholars, and the very foundations of Western intellectual values. Smith objected, too, that by hosting such a project, the university was complicit in the United States' dangerous and counterproductive foreign policy. He wrote, "even from the political and strategic point of view, such 'research' is self-defeating. The immense failure of the United States throughout the world to win the confidence, friendship, and cooperation of other peoples ... [is] in part related to the very attitude which this ... project typifies." He elaborated, "To treat people as pawns in the pursuit of selfish ends is inevitably to alienate them."[11]

Earl H. DeLong, the director of research at SORO, crafted a seven-page letter that painstakingly explained his position on the matter. DeLong had argued since the 1930s that scholars had an obligation to apply their expertise to the service of state and society. After completing his PhD in political science at Northwestern University in 1934, DeLong joined his alma mater's faculty. An advocate of enhancing government efficiency by streamlining bureaucracy and creating an expert civil service, he dedicated his early research to reforming the federal and state judicial systems.[12] When the United States entered World War II, DeLong endorsed the American Political Science Association's suggestion that, in wartime, scholars should eschew their "customary individualism" to offer their services to the state. He promptly left Northwestern for Washington and never returned to purely academic life. By the time he received Smith's letter, DeLong had spent almost twenty years in government service as an administrator and analyst, first for the Civil Service Commission, and later for the Defense Department and the Central Intelligence Agency. The problem of expertise was one on which he had ruminated for decades. Like elite social scientists Harold Lasswell and Max Lerner, who in 1950 called for scholars to create policy sciences that would enhance policy by improving the data available to policymakers, DeLong advocated a model of the social scientist as technical adviser and service intellectual. In a 1959 publication, he argued that the government should create a cadre of senior administrators who could serve as interpreters between researchers and policymakers.[13] Because DeLong fancied himself just such a middleman, his confrontation with Smith gave him the opportunity to prove his mettle.

DeLong argued that in order to maintain the proper relationship between expertise and democracy, social scientists should restrict themselves to the production of knowledge. According to the political scientist, SORO researchers identified facts, principles, and theories, but politicians, policymakers, and military bureaucrats decided if, where, and how those findings would be used. DeLong explained that Prosyms was "strictly a matter of preparation for the contingency of war. The military application of the product of this study will be developed by the U.S. Army for its own guidance and use only in the case of the occurrence of war." Furthermore, what Smith interpreted as manipulation was in DeLong's view an ordinary study of "the process of human communication." Should the United States and Pakistan "meet the catastrophe of a war which intermingled" their interests, "there would be occasion when we would have the need to communicate with them. This process of communication is part of the dynamics of society." DeLong's words weren't mere rhetoric. One Prosyms staff member, Imogene E. Okes, had earned her master's degree in communications for research she conducted for Prosyms Thailand. DeLong admitted that Prosyms' results might be used to influence people, but that possibility alone, he argued, did not justify the prohibition of research. He explained that "it is the *use* which should be judged by the moral imperatives, not the *study* of a social process which may be used" for good or ill.[14]

DeLong's perspective was in part shaped by his long experience as a civil servant charged with executing the orders of changing political appointees. The civil servant's duty, he argued elsewhere, was to "carry out skillfully and promptly whatever policy and program the responsible heads of the executive branch want," and to do so with political neutrality. But DeLong's separation of knowledge from action was no radical departure from the Western intellectual tradition. He was invoking a centuries-old axiom: scientifically derived truths were, by definition, neutral and amoral.[15] By questioning Prosyms' propriety, DeLong implied, Smith was disputing a fundamental tenet of the scientific tradition.

DeLong's separation of knowledge and its application was predicated on a second axiom: a political system wise enough to ground its policies on scientific knowledge was by definition ethical. Unsurprisingly given the circumstances, he explained that scientists were obliged to serve their government, so long as their research was "consistent doubly with the welfare of mankind and the security of the nation." DeLong did not see the need to explain how that proviso was met. It was inconceivable to him, as it was to many in an era of patriotic anticommunism, that human welfare and national security could be working at cross-purposes in the United States. The government might carry out its objectives a bit clumsily at times, he admitted, but that did not change his faith that American liberal democracy "preserves our intellectual independence, our freedom of conscience, and the opportunity to respect and maintain our moral values." In the context of the Cold War, supporting national security was tantamount to supporting freedom. Should democracy collapse because of scholars' failure to support it, there would be none of Smith's precious scientific and moral liberties to protect. This was not, DeLong insisted, a perversion of academia by military interests. Blind to the fact that Smith was accusing SORO of helping to militarize American foreign relations, DeLong insisted, "we do not consider that assistance to the needs of the military arm of our democratic state is in any sense whatever the sale of the University's soul," for at SORO, "there is not one shred of unconscionable compulsion on us to do anything in which we have doubt as a matter of intellectual or moral propriety."[16]

For DeLong, Smith's challenge to his vision of the role of experts in American government was more consequential than the questions he raised about the university's relationship to the national security state. DeLong built his defense of Prosyms on three decades of political thought that, by 1960, had hardened into a deep faith in the symbiosis between science and democracy, which was defined in Cold War fashion as the nonideological and morally relativist quest for political consensus. By the 1940s many scholars—Harold Lasswell, Karl Popper, Sidney Hook, and Robert K. Merton were among the most famous—had constructed models of the interdependence and harmony of science and democracy that were based on the polar opposition of liberal democratic and totalitarian sociopolitical systems. Like idealized democratic citizens who made political decisions consensually, the scientist sought truth through open-minded discussion. The good scientist, like the good democrat, approached his subject with cool disinterestedness, liberated from the taint of values, morals, or prejudice. He rejected tradition and dogma in favor of clear-eyed investigation and discussion. According to this tradition, science and American democracy could be one and the same. By transcending interests, values, and ideology, scientists protected and enhanced democracy.[17]

DeLong was not an avid student of political theory. But the notion that good science and democracy created and sustained one another was common enough in American social thought that DeLong could gesture toward an armory of intellectual defenses for SORO's work. Smith had objected that Prosyms "seem[ed] in radical violation of the moral imperatives of the Judeo-Christian tradition," as well as the "secular moral tradition of our society stemming from Greece and Rome." But according to the same intellectual tradition that held science and democracy to be analogues, Smith's arguments, which appealed to a fixed ethical system, smacked of absolutism and thus trod close to totalitarianism. In his rebuttal, DeLong suggested that Smith was no different from the totalitarians that SORO had dedicated itself to fighting. He equated Smith's claim with scholastic philosophy, the pinnacle of religious oppression of free inquiry. Project Prosyms, DeLong explained,

> has the prospect of applied value in those areas where military need and moral values coincide. It also has the possibility of applied values in those areas where they do not coincide. If it is contended that this latter possibility debars a university from conducting this study, this, in the guise of morality, is an invasion of the independent realm of intellect which is more worthy of the time of Galileo.

According to DeLong, Smith's moralistic attack on expertise not only imperiled social scientists' academic freedom and U.S. national security. It threatened to plunge science and society back into the absolutist oppression of an earlier, unenlightened era.[18]

DeLong's confidence in the righteousness of democracy was so complete that he never betrayed any concern that military patronage might imperil the value-neutral production of knowledge, let alone democratic policymaking.

Totalitarian societies such as the Soviet Union by definition controlled the activities, and even the thoughts, of their citizens. It was inconceivable to DeLong that the U.S. government could do the same. So long as the researcher was not coerced into violating his scientific method or his personal ethics, patronage did not threaten academic freedom.

For DeLong, freedom from value commitments was paramount in good science. But a potential obstacle lurked in the symbiosis between science and democracy. An implicit commitment to the American political system might appear to challenge the value neutrality of science. Prosyms, after all, seemed to champion the U.S. political system. Ironically, the common solution to this problem lent additional legitimacy to DeLong's strict separation of means from ends. By equating science and democracy, scholars defined democracy as a *process* rather than a goal. Just as midcentury social scientists offered a definition of good science that focused on method, they defined American democracy as a pluralistic process. Interest groups competed and forged consensus without imposing their values on each other. The state itself, according to this model, was neutral. The equation of science and democracy refocused attention away from the values inherent in political goals—indeed, in the state itself—toward the methods of political systems. By the 1950s, political scientists rarely discussed the *ends* of the U.S. political system beyond a vague commitment to advancing human freedom. Rather, they focused on its means—the open consideration of ideas.[19] This strict separation of means and ends enabled social scientists to harmonize their dedication to value-neutral research with their commitment to American democracy. Thus could they serve the national security state with a sense of righteousness and faith in their disinterestedness.

Of course, because it provided manipulative messages to the army, Prosyms did not bear even a passing resemblance to a democracy in which the public played a role in decision making. But that disjunction, too, was of a piece with the symbiosis of science and democracy. With his background in public administration, DeLong was, like many midcentury social scientists, deeply suspicious of truly participatory politics. The rise of fascism, the popularity of McCarthyism, the international prestige of the Soviet Union, and the growth of "people's democracies" in the third world spurred social scientists to rethink the meaning of democracy. Popular participation in politics seemed to lead not to pluralist politics in which an educated public made rational decisions for the greater good, but to irrational, ideological, and dangerously authoritarian polities. Surveying the status of democracy around the world, American social scientists downgraded the importance of public participation in it. As Stanford University political scientist Gabriel Almond explained, "If interest, knowledge, and constant participation on the part of the mass were our criteria . . . we would have to write off all historic democracies as something other than democratic." The problems confronting modern polities, it seemed, were too complicated to be grasped by the majority of citizens. As Almond and Sidney Verba argued, for democracy to work, "the ordinary citizen must turn power over to elites and let them rule." Yet democratic stability required that citizens trust political elites to represent their interests. Expert input helped create that trust. Scientific knowledge—itself pluralist, nonideological, and consensual—was a safe substitute for public participation. Democracy worked best when political elites made policy decisions with the aid of expert knowledge. Champions of the model of the service intellectual, from Earl DeLong to more elite scholars such as Paul Lazarsfeld and Edward Shils, advocated a processual vision of democracy in which benevolent elites relied on expert input to reach rational consensus for the greater good. DeLong went so far as to call for the imposition of a "discriminating selection process" across the entire civil service system, ensuring that elites at every level of government had a cadre of expert administrators to direct and implement their policies and that amateur participation in politics was kept to a minimum. The symbiosis of science and democracy amounted to an embrace of elite rule wisely guided by instrumental social knowledge.[20]

Service intellectuals emphasized value neutrality, for by adhering to it, they neutralized the problematic role of expertise in democratic politics. So long as scholars did not cloud their judgment with their idiosyncratic moral commitments, they ensured that a plurality of viewpoints would be considered when searching for consensus. And since Western democracies were allegedly enjoying the "end of ideology," in which consensus on the primary goals of public life had been reached, questions of value should not often intrude into political debate. These convictions animated social scientists, from the rank and file of the gray area to scholars working in elite research institutions. MIT political scientist Ithiel de Sola Pool went so far as to write off the problem of values altogether. Americans had a simple choice, he explained, "between policy based on moralisms and policy based on social science." The right selection was obvious. With the methods of science as its backbone, elite-led democracy would be sound, legitimate, and consensual.[21]

For DeLong and other service intellectuals, the gray area between academia and the national security state was a safe zone where the disinterested consensus on which science and political life were built counteracted the threat that expertise posed to democracy. The political scientist's faith in the mutuality of the processes that defined science and democracy provided him with a reliable tautology: social science protected democracy, and democracy safeguarded social science. The path from knowledge to policy could be navigated with ease.

DeLong's position also obscured the processes and more pernicious consequences of militarization in both social science and American statecraft. To shield SORO behind the symbiosis of science and democracy, he had to argue that its work was, in fact, scientific. (That the policies SORO supported were democratic went without saying.) Social scientists and policymakers assumed that objectivity trumped the potential for scholarship to become militarized; this, in part, was what made expertise attractive to Americans in the Cold War. But DeLong's argument was more specific and far-reaching. Like his fellow Sorons, he viewed SORO's work as an exciting scholarly pursuit; Prosyms was cross-cultural research first, and only incidentally of use to the military. Neither was the military's desire for such information, nor its willingness to use it, evidence that SORO was abetting the extension of military power abroad. As DeLong had explained to Smith, Prosyms was a cautionary measure—preparation for a war he hoped would never be waged. DeLong's argument seemed to exonerate the state from responsibility for an increasingly militarized national security policy. Should the army be forced to use Prosyms, he implied, it would be the fault of the communists, not the result of narrow American self-interest. Like most of his fellow Americans, DeLong believed that war, and by implication the American investment in national security, was imposed upon the nation by external belligerents.[22] Americans were victims of Soviet aggression; there was no need to answer Smith's charge that they were imperialists.

The argument that science and democracy were symbiotic sidestepped the political and moral consequences of SORO's research, concealing the manipulative and antidemocratic potential of the knowledge produced by the national security state's social scientists. Armed with the midcentury faith in the mutuality of science and democracy, DeLong felt that he and his research staff produced knowledge for the security of the nation and the greater good of the third world. Researchers in the gray area, he believed, had surmounted the tensions at the heart of social science to provide a value-neutral tool for an elite-guided democracy at home and well-intentioned, peaceful American-led order abroad.

Jeanne S. Mintz and the Importance of Seeing "Eye to Eye"

Jeanne S. Mintz endorsed a position on the relationship between science and democracy that on the surface appeared to mirror what DeLong prescribed for a service intellectual. Like DeLong, she embraced science as an apolitical policy tool. Mintz, who worked as a senior research scientist at SORO from 1964 to

1966, was drawn to contract research by her ambition to apply her knowledge to the improvement of American foreign and defense policy. But unlike DeLong, who professed agnosticism about the application of his knowledge, Mintz lent her expertise only to causes she deemed ethical—the termination of European imperial rule and the expansion of democracy, vaguely defined as the antithesis of communism, in the new nations.

Mintz's dedication to political causes began during World War II. While an undergraduate at Brooklyn College, she volunteered for the Queen Wilhelmina Fund for Dutch war relief. After graduating, she took a policy research position with the Dutch Indies government-in-exile. Once she became aware that her employers did not intend to liberate Indonesia from their rule at war's end, however, she found she could no longer work for them. Realizing "that the Dutch and I no longer saw eye to eye," she explained, she joined the leaders of the Indonesian independence movement. From 1947 until 1951, Mintz worked as a press officer and research analyst for the Indonesian delegation to the newly formed United Nations. Mintz was both an advocate of and active player in the Indonesian transition from colony to nation. When the Dutch transferred sovereignty to Jakarta in 1949, the new nation's foreign minister called her to the capital city to establish and train its foreign ministry.[23]

Mintz's work established her as an expert on Southeast Asian affairs and whetted her appetite for the study of political science. She left Jakarta in 1951 for Harvard's Graduate School of Public Administration. There, she studied under Rupert Emerson, a member of the Department of Government and a specialist on Pacific colonial politics. Emerson had become a committed anti-imperialist in the 1930s, arguing that political science should help newly independent states build viable political systems.[24]

Mintz, too, saw in political science a tool for nation building and postcolonial stability; she remained so active in policy work while pursuing her PhD in government and political economy that she did not receive her degree until 1964. While completing her course work at Harvard, she examined Indonesian economic development as a research analyst at the MIT Center for International Studies. For much of the 1950s, she served as the director of program development for the Asia Society, a New York–based philanthropy and advocacy organization with clandestine ties to the CIA. Perhaps unaware of the foundation's CIA link, she designed public outreach programs, delivered public lectures, and regularly appeared on television as a Southeast Asian expert. In 1959, she collaborated with RAND consultant and New York University professor Frank N. Trager on a study titled *Marxism in Southeast Asia*. Like Emerson, Mintz remained a staunch anti-imperialist, a position that informed her scholarly work. Although most of her publications were positively received in the political science community, Harry J. Benda of Yale University complained repeatedly that Mintz's anticolonial stance made her too quick to blame the Dutch for Indonesia's political and economic problems.[25]

Although she may have allowed her political views to color her research, Mintz had something in common with the staunch neutralist Earl DeLong—a dedication to Project Prosyms. In 1960, SORO invited her to serve as a consultant for a Prosyms study of Indonesia. Although she was burdened with other responsibilities at the time, Mintz joined the project out of intellectual interest. One of her duties included writing "injunctions," or dos and don'ts, for American psychological warriors. Her suggestions included statements such as, "Do remember that more Indonesian enlisted men are illiterate than otherwise," and "Do *not* forget the importance of ethnic and regional loyalties among the officer corps." Mintz heartily endorsed this aspect of Prosyms. She wrote to John Houk, the project's director, "I think this compilation of injunctions one of the most useful contributions that I or any other consultant can make to the project." She was so supportive of it, in fact, that she provided SORO with over sixty extra injunctions free of charge.[26]

But seven months after joining the project, Mintz began to have reservations about its methodology. Prosyms consultants designed psychological appeals—persuasive messages directed at specific target populations—but the study design did not include plans to test them on Indonesian audiences. Rather, consultants assessed each others' appeals. Mintz completed her evaluations, but she refused to allow SORO to pay her for her time. When a SORO secretary urged her to accept a check so as not to confuse the organization's bookkeeping, Mintz explained, "I have such serious misgivings about the usefulness of this particular assignment that I simply cannot take the taxpayers' money for it." The more time Mintz spent on Prosyms, the more concerned she became about its scientific soundness. She objected that the definitions of particular Indonesian audiences were too crudely drawn, based on the faulty assumption that Indonesian society could be broken into "a series of fairly homogenous strata," when in fact alignments among ethnic, occupational, and political groups were complex and in tremendous flux. Some of the appeals she had been asked to evaluate were so flawed that she noted to herself, "Were some of these slipped in as gags, or to see if we were awake?" Her concern about the methodological design of Prosyms led her to contact officials at the Defense Department to discuss it.[27] She ended her consulting relationship with SORO shortly thereafter.

Mintz's anxieties about Prosyms were based neither on a concern that psychological warfare or military-funded communications research was immoral, nor on reservations that it drew scholars too close to the national security state. She did not see in the study any of the manipulation about which Wilfred Cantwell Smith had agonized. In her eyes, Prosyms was designed to prevent communist infiltration of independent nations; it was a fundamentally anti-imperialist, pro-democratic project well in keeping with her political values. She participated willingly in the creation of psychological appeals designed to promote conflict among military officers, alienate the military from civilians, and encourage enlisted men to commit sabotage. Mintz betrayed no concern that U.S. involvement in such activities might be unethical. American psychological warfare planners had long insisted that their propaganda was always based on facts—believed to be neutral by definition—and was thus immune to the charge that it constituted manipulation.[28] DeLong had argued the same in his letter to Smith in 1960. For Mintz, the study's shortcomings lay not in its political implications, but in its scientific deficiencies. She was dedicated to producing what she and many of her colleagues in the policy research community viewed as scientifically unassailable work of use to American policymakers and soldiers. She would tolerate nothing less. Prosyms' director spoke to her concerns when he wrote to her, "I know you know that we are attempting, as scientifically as our own experience and training will permit, to conduct useful research under the assignment and limitations under which we necessarily work."[29]

She did understand, for she joined SORO three years later. In 1964, after she completed her degree, the research office offered her a "shockingly well-paid" job as a senior research scientist. Mintz regarded it as a matter of course that although her area of scholarly expertise was Indonesia, she had been hired to perform research on Vietnam. She wrote to her adviser at Harvard, "Washington, as you well know, is a strange place and my new assignment there is apparently no stranger than some other things that go on there in the name of research." He responded encouragingly: "When I see the situation in Vietnam all turning bright and cheery I will know that you have been hard at work."[30]

Mintz quickly settled into SORO's mission of combining social-scientific and military expertise. She began work on Project Succindex, the code name for a research study with the cumbersome title "Effectiveness Measurements of U.S. Overseas Counterinsurgency and Country Modernization Programs." Succindex was designed to create a "success index," a qualitative model that would measure army progress toward counterinsurgency and development goals around the world. When American involvement in Vietnam escalated, Mintz tailored Succindex to gauge American success there. At the request of Seymour Deitchman, the director of counterinsurgency research in the Defense Advanced Research Projects Agency, she spent the spring of 1965 interviewing American personnel in the armed services, the Central Intelligence Agency, and the U.S. Agency for

International Development who had recently returned from extensive tours of duty. Based on these interviews, supplemented by research in classified Pentagon files, Mintz assessed the strengths and weaknesses of the American effort.[31]

Succindex required Mintz to traverse the boundary between the scholarly disinterestedness upon which her report's authority would rest and the inescapably political nature of her subject. Her colleagues could have criticized her report for transgressing the rules of social-scientific engagement, for it was highly critical of the American effort in Vietnam and suggested significant policy changes. Mintz argued that the evidence she had gathered pointed to an indisputable fact. "This is a political war," she explained, "a war for popular support. Therefore, political ends must shape military actions and not the reverse." American success would be decided not by bullets and bombs, but by bolstering popular support for democracy and capitalism among the Vietnamese peasantry. Mintz stressed that the American government could only achieve this goal by fully integrating its military and civil forces on the ground. She offered a blunt conclusion: "The present deployment of US and GVN [Government of Vietnam] resources is wrong," and she accused the army of fighting a war without a "doctrine, a concept for victory and an overall plan."[32]

In spite of its critical tone and its stark insistence on a fundamental reorientation of Pentagon policy, Mintz's report met with remarkable support from some senior policymakers. George A. Carroll, a White House staff member, informed Mintz's superiors that the report was, without doubt, the "best thing I have seen produced" by SORO. McGeorge Bundy—a senior national security adviser, an architect of the Johnson administration's escalation strategy, and soon to be one of its critics—requested a copy of the report. And Colonel Edward Lansdale, senior liaison to the U.S. Mission to South Vietnam and a top counterinsurgency expert, endorsed Mintz's conclusions as "ageless."[33]

Mintz's audience of policymakers and policy analysts did not question her critique of American policy, nor did they accuse her of politicizing her research or overstepping the bounds of her technical expertise. Mintz, members of the Johnson administration, and the military men directing the effort in South Vietnam might disagree over the proper balance of political and military initiatives, but they all agreed on their primary goal. When it came to the ends of American policy in Southeast Asia—a South Vietnamese nation liberated from communism by U.S. forces—Mintz and the Johnson administration saw "eye to eye." She understood her commitment to a "free" Vietnam just as she had her allegiance to Indonesian independence: not as a political or partisan position that endangered her social-scientific neutrality, but as a fundamentally righteous embrace of democratic goals, defined principally as the extension of political justice and social welfare through the eradication of communism. Mintz, like DeLong, subscribed to a model of elite-directed democracy. She was not even particularly critical of Indonesian president Sukarno's "guided democracy," which replaced the young nation's short-lived parliamentary democracy with a system of autocratic, personalized rule in which public participation was limited and political oppression common.[34] Yet she differed from DeLong in important ways. As her work for Succindex showed, she believed that scientific research should be simultaneously instrumental and critical. With expertise came responsibility and accountability to the ends to which research might be applied. For Mintz the best expertise was based on both scientific rationality and an unwavering commitment to certain fundamental values.

Even so, Mintz, like DeLong, maintained a methodological cleavage of fact and value. While she saw her research agenda as directed by values, within the bounds of individual research projects she strove to ensure that her work was unassailably objective—that it revealed verifiable truths. Mintz was not unique in her commitment. As Harold Lasswell explained, sound policy research "calls for the choice of problems which will contribute to the goal values of the scientist, and the use of scrupulous objectivity and maximum technical ingenuity in executing the projects undertaken."[35] The problem with Prosyms Indonesia was its failure to reflect the social structure of Indonesian society accurately. The problem with U.S. policy in Vietnam was that it was improperly suited to the situation on the ground. Mintz's work on Succindex underscores the ways in which advocacy of the status quo made value commitments appear neutral and scientific. Succindex may have offered conclusions critical of U.S. policy. But as an objective social-scientific project that limited its criticism to the method of U.S. actions in Vietnam, it bestowed scientific authority upon the larger political status quo: the Cold War commitment to the containment of communism through American military and political intervention. Mintz dwelt comfortably in the world of contract research, where the ends of the national security state were in harmony with her own values. As a scientific advocate for elite values, Mintz easily managed the tensions between expertise and democracy. Furthermore, she thrived in her hybrid role, betraying no anxiety about her close relationship to the concerns of American national security.

Robert Boguslaw and the Tribulations of "Voyeuristic Positivism"

Despite their differences over the political role of the social scientist, Mintz and DeLong were united in their endorsement of a democracy that relied more on administrative elites and experts than on popular participation. The sociologist and systems analyst Robert Boguslaw, like his colleagues Mintz and DeLong, sought to bring objective knowledge to bear on political decision making. Yet throughout his career, he argued that the tension between expertise and democracy was best resolved by rejecting value neutrality and openly embracing the political nature of expertise. Fact and value, he insisted, could not be separated; doing so made science antidemocratic.

Boguslaw's social science was a deeply moral and political crusade. His work was marked by a profound interest in bringing knowledge to bear on the practical problems of modern social life. He explained, "I have always felt that 'earning a living' was not enough—that somehow I would like to leave the world a better place than it was when I found it." Like Mintz, he saw more opportunities to do so by working in the gray area where knowledge met politics, rather than in academe. After earning his PhD in sociology from New York University in 1954, Boguslaw joined RAND's systems analysis staff. He spent eleven years at RAND and its affiliate Systems Development Corporation (SDC). Boguslaw maintained that it was far from unusual for someone dedicated to solving social problems to be a systems analyst for the military. His national security work, like Earl DeLong's, was motivated by the American encounter with fascism. Although Boguslaw abhorred the military as "a specialized institution for mass violence," he emphasized that he could not ignore its positive role in world history, as evidenced by the defeat of totalitarians such as Hitler and Mussolini. Like his colleagues at SORO, Boguslaw argued that social science could reform the military, replacing its instruments of destruction with a socially constructive and progressive international mission—the peaceful expansion of participatory democracy.[36] The military, for Boguslaw, need not necessarily militarize the social sciences; rather, the social sciences could civilianize the military.

That, however, was not the social science Boguslaw found at RAND and SDC. While working on arms control research, he witnessed firsthand the irrationality of the intellectual concepts fueling the Cold War, particularly RAND's favorite brainchild, mutually assured destruction. The systems approach to deterrence was logically sound, he admitted, yet it was utterly detached from basic human values. Experts' narrow focus on military hardware—on means, rather than ends—left no room for policymakers to entertain the possibility of nuclear disarmament.[37]

He thought that SORO might challenge RAND's hold over national security planning by introducing a competing paradigm of policy research— empirical, comparative, interdisciplinary studies of social and political change. Boguslaw joined SORO in 1965 to work on Project Camelot, one of the most infamous Cold War social science projects. A long-range, ambitious study of the causes of social revolution, it sought to create a behavioral scientific model that, in order to circumvent revolution, would identify when and why nations underwent violent change.[38] For Boguslaw, Camelot offered something that RAND's systems approach to policymaking did not. The long-term comparative study of revolution would replace RAND's hyperrational social engineering with a finely grained appreciation for social facts and processes on the ground. Furthermore, Boguslaw argued, it could democratize American foreign and military policy, in effect replacing DeLong's and Mintz's elite-guided system with a pluralist, participatory one. Despite its military patronage, Boguslaw pointed out, the study was unclassified and therefore open to the participation of university scholars. It boasted a staff of researchers and consultants that created what he considered an open intellectual community—a cohort of academics, including Johns Hopkins sociologist James S. Coleman and Harvard economist Thomas Schelling, joined by defense researchers. Boguslaw hoped that Camelot could counteract the authoritarian tendencies of the political elites who ran the national security state.[39] By enabling experts to offer alternative prescriptions for U.S. policy, Camelot could encourage policymakers to incorporate a diversity of voices into decision making, challenging the political status quo and producing a more pluralistic approach to foreign and military policy.

Boguslaw argued vehemently throughout his career that he had joined the research institutions of the national security state to democratize them. He saw himself not as a detached policy analyst who carefully separated research from application, but as an intellectual descendent of Charles Beard, John Dewey, and Robert Lynd—men who argued for the application of relevant, empirical knowledge to public life. Like a small number of sociologists in the 1960s, Boguslaw was an outspoken critic of value neutrality in social research. He argued that removing one's values from social inquiry was impossible, for a scholar's moral compass directed him to the very questions he asked. But more important, he claimed, value neutrality was senseless. It stripped social science of all its power. Echoing his fellow sociologists Alvin W. Gouldner, Irving L. Horowitz, and C. Wright Mills, Boguslaw argued that the scholar who thought he had removed the taint of values from his work simply reproduced the status quo. By avoiding analyses that touched on sensitive or controversial topics, he implicitly supported the values of ruling elites. Boguslaw accused his contemporaries of toiling in "a morass of inconsequentiality" by "rigorously avoiding analysis of critical social and political issues." For Boguslaw, the quest for value neutrality consigned social science to irrelevance.[40]

The attempt to achieve value neutrality also made scholarship dangerous to participatory democracy. Unlike Mintz and DeLong, Boguslaw believed that knowledge was influenced by the matrix of power relations in which it was produced, and furthermore, that it was itself a form of power. He argued that social scientists who embraced value neutrality bequeathed their intellectual power and political authority to ruling elites. In 1965, the same year he joined SORO, Boguslaw completed his most important work, *The New Utopians: A Study of System Design and Social Change*, for which he won the C. Wright Mills Award from the Society for the Study of Social Problems. In it he argued that systems designers built models that, as a result of designers' attempts to be value neutral, reified the values of ruling elites and implicitly supported the status quo. Echoing Jacques Ellul's 1964 critique of RAND's socio-technical systems—he argued they eroded human agency by taking on a life of their own—Boguslaw charged that systems analysts removed political agency from the public and invested it in themselves and their patrons. They forced elites' values upon a public that might not subscribe to them and could not recognize or challenge them, masked as they were by automated systems running on hyperlogical models obscured by technical jargon. Systems analysts, Boguslaw concluded, left Americans "occupying the role of bystander" in their social and political lives. Ostensibly value-free social science was not simply technocratic, he insisted; it was totalitarian. Boguslaw argued that a government aided by such technical expertise was "potentially much more authoritarian than that of any despot in modern history." Value-neutral researchers such as DeLong might claim that they were engaged in an open-minded, communitarian pursuit of truth that ultimately contributed to human freedom. But in fact, Boguslaw insisted, they toiled "on behalf of entrenched existing power centers."[41] Value-neutral social science, far from protecting American democracy, threatened it.

Boguslaw's attack on value neutrality was at base a critique of the expert-directed democracy championed by many twentieth-century social scientists, including most of his colleagues at SORO. For Mintz and DeLong, the affinity between science and the state ensured rational politics. For Boguslaw, it threatened "creeping totalitarianism"—the expansion of elite bureaucratic and technological control over the thoughts, actions, and values of all citizens, scholars included. As political and intellectual power became further embedded in the large bureaucratic and technical systems on which American governance rested, he argued, "the shape of power is becoming more and more obscure." Rather than abetting the extension of bureaucratic power, he called for social scientists to lay bare its operations to the public. Recalling the Deweyan commitment to educated public participation in politics and Mills's exhortation that intellectuals speak truth to power, Boguslaw argued for a science of "radical social action" that could challenge the national security state's undemocratic hold on power. Social science could offer reasoned politics. It could predict the outcomes of certain choices, helping the public to make enlightened judgments about the ends they desired and the means to achieve them. But even further, Boguslaw's social scientist would protect participatory democracy by using his analytical skills to ensure that no single interest group amassed too much control over the institutions, intellectual foundations, and values of American society. The social scientist's duty was to encourage a truly pluralist exchange of ideas—unlike more radical sociologists of the generation, Boguslaw was no critic of democratic pluralism—by keeping power relations in plain view. Boguslaw argued that "to be a scientist . . . must ultimately involve being a committed person—a person who is ready to confront clashes of values and search for a meaningful philosophy of life."[42] The scientist committed to human progress combined his expertise with his conscience, producing scientifically sound *and* relevant, accessible knowledge.

Much of Boguslaw's written work railed against the detached expert who resided in a "protected harbor of passive, voyeuristic positivism that disclaims responsibility for social action." And as much as he decried the cleavage of fact and value in Pentagon social research, Boguslaw found its root cause not in political circumstances, but in social scientific hyperprofessionalism. He agreed with DeLong's antitotalitarian prescription that "the search for truth . . . requires the right to dissent from existing dogma." But DeLong identified dogma with the advocacy of universal values, whereas Boguslaw argued that "scientific societies and scientific journals are notorious for their insistence upon dogmas of all kinds: the dogma of acceptable methodology, the dogma of report format, the implicit dogma of acceptable areas for investigation." Far more than any patron's dollars, professional standards constrained researchers' intellectual freedom and the political potential of social knowledge. Academics' reliance on the financial resources of the ivory tower and on journals to publish results, for example, pressured them to appear disinterested. Like Dewey, Beard, and Gouldner before him, Boguslaw charged that the demand that social science be unbiased led scholars to avoid studying relevant problems for fear that they would create controversy and consequently lose funding or the chance to publish. The "ethical" principle that condemned bias, he sneered, might be phrased as: "Never engage in a study which deals with nontrivial aspects of social and political life."[43] In opposition to scholars who thought that the source of investigational bias was external to research, Boguslaw believed that politics—and thus values— were always present in scientific work. In the name of participatory democracy, scholars must bring those values into the open.

Although Boguslaw assailed DeLong's value neutrality and Mintz's scientized advocacy of the status quo, the three Sorons shared an important common ground. Like nearly all midcentury social scientists, Boguslaw believed that the scientific study of social phenomena was the path to truth, and he embraced the idea that social and political progress occurred through the application of science to society. His adherence to objectivity and scientific progress offered enough middle ground to make him a highly respected member of SORO. When the research office underwent a major reorganization in early 1966, he was named director of its Social Science Research Division, the unit responsible for all SORO research projects, including those conducted at its field units in Panama and South Korea. And he had enough credibility and authority among Washington policymakers that the State Department's Foreign Service Institute hired him to teach an intensive course for high-level government officials titled "Cuba from a Distance."[44]

Although he was accepted by both social scientists and policymakers, Boguslaw found that his hopes for bringing a plurality of voices and participatory democracy to the national security state were too optimistic. Shortly after he joined SORO, the Defense Department canceled Project Camelot. As the next chapter describes, the study had sparked a minor diplomatic crisis when Chilean scholars learned of it, and of its Pentagon sponsorship. In the United States, a small group of outspoken academic social scientists attacked the project as an egregious example of the Pentagon's militarization of social research. Boguslaw, however, interpreted Project Camelot's abrupt cancellation not as an indication that the project was intellectually or ethically flawed, but as confirmation that the powerful figures who controlled the national security state would not allow a study with such radical democratic potential to move forward. Unclassified and open to collaborators from across universities and government-funded research institutes, Camelot "carried the implicit threat of uncontrollable access to information and its uncontrollable dissemination." In his mind, had the study succeeded, it would have challenged the status quo and increased public participation in foreign policy.[45]

Disillusioned with SORO in the wake of Camelot's cancellation, Boguslaw left the research office in mid-1966 for the Department of Sociology at Washington University in St. Louis. His new intellectual home suited him well—the department was a hotbed of social-scientific radicalism. Although he left full-time government research, Boguslaw never surrendered his hope that contract research might successfully serve the public interest. He continued to perform work for the federal government and to consult at SDC, although he largely withdrew from national security research. He never accomplished his goal of creating a publicly accessible scientific basis for participatory democratic action—virtually none of his work was intellectually accessible to the public, and he turned increasingly to existentialist philosophy to understand the role of knowledge in public life. As one reviewer of his later work explained, while Boguslaw offered a trenchant and important critique of expert social planning, he discussed his topics at "such an abstract level that it is difficult to relate them to real-world experiences," choosing instead to launch into "exegeses of Sartre and Althusser." While his work drew on a popular school of philosophical thought, his inscrutable language and abstract defenses of democracy were not conducive to attracting a broad readership, let alone enhancing democratic participation.[46]

Neither Boguslaw nor other critics of value neutrality, such as Mills and Gouldner, solved the problem of the relationship between expert knowledge and democratic action. For Boguslaw, as for most midcentury social scientists, values and goals had no scientific justification. They were "simply prime factors." The *is* of scholarship could never objectively prescribe the *ought* of political action. But if fact and value could not be separated—if the social sciences were inherently normative—there was little to ensure that value-committed scholarship qualified as democratically reliable expertise. While Mintz's and DeLong's solutions to the problem of expert knowledge in a democracy privileged elite governance at the expense of public participation, Boguslaw's position challenged the authority of expertise itself. If knowledge was not disinterested, but rather was laden with political and moral commitments, then what was to distinguish a credentialed expert's advice from political advocacy or propaganda?[47] Boguslaw's normative science protected participatory democracy, but it could threaten the very foundation of expert authority.

It also masked the central role militarization played in his philosophy and career. The sociologist criticized the national security state for mobilizing expertise in an antidemocratic manner. Yet the fact that he turned to the institutions of the gray area to avoid working in "a morass of inconsequentiality" and to "leave the world a better place" signaled how deeply militarization shaped his sense of agency. As Catherine Lutz argues, the Cold War changed the meanings of democratic citizenship by centralizing state power and containing political and intellectual dissent.[48] Boguslaw's experience indicates that even dissenting intellectuals who tried to challenge militarization's constraints could be blind to its ubiquity. By claiming to speak truth to power from within the military-industrial-academic complex, Boguslaw located the center of social research and democracy within the institutions of the national security state. Ironically, the Soron who was perhaps most committed to challenging the political status quo in American politics reinforced it.

Militarization Ascendant

Scholars who worked in the gray area between the ivory tower and the national security state, like generations of American social scientists, confronted a quandary: was science inherently neutral, entering the realm of politics and power only when applied, or was scholarly neutrality itself a fiction? At stake in their answers were the meaning and purpose of expert knowledge and American democracy. Was democracy best promoted by a cadre of service intellectuals like Earl DeLong, who produced objective truths but left ends, goals, and application to political elites? By scientific advocates like Jeanne Mintz, scholars who argued that with their expertise came a responsibility to work in Washington for ends that they deemed just? Or by radical social actionists such as Robert Boguslaw, who openly advocated specific ethical values based on the belief that knowledge itself was fundamentally political? Within the military-industrial-academic complex, the problem of the relationship between expertise and action, science and democracy, was fractured into a spectrum of coexisting positions. For Boguslaw, knowledge was fundamentally political; democratic politics could not be reduced to science. Democracy was not a vague quest for the expansion of human freedom, but an open and ongoing debate about social and political values among an educated public. But DeLong and Mintz believed that elites, aided by value-free expertise, could strip subjectivity from political life, rendering politics apolitical. In typical Cold War fashion, democracy meant the gradual, orderly expansion of a vaguely defined human freedom under the wise guidance of policy elites.

Despite these differences, the three Sorons shared a consensus about militarization. Unlike Eisenhower, Sorons worried not at all that their work threatened the rightful distribution of political power. Mintz's relationship to the national security state was perhaps the most honest; she never felt the need to justify her work. Boguslaw's position, by contrast, seemed almost hypocritical; he simultaneously attacked and served the state's ends. Regardless, all three accepted and abetted the permeation of national security concerns in their work. And Boguslaw and DeLong, in particular, also hid from themselves their own complicity in the militarization of American politics and foreign policy.

Boguslaw's argument that scholarly neutrality was little more than a pseudo-scientific endorsement of elite values held little traction among social scientists and the American public until the second half of the 1960s. Instead, DeLong's ideal of the service intellectual motivated social scientists until the height of the Vietnam War. Whereas Boguslaw obscured militarization behind his radical politics, service intellectuals obscured it behind technique. This phenomenon reached its acme, as Sharon Ghamari-Tabrizi writes, in the work of RAND analyst Herman Kahn, whose infamous *On Thermonuclear War* framed nuclear holocaust "in the bloodless dialect of probabilistic risk assessment." This proclivity was common at SORO, albeit in less grandiose fashion. The service intellectual's obsession with technique animated Doris Condit's Project Numismatics, which sought to streamline American intervention in third world conflicts by correlating complex political, military, and social psychological variables with the outcomes of various counterinsurgency efforts. It drove SORO director Theodore Vallance's quest to render propaganda scientific by breaking psychological warfare campaigns into a systematic series of dependent and independent variables. And it resulted in products like Soron Albert Frances's 1967 dissertation, a seven-hundred page behemoth with the inscrutable title "Structural and Anticipatory Dimensions of Violent Social Conflict," which proposed to systematize the social science of violent revolution.[49]

The democratic theory on which the symbiosis of science and democracy rested also extended the militarization of American foreign policy. According to many Americans, the nation's rational, pluralistic democracy guaranteed its stability. The flip side of democratic stability was communist revolution. Much of SORO's research, including Project Camelot, was based on a handful of popular hypotheses about the causes of violent social and political change. Social scientists believed that revolutions were often instigated by marginalized people suffering from anomie. According to scholars like Daniel Lerner and Seymour Martin Lipset, anomie was endemic in the modernizing nations where the transition from rural to urban life, and from tradition to modernity, uprooted people from old social bonds. If enough people became marginalized, they threatened social and political stability. Social scientists reasoned that the United States had successfully avoided this unhappy state in its own history because of the rich pluralism of its public sphere and its commitment to democracy as a process. SORO consultant Ted Gurr suggested that nations threatened by marginal groups should seek to reintegrate them into mainstream public life through Americanesque civic groups. From these insights came a SORO study called Project Leader, for which researchers studied the personality qualities that gave certain foreign youth the charisma and political acumen to lead anticommunist youth groups.[50]

Yet for all their interest in remaking the third world in America's image, social scientists also lent credibility to the American tendency to see the United States as profoundly separate from the rest of the world. Harry Eckstein, a pioneer of the scientific study of limited war and a senior adviser to SORO, asked in the early 1960s, what is it that makes democracy stable? Looking around the world, he decided that the United States was the only truly stable democracy. He hypothesized that the nation was built on such a careful balance of different systems—political and social, personal and psychological—that its replication elsewhere was quite improbable. Eckstein theorized that in order to achieve stability, a nation's political system had to match its social system. An authoritarian people, in other words, might in fact need an authoritarian government.

This conclusion seemed to indicate that all men were not "natural democrats." As a result, Eckstein explained, the American hope that the world was turning to democracy might be ill-founded; in some nations, the heavier hand of military government might be justified. He wrote, "For our own world we need a more pessimistic approach to democratic government, . . . one which directs attention to those calamitously improbable combinations of circumstances which actually make democracy work."[51]

In other words, cutting-edge social theory indicated that American democracy was unique and that other nations might only be able to approximate it. This scientifically validated bifurcation helped make possible what Marilyn Young has aptly called the "solipsism" of American Cold War policy, a policy driven by the idea that America is historically exceptional, politically powerful, and internationally unaggressive. It was a short step from Eckstein's argument to a scientific justification of American military policy toward much of the developing world. For all their democratic rhetoric, American policymakers and social scientists frequently supported military dictatorships and other autocratic regimes. Yet, if all men were not natural democrats, perhaps some were naturally subservient to autocrats. Democratic politics could not be forced on undemocratic peoples. In fact, Eckstein argued, the most stable system of all governments was a relatively permissive dictatorship—a polity not so overbearing that people experienced the anomie of being excluded from public action, but not so permissive that political life became chaotic and unstable.[52]

Boguslaw, of course, would have none of Eckstein's argument. But even so, he applied himself to Project Camelot—a study that drew extensively on the Princeton political scientist's work—with zeal. And indeed, it was that project's fate that would begin to unravel the symbiosis of science and democracy. Just as important, it would challenge social scientists' easy, often unconscious, embrace of militarization. Boguslaw's arguments for radical social action, however, would have nothing whatever to do with that sudden development.

DEEPER SHADES OF GRAY
Ambition and Deception in Project Camelot

Galvanized by researchers' sense of America's democratic righteousness, SORO charged ahead in late 1964 with a bold new attack on the problem of communist insurgency. Combining insights from anthropology, psychology, political science, and sociology, the research office promised to unearth the fundamental causes of communist revolution and prescribe antidotes to them. Researchers informed their sponsors that they should "anticipate the possibility of spectacular results."[1]

SORO's staff hailed this multiyear, multimillion-dollar unclassified investigation as the Manhattan Project of social science. Promising a breakthrough in "peace research," Robert Boguslaw described it as "an attempt to find nonmilitary and nonviolent solutions to international problems." Sorons hoped that social science would inject reason and rationality into American relationships with the third world. The study's name—Project Camelot—captured its reformist ambitions. Invoking the title of a 1960 Broadway musical hit based on the legend of King Arthur, social scientists associated their research with the mythical court's imagined world of truth, justice, and prosperity. SORO's director, psychologist Theodore Vallance, explained that Project Camelot stood for "the development of a stable society with domestic tranquility and peace and justice for all."[2]

Tranquility and peace, however, did not lie in Project Camelot's future. In the summer of 1965, months before data collection was scheduled to begin, the study triggered a minor international crisis. Scholars and government officials in Chile learned that the research was sponsored not by a university or a research foundation, but by the Defense Department. A study that Americans deemed peace research appeared to Latin Americans as a prelude to American military invasion. Chilean politicians and scholars charged that the Pentagon had enlisted social scientists in an international "shadow-army" of spies and guerrillas. That allegation spread around the globe, appearing on the front pages of newspapers from Montevideo to Belgrade to Addis Ababa.[3]

Social scientists and historians have frequently treated the Camelot incident as a crucial turning point in the history of military-funded research; Camelot's denouement, so the argument goes, was the moment when the Cold War intellectual consensus exploded and the gray area between academe and the military became inhospitable, if not uninhabitable. Ron Robin, for example, characterizes the Camelot episode as a "Paradigm Lost." In its wake, he asserts, the Cold War "supernarrative of behavioralism as an extension of the natural sciences appeared to self-destruct."[4] In fact, the tale is significantly more complicated. Camelot's critics hoped to draw attention to the problems of militarization in social science and American foreign affairs. But the Camelot fiasco would result in remarkably few changes to the gray area. Nor would it do much to rein in the Pentagon's influence in Washington. Camelot drew embarrassing public attention to a long-simmering problem in Washington as the State Department and the Pentagon wrangled over which agency was best equipped to manage American foreign policy. Civilian government officials responded to Camelot with outrage, charging that its existence proved their worst fears: the Pentagon was attempting to seize control of foreign policy making from the State Department.

It seemed, for a time, that Camelot offered scholars and government officials the opportunity to address the Pentagon's growing influence over science and national security. Instead, they sought bureaucratic solutions to the conflict. These solutions would affect social research, but in ways far more subtle than any paradigm shift. Faced with the reality that the State Department might derail their research, scholars allied with the Pentagon. Their actions, ironically, enhanced the militarization of social science and foreign policy.

Project Camelot's Ambitious Rise

In its rhetoric and design, Project Camelot captured the confidence and optimism of postwar American social science. Promising to unite cutting-edge social theory with Cold War military strategy, it was the ultimate incarnation of the gray area. Its designers believed they would soon offer the U.S. military scientific tools to engineer third world stability and democracy. Camelot was, of course, only a code name. The project's official, if rather cumbersome, title—"Methods for Predicting and Influencing Social Change and Internal War Potential"—revealed its ambition. It promised to create a dynamic computerized model of the mechanisms of social change—a model capable of forecasting how and when any nation would undergo violent change. By the early 1960s, modernization theory was as popular in Washington as it was in American social science. To many policymakers, instability and post-independence nation building appeared to go hand in hand. To circumvent the volatility that bred communism, Camelot's planners reasoned, they needed to know more about when internal wars break out, why, and what measures the U.S. government could take to contain unrest. Armed with a computer model that would "let the experimenter see the [revolutionary process] unfold before his eyes," Camelot would do just that.[5]

The project would start with the basics of social theory. To predict social change, researchers first needed to enhance their theoretical and empirical grasp of social conflict, an area of research still in its infancy. They planned to spend a year constructing an analytical model of social change that identified which "social variables"—rates of urbanization, achievement motivation, and other indicators of modernization—most directly correlated to insurgency. Camelot's planning staff grounded the project in academic research at the forefront of political development and internal warfare studies. The names of scholars like Gabriel Almond, Sidney Verba, and E. E. Hagen graced the footnotes of its research design. Princeton political scientist Harry Eckstein's theory of revolution formed the backbone of Camelot's analytical framework. He argued that a systematic understanding of revolution could only be reached once scholars learned to differentiate the "precipitants" of revolution—those events that spark violence, such as economic deprivation or communist agitation—from its "preconditions"—the deep structural causes of revolution, like social inequality and political alienation.[6]

Once armed with their analytical model, researchers would begin testing it against empirical data. First, they planned to write twenty-one historical case studies of internal conflicts, ranging from the Argentinean Revolution of 1943 to the 1960 military coup in Turkey. After using their historical case studies to further refine their analytical social systems model, they would spend two years conducting five in-depth field studies of contemporary societies susceptible to revolution. Sorons considered Bolivia, Colombia, Paraguay, Peru, and Venezuela likely candidates for field research, but they contemplated stationing researchers in Africa and Asia as well. Finally, after using these field studies

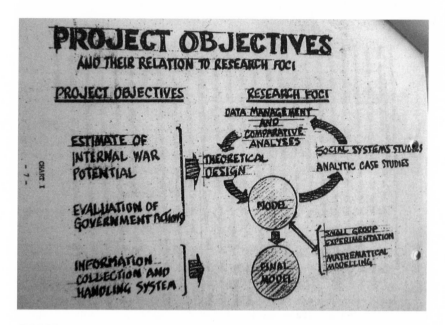

FIGURE 1.   SORO's illustration of Project Camelot's iterative research process. SORO, "Project Camelot: Design and Phasing," February 1, 1965, p. 5.

to refine their social systems model yet again, they would complete the project with a "one-country study"—an intensive field investigation of a nation facing a serious communist threat. The one-country study would serve as the final test of Camelot's predictive and prescriptive accuracy.[7]

Camelot's planners boasted that the study would effect a "quantum jump" in social research and military advising. Vallance explained to his staff that he expected the study would help the United States and indigenous governments improve their abilities to "undercut the forces of insurgency and, at the same time, maintain a good rate of social, economic, and political development." Camelot would prove the value of militarily-relevant social science to both soldiers and scholars. It would accomplish the perfect union of scholarship and operations, and further the cause of peace in the process. As one official briefed on the project explained, "Intellectually, Camelot reflects the faith that research can, in the immediate future, arrive at generalizations about complex social matters that are abstract enough to have serious theoretical significance and still retain immediate practical utility."[8] The study was a test of the viability of the gray area itself.

Unlike other SORO projects, Camelot drew elite social scientists into the research office's orbit. As the process of designing the study got under way in the fall of 1964, Vallance traveled to Columbia, MIT, and Harvard, as well as the Russell Sage Foundation, the Ford Foundation, and the Social Science Research Council, to discuss the project. He boasted that he had circulated SORO's early research plans among "65 of the best and best-known members of the social science fraternity."[9] By the following spring, Vallance arranged for Eckstein, William Kornhauser, and Charles Tilly to spend a month in residence at the research office in the summer of 1965. Johns Hopkins sociologist James S. Coleman planned to spend the entire summer there, designing the mathematical models for Camelot's computer simulations.[10] The Army Research Office, too, sought to enhance Camelot's academic credentials. It contracted with the National Academy of Sciences, an honorific society composed of the nation's most distinguished scientific minds, to create an advisory committee of elite scholars who would also oversee Camelot's design and management.[11]

Vallance and the AU administration were optimistic that Camelot's scholarly standing would earn SORO a new, more academic reputation free from the martial and "clandestine implications" of the term Special Operations. The research office was in the process of rolling out a new journal. Titled *Conflict: A Quarterly Journal of Revolution and Social Change*, it was designed to provide a common ground for scholars, contract researchers, policymakers, and military men engaged with the problems of "radical social change in the world today." Its inaugural issue included an article on Vietnam by Henry Cabot Lodge, as well as contributions from U.S. Information Agency officials and Sorons. The journal reflected SORO's long-standing conviction that counterinsurgency was a subject as much scholarly as it was martial. In a piece introducing the new journal, Vallance opined that "the term *counterinsurgency*—however it may be defined—will never adequately describe the measures required to usher in change with a minimum of upheaval. The subject of our inquiry in fact is the entire range of problems and processes which can cause disequilibrium within or between societies—not merely the military or political consequences of those problems." Such problems transcended the military research communities. Counterinsurgency was merely "the rubric under which fall [*sic*] the study of processes of large-scale social change," processes of immense interest to academic social scientists.[12] To augment SORO's growing public and scholarly presence, Vallance also suggested that American University and the army consider renaming SORO the "Social Science and Operations Research Office."[13]

Vallance turned to academia to staff Project Camelot's top position, hiring Brooklyn College sociologist Rex Hopper to direct the study. An expert on Latin American revolution and an experienced field researcher, Hopper had also taught at universities in Mexico, Argentina, and Paraguay. Like many of his colleagues at SORO, he found his way to social science through a youthful dedication to social change and humanitarian work. He first traveled to Latin America in the 1920s as a missionary, but discovered that such a role failed to satisfy his ambition to improve social and political conditions. After earning a PhD in sociology at the University of Texas, he returned to Latin America in the 1930s as a scholar of revolution and social change.[14]

As social change in the United States and abroad seemed to accelerate in the 1960s, Hopper approached his subject with a growing sense of urgency. He took a year of sabbatical from Brooklyn College to work on Project Camelot, but soon resigned his tenured faculty position to devote himself permanently to the study. Hopper's interest in revolution was not merely academic. By the early 1960s, he worried that the United States might be on the road to revolution. His studies of Latin American society had convinced him that violent social and political changes were preceded by the "emergence of a numerically significant, economically powerful, intellectually informed" group. He feared that such a group was beginning to form in the United States as the government—especially the military—relied increasingly on computers and systems analysis. This "cybernation," he argued, would place a small, privileged elite in power and leave average Americans politically alienated and economically obsolete. The world's greatest democracy could fall into "militarized and cybernatized totalitarianism."[15] The director of the military-industrial-academic complex's most ambitious study of counterinsurgency was motivated by his own fear of the garrison state.

Hopper's colleagues at SORO may not have been inspired by the specter of impending revolution in the United States, but they were galvanized by the hope that they could demilitarize American foreign policy. Echoing Boguslaw, Camelot consultant Jessie Bernard explained that the driving force behind the study was the conviction that "the goals sought by violence [could] be achieved by non-violent means."[16] Bernard, Hopper, and the other scholars who signed on to Project Camelot shared the conviction that had animated Sorons since the research office opened in 1956; as counterintuitive as it might seem, they argued, they could replace armed intervention with peaceful social engineering. The military's experts could disarm the military itself, reinventing it as a pacific instrument of modernization.

Camelot's Precipitous Fall

Project Camelot never came close to achieving social scientists' dreams. Three months before research was scheduled to begin, it sparked a diplomatic uproar. In the spring of 1965, University of Pittsburgh anthropologist, Camelot consultant, and Chilean native Hugo Nutini traveled to Chile on personal business.

Acting without the Pentagon's knowledge, he contacted over a hundred scholars, university administrators, and government officials to gauge their interest in the study. Rather than disclosing its Defense Department patronage, however, he claimed that the National Science Foundation was funding the study. He also allegedly informed his contacts that Seymour Martin Lipset and Robert K. Merton were members of the research team. Nutini's deception was flagrant. According to Gabriel Gyarmati, the director of the Sociological Research Center at Catholic University in Santiago, Nutini gave him a doctored version of Camelot's planning documents in which "references to U.S. Army . . . were crudely inked over and written above [them was] 'social scientists.'" Nutini's deception was also astonishingly transparent. Gyarmati reported that "by holding the paper up to the light it was possible to read the original wording."[17]

Not surprisingly, Nutini's fraud quickly caught up with him. Camelot's Pentagon sponsorship was no secret in the social science community. Because SORO and the military conceived of it as a project as much scholarly as martial in its orientation, it was unclassified. Hopper had publicized the study's planning documents widely, inviting dozens of Americans and a handful of foreign social scientists to join the project as consultants. Nutini had the misfortune to contact one of them while in Chile. Scandinavian sociologist Johan Galtung, in Chile in 1965 as a visiting professor, had rejected Hopper's invitation. He had objected to Camelot's implicit assumption that the American military could be a force for social progress. Nutini's lies gave Galtung the opportunity to publicly expose the study's flaws. Armed with his unblemished copy of SORO's planning documents, Galtung revealed Camelot's military sponsorship to Chilean scholars and government officials. Predictably, most were outraged. On June 12, the communist newspaper *El Siglo* took the story public in a front page story headlined "Yankees Study Invasion of Chile." Within the week, President Eduardo Frei denounced Camelot as an example of "unwanted and unacceptable interference in national life," and shortly thereafter, the government banned Nutini from Chile by invoking a law denying entry by "politically undesirable individuals." The outcry over what the Chilean press on both the left and the right called a "Pentagon plot" quickly captured the attention of the American embassy. On June 14, American ambassador to Chile Ralph Dungan fired an angry confidential cable to Washington demanding to know what the project was, who had sponsored it, and what Nutini was doing in Chile promoting such a "politically dangerous" Pentagon-funded research project without the embassy's knowledge.[18]

For the next two weeks, Dungan continued his tirade against Camelot in daily cables to his superiors. In Washington, State Department officials insisted in closed-door meetings that the Defense Department be held accountable for the foreign relations crisis in Chile, and the Defense Department attempted to

FIGURE 2.   Rex Hopper poses with a Chilean newspaper published in the days after Project Camelot's exposure. The headline reads, "Here Is the Proof of Yankee Espionage." Courtesy Janet Holt.

keep the incident out of the American press. But the Pentagon refused to take the blame for events in Chile. Its officials insisted truthfully that they had no plans to conduct research about Chile and that Project Camelot had not even begun. They claimed, perhaps less truthfully, that neither they nor SORO had authorized Nutini to contact Chilean nationals (some evidence indicates that SORO had provided Nutini with funding for his trip). And they reminded the State Department that its officials had already been briefed on the project—a State Department representative had a seat on Camelot's planning staff.[19]

State Department officials felt that they had reasonable cause for concern. Less than a month before Galtung exposed Camelot in Chile, the department had intervened in Camelot's study design when SORO proposed the French Canadian separatist movement as one of the project's historical case studies. In a confidential letter to the army's head of research and development, the State Department's assistant secretary for European affairs explained, "Canadians are always very sensitive to any implication—intended or not—of United States interference in things Canadian." A military-sponsored study of one of their most sensitive political problems was sure to damage U.S.-Canadian relations. In order to protect U.S. national security, the State Department urged the army to leave the Canadian issue alone. The army relented, and SORO dropped the Canadian case study from Camelot's design.[20]

Chilean officials reacted to Camelot just as State Department officials had predicted the Canadians might. Less than a week after *El Siglo* revealed the study, the Chilean Chamber of Deputies launched an investigation into whether Camelot infringed on Chilean sovereignty.[21] While U.S. military officials were willing to admit the impropriety of studying their modern neighbor to the north, they viewed Chile and other Latin American nations in very different terms. Pentagon officials accused Dungan and his colleagues of playing right into the hands of the Chilean communists that Camelot was designed to contain. In memos to State Department and White House officials, they defended Camelot as a scientifically sound, unclassified research study designed to assist "free nations." The State Department, they insisted, had been duped into thinking otherwise by Chilean leftists.[22]

With the Pentagon defending Camelot and unwilling to admit responsibility for the Chilean uproar, someone from the State Department (possibly Dungan himself) leaked the story to the American press. The informant blasted the project, calling its goal of scientifically engineering foreign relations "naïve and sometimes alarming," and characterized one State Department official's response to the project as one of "open-mouthed amazement." The tactic worked. On June 27, Camelot and the feud it sparked between the Pentagon and the State Department became front-page news in the United States. Congressional interest followed almost immediately. Three days after the story broke in American newspapers, Senator Eugene McCarthy demanded a congressional investigation into the episode and, more seriously, into whether the army had "intruded itself into the field of foreign policy without authority." He insisted that Congress examine the relationship between the Departments of State and Defense. The same day, the House Appropriations Committee promised a full inquiry into the Defense Department's behavioral research projects. An irritated President Lyndon Johnson, busy with the more pressing problem of Vietnam, instructed Secretary of State Dean Rusk to resolve the Camelot issue quickly. With Congress, the White House, and the press asking embarrassing questions, the Defense Department worked damage control. On the morning of July 8, hours before a congressional inquiry into Camelot was scheduled to convene, Secretary of Defense Robert McNamara announced abruptly that the Pentagon had canceled Project Camelot.[23] The study was dead before it began.

In the years after Camelot's cancellation, the project became synonymous with the outlandish and scientistic pretentions of Cold War social research. But

Camelot's sudden cancellation had little to do with its intellectual content. As Harry Eckstein argued of revolutions, cataclysmic events have both precipitants and preconditions, and Camelot's demise was only a precipitant in the growing conflict over militarized social research and foreign policy. As the Cold War blurred the lines between the martial and the diplomatic and the Pentagon encroached into foreign affairs, the relationship between the State Department and the Pentagon had grown increasingly antagonistic. The public outcry in Chile gave the State Department some much-needed ammunition to counter what many officials considered to be the military's unrelenting effort to use social science to legitimate the militarization of American foreign policy. Project Camelot was a casualty of the turf war between the Departments of State and Defense over which agency was best equipped to defend American national security. It was also a battle over what kind of expertise—scientific and militarized, or diplomatic and interpersonal—was best suited to international relations. And at its root, it reflected growing concern among American policymakers that the militarization of American foreign policy was beginning to threaten American national security and the nation's global reputation.

The theory that foreign policy should flow from the State Department to other federal agencies was a far cry from practice in the Cold War as the Departments of Commerce, Labor, Agriculture, the Treasury, and Defense became active players in international affairs.[24] One Senate report concluded in 1960 that, while the president had historically turned to the State Department to create foreign policy, "today, the sphere of the State Department is far narrower than the full range of contemporary foreign relations. As an organization, the State Department can now claim no greater concern in certain aspects of foreign policy than the Defense Department." And as the National Security Council took on an increasing responsibility for foreign policy during and after the Kennedy administration, the State Department's power diminished further. By the early 1960s, the State Department appeared to many in Washington to be an ineffectual bureaucratic behemoth. According to the media, Kennedy referred to the department as "a bowl of jelly," and he claimed with exasperation that he and his staff accomplished "more in one day than they do in six months." The Defense Department, too, had become a more proactive force in foreign policy making. Project Camelot was just one example of the department's turn to experts for advice in international affairs. Foreign policy experts worked in the Office of the Secretary of Defense, and military educational institutions increasingly offered students instruction in foreign affairs. By the time the Camelot story made news in the United States, the idea that "Defense, not State, really runs foreign policy" was widespread.[25]

Part of the State Department's problem was financial. While the Pentagon commanded over $20 million for social research contracts in 1965, the State Department spent only $125,000. Over a month before the Chileans discovered the study, State Department officials discussed the possibility that they might "use the Camelot occasion to communicate our discontent with the project *as research* and furthermore our more general discontent with the Defense Department's unrestrained expansion of its research activities into areas of central interest to State." Nutini gave them the opportunity they sought. Telegrams between Ralph Dungan and agency officials in Washington admitted candidly that the department resented the Pentagon's research budget. Officials worried that the Pentagon's largesse would "create a dollar competition for top notch personnel" that the State Department could never hope to win. The State Department was not worried about losing access to researchers' expertise; rather, officials worried that the Pentagon was using research to legitimize its encroachment into foreign policy. In a letter to Deputy Secretary of Defense Cyrus Vance, Dungan was blunt: "On one point I want to be completely clear. As long as I am in this position I intend to operate in a way which insures that primary responsibility for foreign policy decision making does not shift to the military services."[26]

For the ambassador, there was more at stake than funding or turf. He wrote a personal letter to Harold Brown, the director of defense research and engineering at the Pentagon, to warn him, "The continued militarization of problems which are essentially of a civil-political character would be disastrous . . . to the long-run interests of the United States." Brown was unmoved. He reminded Dungan that "the 'war of liberation' technique deliberately makes the boundaries among political, economic, social, and military matters vague." Thus, he said, the military, not the State Department, was responsible for overseas internal defense missions. Dungan objected to such an expansive view of internal defense. He remarked snidely, "If internal defense means dealing with the complex of social, political, and other matters, I am appalled and suggest maybe that you will want to start paying the rent at 21st and Virginia," the State Department's address.[27]

By drawing on scientific expertise to manage issues of American foreign and military relations, the Pentagon challenged the State Department's approach to foreign policy. As one observer noted, the agency's resistance to Project Camelot reflected "a latent State Department preference for politics as an art rather than politics as an object of science." State Department officials objected strenuously to Camelot's assumption that complex matters of foreign relations could—and should—be reduced to social scientific principles. Walt Rostow's position on the Policy Planning Council notwithstanding, many State Department officials viewed the attempt to scientize politics as wrongheaded and dangerous. Dungan wrote to Defense officials, "If you have a million and a half dollars to throw around, I could use a couple of political officers who would be worth much more than all the model makers that you could assemble." To his colleagues in Washington, he elaborated, "I think that someone in the Pentagon has gone completely crazy." He explained that he was alarmed at the volume of "over-funded, not very intelligent people, in and out of uniforms, but all funded by the military services" using social science research as a pretext to interfere in foreign policy and damaging foreign relations in the process. Camelot's ambition to turn diplomacy into applied science, and a militarized one at that, threatened American national security.[28]

But outside the State Department, the hope that politics could be an object of science was widespread. Unsurprisingly, social scientists criticized the State Department's approach to foreign policy as outdated. Called to testify before Congress about the federal government's use of social research, political scientist Gabriel Almond asserted that the department was "unduly skeptical and unduly slow in carrying on social science research." He elaborated, "I believe they are a backward agency, as far as their relationship with science is concerned." Elected officials concurred. After investigating the circumstances surrounding Camelot's cancellation, a subcommittee of the House's Committee on Foreign Affairs concluded that the State Department was to blame for the military's dominant role in both social research and foreign policy. Its conclusion was damning: "The civilian authorities charged with the conduct of our foreign policy have not succeeded" in properly mobilizing the social sciences for American national security.[29] Most policymakers and researchers agreed: the State Department had given the military no choice but to develop foreign policy expertise itself.

It was no secret in Washington that the State Department was using Camelot to rein in the Pentagon's increasing influence over foreign affairs. But the State Department's political maneuvering drew attention away from the militarization that Dungan had hoped to address. Social scientists at the National Academy of Sciences expressed frustration that "the behavioral sciences were regrettably caught in the middle of a conflict between the State Department and the Department of Defense." Seymour Deitchman, the head of counterinsurgency for the Pentagon's Advanced Research Projects Agency, described the State Department leak as part of "a carefully oriented sequence" that reflected a broader, "bureaucratically oriented malevolence" toward the Pentagon. In one congressional investigation of the study, Congressman Peter Frelinghuysen posed a rhetorical question to the army's head of social science research: Was the episode not, he asked, "an opportunity for the State Department to get back at what they basically are not enthusiastic about?"[30]

Yet whether Camelot could improve American foreign policy became irrelevant when it threatened to damage the nation's reputation abroad. The uproar over the study in Chile signaled that even if social science might one day prove a boon to American national security, it could also damage foreign relations. Unfortunately for the United States, Camelot's cancellation in early July did little to quell foreign concern. Throughout the summer, popular Chilean news radio programs broadcast reports alleging that the Americans were engaged in espionage efforts with the goal of carrying out a coup d'état.[31] In Cuba, state radio stations reported that a U.S. spy ring had been exposed in Chile. And U.S. embassies from Caracas to Zagreb fielded questions about Camelot from the press and concerned government officials.[32]

Camelot also damaged the Pentagon's and the State Department's reputations at home. By mid-July, Secretary of State Dean Rusk had been forced to testify about the study at a House Committee on Foreign Affairs hearing. Meanwhile, the press attacked the Pentagon for pursing an expensive, "substantially useless" project. The *Washington Daily News* mused, "We don't know why the Army nicknamed the Chile project Camelot—but in French the words means [*sic*] 'peddler of cheap merchandise,' in which case it was well-named."[33]

Recognizing the need to put a stop to domestic investigations of Camelot and its causes, President Johnson directed the State Department to assert control over the Pentagon's foreign area research program. On August 2, he empowered Rusk to "establish effective procedures which will enable you to assure the propriety of Government-sponsored social science research in the area of foreign policy." Johnson's directive authorized the State Department to initiate a project-by-project review of all government-sponsored social research into foreign areas. Dungan wrote excitedly to a colleague in Washington, "Would it be too much to hope that [this] represents a real public assertion of State Dept. control in areas of [foreign relations]?" To some observers, the order resolved the departments' public battle over turf. Overlooking the fact that the State Department had little interest in supporting the application of social science to diplomacy, the *New York Times* editorialized, "One might say that the social sciences, as Clemenceau said of war, are much too important to be left to the generals." The newspaper pronounced hopefully that henceforth, foreign relations would "be left to the State Department, where it belongs."[34] Perhaps the White House would rein in the militarization of American foreign affairs.

From Two Masters to Many

Most social scientists, however, were unmoved by the assertion that Camelot signaled the dangerous reach of the military's power. Instead, many reacted with outrage to Camelot's cancellation and Johnson's orders, which they interpreted as an unfair referendum on the value of their expertise. Political scientist and unapologetic cold warrior Alfred de Grazia was one of the first to respond to the episode in print, and he was not shy about assigning blame widely for the debacle. He charged that Johan Galtung had colluded with the enemy, "egg[ing] on a Chilean communist paper to agitate South American anti-yanqui jingoism." The State Department and "Generalissimo McNamara," too, played directly into Chilean communists' hands by canceling what de Grazia called a "skillfully manned, well-planned" project of profound political and scientific utility. Outraged by the State Department's argument that the Pentagon had no business sponsoring such vital national security research, he asked his readers, "Are Cuba and Santo Domingo, Lebanon and Vietnam, and other cases too, going to stand as historical proof that the Army can send men in to be killed but cannot help anyone go in and forestall by preventive understanding the occasions of killing?"[35]

Scholars less hawkish than de Grazia supported Camelot's intellectual and political mission. Leonard E. Schwartz, a public policy expert, described it as the kind of "peace research" and "action-oriented" study that the Cold War required. He argued that Camelot "constitutes a model combining action and scholarship that deserves careful consideration for further emulation not preemptive rejection." William Goode, a sociologist and former student of Rex Hopper, agreed. Although he had declined Hopper's invitation to join the project, he wrote after its cancellation that he was "convinced Camelot was intellectually the most significant research project under way during the past decade. Even now, I would accept its challenge and devote the next ten years of my professional life to its execution." Gabriel Almond endorsed the project as "a straightforward basic study of social systems [and] social stability."[36]

Like most Sorons, Camelot researchers and their defenders were firm believers in the symbiosis of science and democracy. The study embodied the liberal democratic faith in the righteousness of scientifically guided policy. Camelot's staff believed they could discover rational, nonviolent solutions to the problems of revolution and violence; they sought to replace insurgency with gradual social change geared toward stability and, eventually, democracy. And they were unapologetic about the study's normative goals. As Hopper explained, the United States "must develop the skills requisite to the promotion of revolutionary social change with a minimum of violence. . . . In other words, we should prevent internal wars if we can." For Camelot's director, as well as for other social scientists confronting daily the prospect of nuclear annihilation and revolutionary unrest, an incontrovertible scientific theory was unnecessary to support the claim that violence was not a social good. Camelot's planning documents cited the work of Pitirim Sorokin, the Russian émigré and Harvard sociologist who had explained in 1925 that "revolution is a bad method for the improvement of the material and spiritual condition of the masses." Camelot may have embraced the Cold War values of the national security state, but for its staff, those values were fundamentally ameliorative and democratic. After interviewing a number of Camelot researchers, sociologist Irving L. Horowitz concluded that its staff largely believed in the "worth of rational persuasion" through science and "saw little difference between scholars engaged in the war against poverty and those directly concerned with the war against violence." By bringing scientific means to bear on morally unassailable ends, Camelot researchers felt that they neutralized any problems of bias raised by their financial affiliation with the national security state.[37]

Nutini's deceitful actions in Santiago enabled many social scientists sympathetic to Camelot's mission to blame the incident on him, freeing them from facing the more difficult questions raised by the study's military sponsorship and political assumptions. Even the social scientists on Camelot's National Academy of Sciences advisory committee, who had asked to be relieved of their duties when they learned of Nutini's actions in Chile, never spoke out publicly against the study's sponsorship and political implications.[38] A few outspoken opponents of Camelot worked concertedly to change that state of affairs. Dale L. Johnson lambasted the study in letters to the *American Sociologist* and the *American Anthropologist*. His research had been interrupted when, in the weeks after Camelot's exposure in Santiago, the Chilean Chamber of Deputies denounced him and described his work on Chilean industrialists as "Yankee espionage." Citing revelations that CIA front organizations like the Human Ecology Fund were funneling money to fieldworkers, anthropologist Marshall Sahlins intimated that Camelot was only one indication of a far-reaching effort on behalf of the American government to use social science as cover for espionage.[39]

But Camelot raised a profound challenge to social science: it threatened to destabilize the symbiosis between science and democracy. Beginning in the late summer of 1965, the study became a touchstone for social scientists who were skeptical of the liberal assumption that science could direct politics. Horowitz worried that Camelot's planners—not to mention their patrons—were victims of the "Enlightenment Syndrome." They shared "a faith in the perfectibility of mankind" and a conviction that "the military [could perform] a major role in this general process." As a result, he explained, they neglected to consider a series of complicated epistemological, political, and moral questions: What relationship should science have to democratic policy? What rights did American scholars have to investigate other societies on behalf of their own government? If scholars did in fact discover how to avert internal war, what right did governments or social engineers have to act on that knowledge? And most fundamentally for scholars, what were the "vital connections . . . between objectivity and commitment" in the context of the Cold War?[40]

If science and democracy were not neatly symbiotic, then contract research threatened to place researchers in an untenable intellectual and professional position. Political scientist Kalman Silvert objected to Camelot researchers' belief that they could operate in an objective and neutral position from the gray area. Full-time government employees, he explained, could not be expected to be objective scholars, and thus were not accountable to the scientific standards of transparency and independence. And there was no confusion among purely academic researchers who were supported by government grants, for their allegiance to science protected them from biasing their research with their patrons' values. But, he insisted, "It is the social scientist working in both fields [government and academe] who is in danger of betraying both of his masters." Horowitz concurred, but saw the problem in even broader terms. Camelot challenged social scientists to ask: "What are and are not the legitimate functions of a scientist?" He directly challenged the symbiosis between science and democracy, charging that "the Enlightenment assumption that people in power need only to be shown the truth in order to do the right thing is unacceptable" in a democracy.[41] But what practical purpose, then, could social science serve? Horowitz's question cut to the core of Cold War social science. The problem was not a new one, but in an age of militarization, the stakes might be high.

Camelot's exposure seemed to call new attention to the complex problem of expertise and democracy in an age of militarization. Yet serious professional engagement with it was quickly diverted by researchers' bureaucratic concerns. The main target of scholars' ire in the wake of Camelot's cancellation was neither Hugo Nutini nor the Pentagon, but rather the State Department. Johnson's order that the State Department oversee foreign area research was vague; if it played its political cards right, the agency could justify investigating *all* social research, private or public, conducted abroad. Even private philanthropies, like the Ford Foundation, were anxious that the State Department's reach could hamper its generous programs. Most social scientists responded with outrage to the idea that a government agency—particularly one widely perceived as hostile to scientific expertise—was charged with policing social research. Even Horowitz, who was quite critical of many scholars' implicit embrace of American Cold War values, argued vehemently against the State Department's new powers. He insisted it was "an act of government censorship" and "a gross violation of the autonomous nature of science." Others disputed the government's ability to protect scholarly neutrality and integrity. As Goode explained, agency clearance would make it appear that scholars were working directly for the government. That made social scientists its "vassals, lackeys, carrying out [its] will. We cannot claim to be independent," he charged, "if everyone knows that our research has been previously 'approved.'" Far from protecting intellectual autonomy and the objectivity of its contract research, scholars argued, the State Department's review abrogated them.[42]

The State Department's attack on Project Camelot further damaged its already poor reputation among social scientists. Called to testify before Congress about the relationship between scholarship and the federal government in the wake of the study's demise, psychologist Arthur Brayfield announced, "I would certainly go strongly on the record that I think the State Department has been in the nineteenth century in its use of behavioral sciences and behavioral scientists." Horowitz characterized the agency's attack on the study as "an expression of the contempt for social science so prevalent among those who need it most." Social scientists accused the department of failing to recognize the value of their expertise, preferring instead to make decisions "through some kind of intuitive and antenna-like process." The department's unwelcome incursion into their affairs solidified many scholars' view that Pentagon involvement in research was comparatively benign. Even vociferous critics of Camelot like Galtung spoke favorably about the military's willingness to support social science research.[43]

To protect their professional interests against the State Department, a number of American social scientists allied with the Pentagon. After it had become obvious to Pentagon officials that the Camelot episode was going to result in increased State Department involvement in the Defense Department's foreign area research program, its officials responded proactively. They again turned to the National Academy of Sciences (NAS). Brown offered the academy's Division of Behavioral Sciences $50,000 to advise the Pentagon on its foreign policy research program, and he asked in particular for advice on the best way to avoid future Camelots. The NAS was happy to comply. It quickly established the Advisory Committee on Government Programs, chaired by Rockefeller University's Donald Young. Its membership included anthropologist George P. Murdock, political scientist Ithiel de Sola Pool, and sociologist Morris Janowitz. Murdock was no enemy of the national security state; during the late 1940s, he served as an FBI informer, outing fellow anthropologists with communist tendencies. Pool, too, had a long-standing relationship with the Pentagon. A vocal supporter of the American effort in Vietnam, he served on numerous military advisory boards and performed contract research for the Pentagon throughout the 1950s and 1960s.[44]

In creating the committee, Brown paid some lip-service to the Pentagon's need for expert social science advice about foreign and military policy. But he made it clear that the committee's first task was to tackle the problem of State Department clearance. Members of the National Academy of Sciences shared the Pentagon's concern. Murdock, who was also the director of the Division of the Behavioral Sciences, feared that if left to its own devices, the State Department would create a "censorship board" that would leave foreign area study "seriously crippled." Frederick Seitz, the academy president, explained to its senior leadership that the new advisory committee would serve as "a deterrent to uninformed or censorial actions on the part of the State Department, which is not highly competent in its comprehension of the behavioral sciences."[45]

The advisory committee enlisted distinguished American social scientists wholesale in defense of the gray area. The Pentagon called on it to solidify the connections between the Department of Defense and academia by creating a liaison between the government and scholars willing to take on sensitive research under contract. And while Brown did not specify the kinds of social research the NAS would be asked to promote, his intent was clear. He placed Seymour Deitchman, the Pentagon's special assistant for counterinsurgency, in charge of coordinating between the Defense Department and the advisory committee. He also requested that the committee advise him about how to make Pentagon-sponsored foreign area research palatable to foreign governments, foreign scholars, and skeptical American academics. "Often," he explained, "the simple manner of phrasing a particular task can make a difference in its acceptability" as a Defense-sponsored project. Seitz supported Brown's vision of the committee's purpose. He instructed its members that one of their duties was to "defend the scientific content of proposed [Pentagon] programs."[46] Eager to circumvent the State Department's encroachment into foreign area research, the NAS itself abetted the militarization of the American scholarly community.

The alliance between the Pentagon and the NAS benefited both parties. Shortly after the advisory committee first convened, Pentagon officials discovered that the State Department was attempting to devise its clearance procedures without consulting the Defense Department or the research community. At Deitchman's urgent request, the advisory committee immediately set about protecting social science and the Pentagon from the State Department. Its members lobbied State Department officials. And they succeeded. After months of discussion, social scientists persuaded the State Department to apply its review powers in a highly circumscribed fashion. In December 1965, six months after Camelot's cancellation, the State Department announced the creation of the Foreign Area Research Council. Located in the State Department's Bureau of Intelligence and Research and staffed by fifteen bureaucrats from each of the department's geographic and functional bureaus, the council would only scrutinize research plans sponsored by national security agencies—the Pentagon and each of the armed services, as well as the U.S. Information Agency, the Arms Control and Disarmament Agency, the Agency for International Development, and the CIA. Research conducted by civilian agencies would be exempt from review. Furthermore, the council would examine only those studies that included foreign travel, contact with foreign nationals, or any other "sensitive" activities. Military-sponsored foreign area research that was conducted in the United States would be free from review, as would research funded by the National Science Foundation and private philanthropies, which supported basic social research projects conducted abroad.[47]

The department's intellectual purview would be similarly circumscribed. Officials were only tasked with assessing the potential impact of research on U.S. foreign relations. They would not investigate the intellectual merits or deficiencies of projects, nor their relevance or importance to the agency that sponsored them. In fact, the State Department did not have the expertise to do so. Few of the agency's staff had any training in or experience with the social sciences. A project's methodology would be of interest only insofar as it involved contact with locals through instruments like ethnography and public opinion surveys. The Foreign Area Research Council's only duty was to weigh the danger to foreign relations posed by each study against its value to American national security. Reviewers asked questions like: If foreign nationals become aware of this project, will they respond as Chileans did to Camelot? Are the study's questions, design, and methodology sensitive to diplomatic relationships, or do they pose an undue risk to foreign relations? To answer these questions, they considered the political climate of the countries where work was scheduled to take place; the inherent sensitivity of the subject matter being studied; the political risks of project sponsorship; and whether the project was or should be classified. As one State Department official explained, "Clearance means only that State has determined that, whatever other merits or deficiencies a project may or may not have, it is not likely to prove seriously embarrassing to the Government."[48]

The review council cleared most projects. In its first two years, it vetted 138 Pentagon-sponsored studies and denied clearance to only four. But it did little to reduce the militarization of social research. In fact, it enhanced the military's control over the design of its sponsored research and the dissemination of its results. Instead of rejecting studies outright, the council typically granted conditional clearance, allowing research to proceed only if agencies increased the project's classification level or avoided contact with foreign nationals. In its first two years, the council imposed extra surveillance conditions on over half the projects it inspected. It also noted that because research contract programs like SORO encompassed a variety of changing research projects, they did not "lend themselves easily to detailed review project by project." As a result, the council did not necessarily review every study SORO conducted.[49]

But with the creation of the Foreign Area Research Council's guidelines, the State Department did gain some control over the Pentagon's research program. The review system gave American embassies a larger surveillance role, for the council typically required social researchers working abroad to clear their visits with ambassadors and chiefs of mission. Most embassies insisted at a minimum that researchers meet with embassy representatives upon their arrival and brief them upon their departure. And in a few cases, embassy officials successfully blocked Pentagon research projects. One month after Camelot's exposure, a number of embassies in Latin America objected to visits by researchers working on contract with the army to study communist subversion in urban areas. Ambassador Lincoln Gordon used the project's political sensitivity to kill the Brazilian portion of the study. He justified his position in a cable to his superiors in Washington, in which he argued that the Brazilian press could too easily use researchers' presence "to blazen [the] prospect [of a] US Marine invasion of Rio, Recife, and Venezuelan and Colombian cities." The project continued, although in a highly circumscribed fashion. After similar objections from the embassies in Bogotá and Caracas, the State Department restricted researchers to conducting their investigations from within the American embassies. Washington officials explained to their ambassadors that, although they too viewed the project as politically explosive, they were "reluctant to block reasonable requests" from the Defense Department for fear of appearing "negative" to social research.[50]

The costs of the State Department's actions were high. By asserting control over social research, the State Department unwittingly drew the social science community's attention away from the problem of militarization in their scholarship and in American foreign policy. Although Project Camelot's sponsorship and political normativity presented social scientists with profound challenges to the idea that they could be rational, neutral advocates for American democracy, the State Department's actions led scholars to ally with their Defense Department patrons. In the process, they would leave Horowitz's questions about the legitimate role of experts, and Dungan's queries about the scholarly and diplomatic dangers of militarization, unanswered.

It seemed, for a time, that Camelot's exposure could inspire social scientists to engage with the process of militarization. They might question under what conditions, if any, it was appropriate for researchers to work for the national security state. Likewise, they might question the military's tendency to equate social change with insurgency. Instead, as the State Department loomed, they left these questions aside. Rather, they asked: How could they meet the government's clear need for foreign area information while preserving their intellectual autonomy and scholarly integrity? Most who weighed in on the issue agreed that scholars had a right, and perhaps even a moral and professional responsibility, to share their expertise with the state. As the International Studies Association president, John Gagne, remarked matter-of-factly at a forum on the implications of Project Camelot's untimely demise, "The government in every respect has got to have more information which is more up to date and more reliable." Even members of the anthropological profession—the discipline most galvanized by the revelations about Camelot—tended to agree that they had a "responsibility to government even if they do not agree with government practices." After all, they depended on federal funding to carry out their research. Similarly, Gabriel Almond summed up the sentiments of many political scientists when he said, "The Camelot problem really is only a symptom of a problem which has been with us and will perhaps be with us on an increasing scale" as the government funds research to fulfill its need for information in an age of global Cold War.[51] Whether or not they were supportive of the goals of the American national security state, most social scientists who participated in the Camelot debate recognized that their professions relied on federal—most often military—funding. And they seemed to find it inconceivable that the government could use their knowledge for nefarious ends. In 1965, a well-advised democracy was still a benign international force.

Confronted with threats to their autonomy from outside their professional communities, social scientists sought to contain the debate about Camelot and project the appearance of professional unity. A forum on the implications of the project held at a joint meeting of the American Anthropological Association, the Washington, D.C., Sociological Society, and the district's Psychology Association in December 1965 was so friendly to Camelot that Sorons who attended later reported that they did not need to speak up in their own defense. When an audience member suggested that military-sponsored research might raise problems of professional autonomy and credibility, reported one Soron, "he was demolished by the panel," whose members included the sociologist and member of the National Academy of Sciences advisory committee Morris Janowitz. Nor did any American professional association ever publicly condemn the project, much to the dismay of Latin American social scientists.[52]

In 1965, American social scientists still largely denied that there were significant problems with the way Camelot's planning documents fused military and social scientific concepts. The few who conceded that such a merger was problematic reduced the issue to one of semantics, rather than recognizing it as a symptom of their work's militarization. Referring to the planning documents that Hopper had distributed to academic social scientists, Almond asked, "Wasn't the naiveté of the Camelot project—the really massive naiveté of the project— that a project called by a code name was sent through the mail to dozens of scholars in this country with the justification of counter-insurgency, in a sense bringing the whole of social sciences under the heading of counter-insurgency?" To a number of Camelot's supporters, that was precisely what had occurred. While planning documents stressed that the study was a theoretical and empirical study of social change, they were also peppered with militaristic concepts and interventionist language. According to the description of the study that Hopper sent to potential consultants, including Galtung in Chile, Camelot's goal was "to predict and influence politically significant aspects of social change." As such, it would in part be used "to assist friendly governments in dealing with active insurgency programs."[53]

Most social scientists who weighed in on this problem reached a conclusion similar to the Pentagon's: language could make all the difference in a project's acceptability. Anthropologist Ralph Beals reported that after the study's cancellation, Camelot's director expressed regret that he did not object when the army introduced the vocabulary of insurgency into the study's plan. Horowitz, too, blamed language, for Camelot's planning documents revealed "an incomplete incorporation of the military and sociological vocabularies."[54] With the problem of Camelot reduced to semantics, engagement with the fundamental issues of intellectual militarization remained muted.

Social scientists also seemed unable to confront the problem of military patronage. Camelot raised enough concern that government contracting could threaten scholarly autonomy that social scientists' professional associations attempted to tackle the problem. But they too failed to find effective solutions. In November 1965, the American Anthropological Association created a committee charged with examining the relationship between the profession and government research sponsors. Most anthropologists strongly endorsed the committee's findings, even though they were internally inconsistent. The committee cautioned anthropologists that national security agency sponsorship might pose challenges to scientific openness. It encouraged them to avoid using their expert status as a cover for intelligence gathering, an activity unrelated to Camelot. But it recommended that, despite the challenges that government funding presented to social research, scholars should make more of their research available to the government.[55]

The anthropologists' solution was a weak one. They enshrined these findings in a new ethical code, ratified in 1967. The code was not binding. Rather, it offered a set of guidelines for practitioners. Even Sahlins, who spoke out vehemently against Camelot and objected to anthropologists pursuing any military-related work, opposed the creation of a binding ethical code. Instead, he endorsed "the principle of letting each man learn to live with himself." This was the favored approach among many social scientists, who feared that binding codes, like State Department regulations, could also infringe upon academic freedom.[56]

Political science, with its long tradition of government service, reached an even less robust consensus about government sponsorship. Political scientists halfheartedly discussed creating ethical codes in the wake of Camelot, but they did not begin serious deliberations on the issue until February 1967, when allegations surfaced that two high-ranking figures in the American Political Science Association had knowingly received funds from several CIA fronts. Even then, most members of the profession remained lukewarm to the creation of a code of conduct. An ad hoc committee created to examine the issue reported that, while "the rapid development of political science research in the past decade or two gives the relationship between government and the profession a salience it has not had in the past," the committee could not make any recommendations for dealing with the issue without "a great deal of work." After another year of investigation, the committee determined that the matter was so complex that the association could not create a code regulating the relationship between scholars and the government.[57] The committee disbanded.

The controversy over Project Camelot had the potential to challenge social scientists to respond as a community to the problem of militarization. But no serious discussion of severing social science from the Defense Department ensued from the Camelot episode. Silvert and Galtung, two of Camelot's most vocal critics, stopped short of any radical proposal to that effect. Defending himself against the accusation that he was anti-American, and quite pragmatic about the dearth of research funding for the social sciences, Galtung wrote that he saw "nothing wrong in general in Defense Department sponsored research" and recognized the central role the military had played in supporting scholarship. And Silvert, despite his own opposition to Camelot, insisted that the military had a legitimate need for social scientific investigations of internal war.[58]

Instead, most social scientists sought more personal solutions to the challenge of serving two masters. Sociologist Herbert Blumer perhaps best voiced the social scientific consensus in the wake of Camelot. He pointed out that while agency-directed research posed a risk to scientific neutrality, scholars could counteract it by personally embracing an unwavering commitment to "the precepts and ideals of science." Sponsors would then have no choice but to bend their needs "to meet the requirements of the scientific ethic rather than the reverse." The researcher who stayed true to proper scientific behavior rose above political and moral bias regardless of who paid for his work. Perhaps the symbiosis between science and democracy was intact after all.[59]

And even if it was not, social scientists refused to countenance intrusion into their disciplines on the part of agencies that did not pay. As Klaus Knorr explained, "scholars are used to extreme independence. They prefer anarchy . . . and are ready to fight any control of research activities as illegitimate invasions of free inquiry"—even their own scholarly communities' efforts toward control. Beals voiced the most common opinion: Social scientists should be free to work for the government so long as research requests "are made in terms consonant with the [social scientist's] professional and academic goals, values, and ethical systems."[60] With no discipline-wide agreement on those goals, values, or ethics, individual social scientists preferred to be left alone to police themselves. Knorr's comments indicated that they were willing to overlook what Beals called "invasions of free inquiry" so long as the invaders were generous patrons.

Deepening Shades of Gray

Camelot's critics hoped to reduce the militarization of social research and foreign policy. But for SORO and other defense research institutes, remarkably little changed in the wake of the Camelot debate. In fact, Sorons continued to pursue Camelot's ambitions despite the study's cancellation. Fewer than two weeks after McNamara axed the study, Brigadier General Walter A. Lotz, the director of army research, stressed to Sorons that "CAMELOT must be buried and referred to in the past tense." But, he insisted, "*all* SORO research was to go on." The study of internal warfare, social change, and counterinsurgency would continue.[61] One of Camelot's aims was "to test whether such a large scale, closely integrated project has a higher probability of pay off than a series of small, loosely related studies." The Chilean reaction to the study delivered an unequivocal answer, and the Defense Department applied its finding immediately. The day after McNamara announced Camelot's cancellation, the Army Research Office instructed SORO to redesign the project by subdividing Camelot's aims into "a number of small interrelated specific studies with limited objectives," which would ultimately lead "collectively to the overall objective."[62] SORO immediately designed a new study titled "Measurement of Predisposing Factors for Communist Inspired Insurgency." Its goals were familiar: SORO would "identify the parameters significant in detecting social unrest which lead to Communist penetration . . . and potential Communist-inspired revolt in the developing nations"; identify the most efficient techniques for containing unrest; and suggest to the army how to apply the results. Over the next few months, Sorons busied themselves fleshing out specific proposals for each of these new, discrete studies.[63]

By January 1966, the army cleared a new slate of studies for the fiscal year that included the resurrected Camelot. The studies reflected the research office's new linguistic discretion. Researchers assigned to "Task PROPOSITIONS" sought to locate "existing social science information relating to political unrest" and develop consistent terminology for insurrection. Those working on "Task LOWAR" examined the impact that various military actions had on incipient insurgencies. And those dedicated to "Task MODELING" were dutifully engaged in an effort to develop a research model "for investigating the dynamics of environmental factors and the effectiveness of governments in supplying the needs of diverse interests of a country."[64]

The obscure language of these tasks reflected one of the most important lessons that the army gleaned from the uproar over Camelot. Eugene Stubbs, who managed SORO's contract for the army, explained to Vallance, "Although the goal of unclassified research that involves many members of the scholarly community remains a good one, the fact that the objectives of this research can be so easily misinterpreted by important people in that community, and by foreign scholars and governments, dictates that a different approach be taken."[65] SORO's profile needed to be lowered. The research office was to avoid catchy project names, and researchers were instructed to carefully avoid giving scholars and foreign officials any impression that their work could lead to American military intervention in third world nations. Over the course of the summer and fall of 1965, Stubbs vetted the language in all of SORO's research assignments and changed those that appeared unduly militaristic. "Task PSYGUIDE," for example, was rechristened "Intercultural Communications." The army extended these new regulations to its other research contractors, including HumRRO, RAC, and the Simulmatics Corporation.[66]

Although the army gave SORO some responsibility for managing appearances in the research office, it did not trust Sorons to maintain a low profile. In the months following Camelot's exposure, the military significantly increased its control over the office's daily operations. In September, Vallance welcomed a new member to his staff. Major John Johns, an official in the army's Social Science Research Division, was assigned as SORO's army liaison officer. Henceforth, a uniformed army man would be an almost daily presence at the research office. The army also muzzled the research office, banning research-ers from speaking publicly about their work or contacting foreign scientists without prior army approval. Vallance supported the new policy. He explained that the military was not attempting to censor researchers; rather, he suggested that "the substance of their studies is more properly to be considered Army information—and therefore privileged." Despite some Sorons' objections that such policies infringed upon their academic freedom, officials maintained them long after the tumult over Camelot had passed. When the army granted SORO a five-year contract extension in 1967, it added a new provision stipulat-ing that no information resulting from SORO's research could be divulged in any format—written or verbal—without prior approval of the army's chief of research and development.[67]

The Pentagon also dramatically increased its reliance on security classification to protect its research programs from public scrutiny. Beginning in July 1965, it mandated that all military-sponsored social research projects that might affect foreign relations be cleared by its office of International Security Affairs, which was responsible for Pentagon foreign relations, before researchers could apply to the State Department for clearance.[68] Furthermore, the Pentagon's director of research sent a confidential letter to all the armed services' R&D offices in-structing them to classify all documents that might imply U.S. involvement in or influence over any foreign government. Brown explained the new regulations as necessary given both foreign sensitivities and the fact that communists were always looking for any propaganda opportunity they might exploit to their ad-vantage. Indeed, in the years after Camelot, social scientists generally agreed that "the easiest way to get a project approved is to promise to classify the results." Brown also suggested that SORO and other institutes use subcontracts to hide their most sensitive research. Highly sensitive research, he instructed, should be done "at second or third hand, by universities and the like, under various sub-contract arrangements."[69]

These events left Sorons feeling disheartened, and some of the senior re-searcher staff quit. Philip Sperling, deputy director of social research, left to man-age social research at the U.S. Agency for International Development. William Lybrand, who had been Vallance's right-hand man since the director had joined the research office in 1962, resigned a few weeks later. Concerned that SORO's future lay not in original research that fused scholarly and national security con-cerns but in more narrow applied work, he informed Vallance: "I do not feel there is a compatibility between my interests, capabilities, and longer range ca-reer plans on the one hand, and the organization which SORO seems certain to become in the near future on the other."[70]

The scholars and government officials who attacked Project Camelot hoped to reduce the Defense Department's influence on social research. They failed. By and large, Camelot's critics inspired the Pentagon to increase its control over its social researchers. The military also further militarized the content of SORO's research. Senior army research officials planning studies of modernization, development, and communism in Latin America explained that because "any contact, no matter how innocuous the research objective, with the civil populace of a Latin-American country by US scientists presents a potentially inflammatory situation," all research should "focus as much as possible on the Latin American armies." They suggested that U.S. researchers use students at the U.S. Army School of the Americas as their research subjects so as to avoid the need for State Department and embassy clearance.[71]

Had Camelot's opponents been aware of the Pentagon's response—which unfolded largely in classified correspondence—to the controversy the study caused, they would have found that their actions produced results opposite to what they intended. Ultimately, the fallout over the study failed to reduce Pentagon research into foreign areas or challenge the Pentagon's hold over American foreign policy. Instead, it rendered research and policymaking more clandestine and more militarized.

FROM DEMOCRATIC EXPERTS TO "AUTOMATIC COLD WARRIORS"

Dismantling the Gray Area in the Vietnam Era

In early 1968, Americans debated the appearance of a new research study with results so "interesting and horrifying" that it accomplished something perhaps no other government-sponsored study of nuclear deterrence had: it soared to number eight on the *New York Times* best-seller list. *Report from Iron Mountain on the Possibility and Desirability of Peace* detailed the secret conclusions of a study ostensibly initiated by the Pentagon in 1963 to determine the social, political, and economic implications of lasting peace in the United States. Leaked by a member of the study group, who claimed that its implications were so unsettling that the Pentagon refused to publish it, the report came to a shocking conclusion: while permanent peace might be possible, it was undesirable. War, the report concluded, "is the basic social system, within which other secondary modes of social organization conflict or conspire." The economy ran on war; the nation's political system was stable only in the face of the threat of future war; and wars were eugenic—they siphoned off antisocial citizens who might otherwise disrupt society. War was the glue that held society together. Lasting peace was a recipe for anarchy.[1]

While a few gullible scholars and government officials were taken in by the publication's conceit, most realized that the report was a hoax. With its hyperlogical endorsement of permanent war and its methodological appendix devoted to a breakthrough innovation called "peace-gaming," it cleverly satirized the work of government-funded agencies like RAND and Herman Kahn's private nonprofit Hudson Institute. Astute academic social scientists pointed out that the report's authenticity was irrelevant. Whether real or not, its political and intellectual implications were deeply troubling. Bruce M. Russett, a Yale political scientist, wrote, "That some people have taken the *Report* at face value makes me worry even more than usually about the quality of the American debate on foreign policy."[2]

Report from Iron Mountain doubtless owed its notoriety in no small measure to its timing. It ascended the *Times* best-seller list in the weeks after the Tet Offensive. The hoax was one of a number of public efforts in the second half of the 1960s to expose the dense ties between social researchers and the national security state. In 1966, the leftist magazine *Ramparts* reported that a defunct Michigan State University technical assistance program funded by the United States and South Vietnamese governments had provided the cover for a Saigon-based CIA counterespionage training unit in the late 1950s. Soon after, MIT's prestigious Center for International Studies admitted that its budget had included a significant infusion of CIA funds since its founding in 1951. That revelation tied well-known American social scientists— including Daniel Lerner, Lucian Pye, and Walt W. Rostow—to clandestine government research. That Americans took notice of such stories indicated the extent to which public concern about the militarization of scholarship and foreign policy had mushroomed. Critics had publicly fingered both the MSU and MIT programs as CIA projects as early as 1957. But it took the American war in Vietnam for those allegations to gain traction. As Americans became increasingly disenchanted with the fact that the war was grinding on with little visible success, and as journalists and activists unearthed evidence that Camelot was just one example of a widespread Pentagon social research program, the criticism directed at the national security state and its social scientists took on a new urgency. Scholars and elected officials warned that the military's contracting system rendered researchers "automatic cold warriors" who unquestioningly did the bidding of their patrons. And by the late 1960s, fewer Americans interpreted researchers' actions as a principled stand against communism.[3]

Although social research commanded a small share of the military's budget, it became one of the principal proxies in Americans' broadening critical engagement with the consequences of militarization. By the end of the decade, Admiral Hyman G. Rickover, a vitriolic critic of Robert McNamara's "whiz kids" and their relentless search for social-scientifically informed counterinsurgency tools, warned that the Defense Department would grow according to Cyril Parkinson's sardonic law of bureaucracies. Echoing Harold Lasswell's warning about the garrison state, Rickover counseled that unless restrained by an external force, the "boundaries of its 'empire'" would expand, dwarfing the rest of the federal government. As the growing U.S. commitment to Vietnam consumed more money and more lives, many Americans worried that the United States was indeed becoming a warfare state.

This transformation seemed spurred in no small part by the military's prodigious research contracting programs. Critiques tying research contracting to the expanding Pentagon "empire" exploded in the late 1960s. Rickover was joined by political scientist H. L. Nieburg, who attacked the growing "contract state" that, he asserted, funneled billions of dollars into the coffers of greedy and increasingly powerful R&D organizations. Likewise, Pulitzer Prize–winning journalist Clark R. Mollenhoff argued that the unchecked expansion of the Pentagon's power over American intellectual life minimized the ability of Congress and American voters to shape foreign policy.[4] The contract state, it seemed, was both cause and consequence of the war machine.

Galvanized by the Vietnam War, many Americans began to take to heart Lasswell's warning about the garrison state. Social scientists, Congress, and a variety of federal officials continued their earnest search for solutions to the challenges posed by the gray area. But they would fail to meet the growing public demand for engagement with the problem of militarization itself. While social scientists continued to debate the epistemological and professional problems posed by the union of expertise and national security, Congress and the Defense Department searched for bureaucratic and institutional fixes. As a result, by 1969, advocates of the Pentagon's contracting programs, both within and beyond government, would cede control of the gray area's fate to student activists and other ardent critics of the Vietnam War.

Taming "Spooky"

Unfortunately for SORO, the revelations about CIA ties to MIT and Michigan State did little to detract public attention from its own research. In early 1966, the *Washington Star* gleefully exposed SORO's Project Simpatico. Code-named before the Pentagon issued its injunction against catchy project names, the project was designed to identify the ways that the Colombian government could enhance its reputation among civilians. The study's directors, cultural anthropologist Howard K. Kaufman and psychologist Norman Smith, designed a battery of psychological tests and questionnaires designed to discover which political leaders Colombian peasants most respected. One questionnaire included questions like, "If a leader of the people should arise, should he be tall, short, white, black, armed, married, over 40 years of age, or under?" Colombians trained by Kaufman and Smith fanned out across the countryside to find the answers. Unlike Camelot, the study had been cleared by the U.S. embassy and the Colombian ministry of defense. But when other Colombian government officials learned of the study's Pentagon sponsorship, they balked. Legislator Ramiro Andrade attacked it as a covert attempt by the U.S. military to intervene in domestic affairs. Simpatico, he implied, threatened to militarize Colombia just as the Pentagon was militarizing the United States. The *Washington Post* soon picked up the story in an article headlined, "Hey Senor! Do You Beat Your Wives Often?"[5] Before the debacle could fade from public consciousness, it was joined by a second embarrassing tale when journalists in Montreal discovered that SORO had considered including a study of Quebec in Project Camelot. An American University official publicly dismissed both attacks as the "erroneous and possibly malicious stepchildren" of the Camelot episode, but the damage to SORO's already tarnished image could not be so easily undone. An embarrassed Theodore Vallance was forced to write a letter of apology to the Canadian prime minister.[6]

As the U.S. military increased its commitment to Vietnam in 1966, Vallance focused on restoring SORO's reputation. The contradictory nature of his efforts reflected Sorons' continuing ambivalence about militarization. Although Vallance supported the army's increased control over the research office's output after Project Camelot's exposure, he simultaneously tried to demilitarize SORO. In a bid to enhance its intellectual prestige and autonomy, he also persuaded the army to capitulate to his repeated requests for institutional funds—money for "long-shot, high risk, high potential" basic studies that might not be immediately applicable to counterinsurgency but could eventually pay off handsomely. The army agreed to allocate 5 percent of SORO's budget—about $135,000 in 1966— to pathbreaking research projects that would be designed by Sorons without the army's oversight or input. SORO's 5 percent budget for institutional research was only half of what more prestigious and well-funded outfits like RAND enjoyed, but, Vallance reasoned, it was a start. To further counter the public perception that SORO was merely a captive arm of the military, he also persuaded American University to give the research office a board of advisers, which included AU faculty and trustees.[7]

Camelot had tainted SORO's name, so Vallance set about rebranding the research office. To make it "less threatening to foreigners" and less attractive to muckraking journalists, he sought a name that was as ambiguous as SORO but also, as he put it, "less 'spooky.'" In July 1966, the army and AU rechristened SORO the Center for Research on Social Systems (CRESS). Its rapid-response counterinsurgency research service, the Counterinsurgency Information Analysis Center, was renamed the Cultural Information Analysis Center. Vallance was still a believer in the promise of the gray area. Seeking an organizational formula that would maximize CRESS's benefit to scholarship and national security, he restructured it, combining its "basic" and "applied" research under the same wing. This tactic, he argued, would prevent "theory-oriented research from becoming esoteric, purposive research from losing objectivity, [and] secondary source research from becoming superficial and unchallenging." Vallance fervently hoped he could finally make CRESS's work institutionally autonomous, intellectually sound, and militarily relevant at the same time.[8]

With the army's approval, the university issued a press release announcing CRESS's creation that portrayed it as a scholarly break from the old, militarized SORO. The administration explained that while CRESS might continue SORO's research, it would be integrated into the university, complementing and extending research performed by AU's academic faculty. Furthermore, the press release indicated that CRESS would also expand its sponsorship to include other government agencies and private foundations. In a *New York Times* article announcing CRESS's creation, American University's provost signaled his optimism about the research office's future. He announced that while Camelot had triggered "a certain demoralization" among faculty and students, with CRESS now subject to greater university control, "we hope to have a considerably warmer relationship between the faculty and the administration." The research center appeared to be back on track; in 1967, it moved to new offices to accommodate its growing staff, which had swelled to over 150 personnel.[9]

CRESS's more scholarly and independent appearance appealed to the Pentagon, but not for the reasons that Vallance or American University officials hoped. The institute's more benign moniker and its advisory board might insulate CRESS from the public scrutiny that had plagued SORO after Camelot. But these accoutrements were superficial. In every material respect, CRESS retained the heavy imprint of its military sponsors. A mere five months after promising funding for independent institutional research, the army terminated its commitment, citing budget constraints. And it maintained its ban on the public release of CRESS research without prior army approval.[10]

In fact, the military increasingly pushed Vallance and his staff toward narrowly applied studies. In the 1950s, the army had turned to contract research in part because at least some counterinsurgency and psychological operations officials believed that independent, scholarly work was necessary to challenge the army's reliance on hardware in the war for hearts and minds. The independence and academic credibility of contract research rationalized the creation of SORO, HumRRO, RAC, RAND, and dozens of other research institutes. But by the late 1960s, it became apparent that the army in fact desired heavily militarized work. CRESS's most successful products, at least as far as its sponsors were concerned, were reports that synthesized library research. Collections of cultural information about communist-threatened minority groups in Southeast

Asia, case histories of insurgencies and counterinsurgencies, and detailed descriptions of communist subversion methods were especially useful in the classrooms at West Point and the war colleges. These studies, of course, continued the militarizing trend of army engagement with the peoples of the third world. A faculty member at the army's Special Warfare School, for example, hailed Task Numismatics, a comparison of fifty-seven cases of insurgent violence, as "invaluable in preparing and teaching area studies." Researchers also earned accolades from their military clients stationed in Asia for a report titled *Working with Peoples in Developing Areas: One Task of the American Soldier Overseas*, which taught military personnel culturally sensitive methods for working with third world allies. Describing the report as "a primer for leadership which ought to be read by every soldier and officer" sent into the field, military officials complimented CRESS on "one hell of a fine job." The military distributed reports relevant to the war in Vietnam to General William C. Westmoreland and his staff. In Saigon, the American forces maintained a library of contract social research useful to psychological operations, civic action, and other counterinsurgency strategies.[11]

By contrast, projects that attempted to bridge social science theory and military relevance met with little success. In response to an army request for a report on the "socio-political structures and dynamics" of African urban, intellectual, and military elites, CRESS political scientist William Hanna penned a report titled *Urban Dynamics in Black Africa*. Hanna had conducted field research in sub-Saharan Africa prior to joining SORO in 1965. Drawing on that experience, he succinctly described the complex social cleavages in a number of African cities, using sociological theories about urbanization to predict the likelihood of communist incursions. The army, however, found Hanna's report far too complex. One officer complained that "the extreme detail of the study would prevent effective, 'in-time' absorption of the material." Its sociological approach was quite simply "of very limited use" to the military. The army promptly terminated the project.[12] Hanna went on with his wife, an anthropologist and fellow CRESS researcher, to publish a book-length academic study based on the same research. But reviewers in elite disciplinary journals like the *American Anthropologist* and the *American Political Science Review* were unimpressed by what they described as the text's superficial and self-evident generalizations. Hanna and Hanna, perched between the military and academia, were unable to satisfy either.[13] Despite Vallance's well-intentioned efforts, CRESS was floundering between the conflicting demands of scholarship and national security. Owing to the public's newfound concern with the Pentagon's empire—both at home, in its domination of research, and abroad in its domination of the Vietnamese—CRESS found its travails again in the public consciousness.

Two Masters, Redux

CRESS's problems were part of a wider phenomenon. The increasingly negative attention directed at the gray area indicated that social scientists were reaping bitter fruit from their newfound political relevance. In the second half of the 1960s, the federal government increased its support for social science R&D as more public problems appeared amenable to social scientific interventions. Between 1960 and 1966, the federal government's contribution skyrocketed from $35 million to $118 million. Much of this money was allocated to domestic agencies, but the budget for foreign research grew as well. In 1967, eleven government agencies spent $40 million on research in and about foreign areas. The Defense Department provided $13 million, far more than any other agency. By contrast, the State Department contributed only $125,000, despite the concerns raised by Project Camelot.[14]

This money brought more scholars into the realm of politics and action. By 1968, nearly 40 percent of all social science PhDs were employed full-time in research and development projects. The contract state, as critics took to calling the gray area, assumed a major role in social science research and employment, with significant consequences for researchers. Sociologist Leonard Reissman and political scientist Kalman Silvert opined, "Today, no chasm separates research activity from policy determination, but instead, the two are part of a single continuum that shades almost imperceptibly from one pole to the other."[15] With utility to the state came a host of implications, some familiar and some new: mission agency funding could distort the direction of research and reduce its quality; it could threaten academic freedom; and in cases of foreign area research, it could render all Americans working abroad suspect, reducing academic researchers' access to information. By the second half of the 1960s, more social scientists worried that national security work could threaten their reputations as value-free scholars. Sorons like Earl DeLong and Jeanne Mintz remained convinced of the righteousness of their efforts, but the confidence of other social scientists dwindled. Their work, they feared, might fundamentally challenge the scientific authority of social research. Many saw themselves as noble and unwitting victims of these events. Sociologists Irving L. Horowitz and Lee Rainwater explained that "in the absence of any popular movement to do the job, social science has had thrust upon it the burden of providing legitimation for rational, non-violent solutions to major problems."[16] Their goals, they still insisted, were virtuous. But the means by which they sought to accomplish them were proving increasingly problematic politically, professionally, and epistemologically. The tidy parallel between disciplinary values and national security interests so common in the gray area of the 1950s and early 1960s was beginning to break down.

In the second half of the 1960s, social scientists commented with increasing frequency on what Reissman and Silvert termed the "third culture"—not quite academic, not quite governmental—that the gray area created. The contract state blurred the lines between science and sovereignty, thrusting upon social scientists a complicated set of epistemological and ethical commitments. And once social scientists began to recognize their research culture as militarized, the gray area became even more problematic. As institutions like CRESS made it increasingly difficult to distinguish public and scientific responsibility, researchers found themselves saddled with what Latin American studies expert Richard N. Adams referred to as "obligations in two distinct social systems: the society of scholars, and the nation." Scholars worried that they had to choose between their patriotic obligations to their government, which seemed to justify the pursuit of secretive research in the context of the Cold War with the Soviet Union and the hot war in Vietnam, and their scholarly obligations to science, which required them to place intellectual integrity before national security and citizenship.[17]

Now it seemed that the third culture was riddled with deep—perhaps unbridgeable—contradictions. As Horowitz explained, contract researchers' desire to satisfy two masters, the increasingly militarized state and the ideally non-militarized practice of science, forced them into a cognitive bind. Government agencies hired social scientists for their credibility, which rested upon the scholarly virtues of openness, impartiality, and independence. But in the context of growing questions about the motives of the national security state, it seemed that government funding might threaten the very qualities that gave social science its credibility. Applied to policy, military-funded social science became "patriotism" and "reform therapy." If the hallmark of a science was its autonomy, policy, which placed "a premium on involvement and influence," could not be made scientific. Lasswell and Lerner's vaunted policy scientist of the 1950s might be a contradiction in terms.[18] If Horowitz was right, the third culture was unviable whether or not science and democracy proceeded in tandem.

But what, then, was the proper relationship between knowledge and political action? Pierre L. van den Berghe, a University of Washington sociologist and expert on South Africa, questioned Horowitz's assumption that the scientific ethic trumped political action. He doubted "that there are any scientific ethics distinguishable from general ethics and political ideology." After all, his own ethics forced him to use secrecy and deceit while working in South Africa to protect his informants against the apartheid government. He admitted, "I would not necessarily disapprove of classified U.S. government-sponsored research aimed at the overthrow of the South African government." The same ethical calculus applied to studies like Project Camelot. Van den Berghe defended the *moral* right of researchers to work on studies like Camelot so long as they agreed with the

foreign policy goals of the federal government—foreign intervention and or-
ganized subversion—and recognized that Camelot had important ideological
and political implications. The criteria of ethicality and legitimacy, he argued,
"should be whether [the social scientist] agrees with the actions and purposes of
his sponsor." Van den Berghe's position echoed that of Soron Jeanne Mintz: all
one could expect of social scientists working on pressing international problems
was a consistency of means and ends and an honest appraisal of the uses to which
one's knowledge could be put. Van den Berghe objected not to the government's
use of social science for clandestine military actions, but to the ability of social
scientists to "rationalize their inclination to follow their self-interest" by deluding
themselves into thinking that they could civilianize military policy or that the
Defense Department shared their passion for knowledge.[19] On this count, van
den Berghe parted ways with Mintz and argued explicitly for the social responsibility of individual scientists.

Social science's policy relevance confronted scholars with a crucial ethical
question: did the obligation to science trump personal values and political responsibility? Or was the scientific ethic merely a rationalization that allowed
scholars to avoid considering the ends to which their work could be put? Klaus
Knorr, director of Princeton University's Center for International Studies, argued that the scientific ethic was too crude a measure for policy work. If social
science could shape global affairs—a possibility that scholars, citizens, and government officials entertained in the 1960s more than ever before—ethics beyond
scientific purity were at stake. Echoing Soron Robert Boguslaw's argument that
ostensibly value-free research in fact reified the values of policy elites, Horowitz
intimated that the core tenet of the scientific ethic might be untenable. Value
freedom was not merely illusory; it was "a rationale for selling information to
the highest bidder . . . a way of saying that facts are for public sale, while values are for private sensibilities." If social science could impact the social order,
science and values could not be separated at any point in the research process.[20]
As Boguslaw had argued from his position at SORO, means and ends had to be
synchronized. Science and democracy were only symbiotic if scholars took great
pains to ensure that their research—and perhaps their patrons as well—served
democratic ends.

This tension arose within a particular historical moment. Social scientists
had long seen the interests of science in harmony with the interests of the state.
Under the rubric of Cold War liberalism that drove SORO's creation, both science and the state strove for the peaceful extension of democracy and human
equality. But as the Johnson administration's foreign policy crept toward the
belligerent expansion of American power, critics unmasked its embrace of
expertise as a crude cover for militarization. With social scientists designing

and supporting ill-conceived pacification projects and fabricating evidence of American success against the Vietcong, government-funded research no longer appeared disinterested or benign. Rather, international relations theorist Hans Morgenthau explained, the Pentagon's social science served as "the ideological defense of a partisan position, an intellectual gloss upon power, made to appear as the objective truth." The problem was not merely the old problematic relationship between social knowledge and political action. Now, knowledge itself was tainted.[21]

During the 1950s and for much of the 1960s, the question of value freedom had seemed to most social scientists a rarefied, self-contained issue of philosophical interest. Scholars like Boguslaw, Horowitz, Alvin Gouldner, and C. Wright Mills pontificated on the subject to little practical result. But in the second half of the 1960s, the issue became profoundly political as a growing number of intellectuals implicated the ethic of value-freedom in the expansion of American belligerence abroad and militarization at home. Anthropologist Kathleen Gough argued that as knowledge became bureaucratized in institutions that were tied to the state—whether universities relying on federal money or contract research agencies created by the Pentagon—scholars became "hired functionaries."[22] Over the course of the late 1960s, many academic social scientists embraced the idea that knowledge was influenced by the matrix of power relations in which it was produced. Knowledge itself, they argued, was a form of power. Scholars could not ignore their social and political responsibility to wield it wisely.

This argument complicated even further another long-standing conundrum: What was the proper function of the social scientist? Outside the Pentagon, playing the role of the service intellectual might be increasingly untenable, but a number of other postures presented themselves. On one side of the spectrum, Silvert insisted that scholars radically limit their participation in policy. Social scientists, he explained, were qualified to "generate data, reconstruct and refocus extant data, and make available descriptive analyses." But they were not qualified to advocate for specific courses of action, for policy questions "are not within the realm of our expertness." Questions about "shoulds" were for citizens, not scientists. The service intellectuals of the 1950s and early 1960s, of course, had offered a similar argument for separating knowledge and action, but Silvert rejected that position, calling instead for a return to independent scholarship.[23]

Silvert's solution provided a technique for avoiding the dangerous political implications of knowledge, but his separation of knowledge from action was ill-suited to an era in which a significant number of social scientists worked in applied areas. Furthermore, Silvert's solution was poorly suited to an intellectual climate in which many social scientists—from the radical Noam Chomsky to the ameliorist Ralph Beals—expressed faith in the potential beneficence of expertise. In the late 1960s, many scholars railed against the posture of Silvert's detached scholar. To Theodore Roszak, Silvert's technical experts merely traded their status as "henchmen of the military-industrial complex" for that of "recluse[s] in an apolitical ivory tower." Silvert, he implied, threatened to make social science irrelevant.[24]

By the late 1960s, a growing contingent of scholars believed that the national security state's experts had realized C. Wright Mill's worst nightmare: the socialization of the intellect indeed betokened the demise of both the critical intellectual and participatory democracy. The debate about the gray area was, at base, a critique of the expert-directed democracy championed by many midcentury social scientists and embodied in Robert McNamara's Pentagon. Traditional Sorons like DeLong had believed in the affinity between science and the state; expertise, they believed, could rationalize and depoliticize politics. But for Boguslaw, Chomsky, and other critics on the left, that perspective threatened "creeping totalitarianism"—the expansion of elite bureaucratic and technological control over the thoughts, actions, and values of American citizens. The garrison state was real, and the national security state's social scientists were its foot soldiers.[25]

Even so, scholars were reluctant to abandon their hope that social science could inform policy. The faith that social science could advance democracy animated many of the Vietnam-era critics of the national security state and its experts, just as it had animated the military's scholars. Boguslaw, Chomsky, Roszak, and other critics affiliated with the New Left argued that social knowledge was most useful when critical of the status quo. But scholars on the New Left failed to solve the problem of the relationship between expert knowledge and democratic action. The discussion of social responsibility, values, and action led scholars back to the point where they began: debating an intractable question of epistemology. And as that debate raged on, Sorons and their ilk at similar institutions continued to ply their trades contentedly for the Pentagon. Militarization was firmly entrenched in the social sciences and the national security state. Epistemological debates were no match for it.

"Civilianizing" the Military-Academic Complex

Epistemology was not the only challenge holding social scientists back. To whom could they turn to support politically sensitive research if not the national security state? Social scientists were in no position to spurn the Defense Department's patronage, and debates about the proper roles of social knowledge in a democratic polity did little to drum up fresh dollars for research. So while the pages of professional journals thickened with articles about the conflicts between science and statecraft, social scientists—including those uninterested in the epistemological problems that galvanized their more scholarly colleagues— embarked on a search for bureaucratic solutions to the problem of militarization. But they fared no better than their epistemologically engaged colleagues. Instead, they engaged in a cacophonous discussion about what kinds of research—pure or applied, grant-based or contractual—could be performed by what kinds of institutions. They reached no compelling conclusion.

Some of their suggestions, unsurprisingly, were self-serving. Clark Abt, founder and head of the for-profit defense contracting firm Abt Associates, argued that organizations like his, which were freed from the narrow boundaries of scholarly discipline, were best suited to perform the most innovative interdisciplinary social science research. Anthropologist Ralph Beals, on the other hand, questioned the ability of for-profit research agencies to perform unbiased research, guided as they were by the profit motive. But even among academic social scientists, there was no consensus on the value of for-profit research corporations. Political scientist Alfred de Grazia argued that the federal government should contract as much social research to for-profit agencies as possible, for they were more efficient than nonprofit organizations and would pay large taxes on their profits. For his part, Eugene Lyons, the social scientist hired by the National Academy of Sciences to survey the relationship between social science and the government in the wake of Camelot, argued simply that research should be done by whatever institution had the most competent staff for the particular problem at hand. Jesse Orlansky, a social scientist in the Pentagon-university consortium Institute for Defense Analyses, reported frankly, "I find it difficult to believe that the location of a research effort is an important question."[26]

Many social scientists found consensus on one point, however: universities should be insulated from government influence; they should accept only basic and unclassified research projects. Abt, Beals, and sociologist Edmund H. Volkart agreed: "The academic community must remain the one place where social science research can be freely undertaken, freely reported, and subject to no substantive controls." Because most social scientists also doubted the competence of in-house social research personnel in government agencies, the argument for protection of the university translated, somewhat ironically, into support for the Pentagon's contract state. Alvin Gouldner, himself a staunch critic of service intellectuals at CRESS and elsewhere, argued that "*all* social research should be given to outside contractors."[27] Throughout the late 1960s, a vocal contingent of social scientists endorsed institutes like CRESS for their combinations of agency relevance (they were created to fulfill the missions of the agencies they served) and credibility (they were technically independent from their client agencies). James S. Coleman, the Johns Hopkins University sociologist who had worked on Project Camelot, argued that federal contract research centers offered the best guarantee of independent, relevant applied research. Psychologists Henry Reicken, Charles Brayfield, and John G. Darley agreed. When asked by Congress what organizations performed the best applied research, they all endorsed HumRRO, CRESS's sister federal contract research institute housed at George Washington University, as "an outstanding example of programmatic problem-solving research."[28]

This consensus, loose as it was, jarred against the fact that a growing number of Americans were coming to associate Pentagon-sponsored social research with the unseemly militarization of American foreign policy. While social scientists debated institutional and epistemological solutions to their relationship to the military, Congress turned its legislative powers to the issue. Senator Wayne Morse, one of the first members of Congress to speak out against the Vietnam War, warned in 1966 that the government was facing a crippling crisis of expertise. As the Pentagon dominated foreign relations research, he warned, it was becoming increasingly difficult for Congress and American citizens to locate sources of independent counsel and criticism. The fear that the Pentagon was controlling intellectual life was not contained within the Left. Republican senator Clifford Case worried that the Pentagon's growing "monopoly on intellectual opinion" would soon result in a dearth of "independent scrutiny by independent academicians, because there are not any more."[29] Social science had come a long way since the late 1940s, when congressional suspicion had cemented its exclusion from the National Science Foundation. Between 1965 and 1967, two different congressional committees held weeks of hearings on the subject of social research. They heard testimony from over one hundred witnesses. A third committee produced a four-volume study on the subject of government-sponsored social research. Each committee hoped to counter the militarization of science and statecraft by "civilianizing" social research.[30] Some elected officials argued that by increasing federal funding for basic social research, Congress could begin to reclaim its power over American foreign policy.

Congress's first stab at the problem followed on Camelot's heels. In 1965, after hearing testimony about the study from the Pentagon, SORO, and the State Department, Representative Dante Fascell's subcommittee of the House Committee on Foreign Affairs pronounced social science "one of the vital tools in the arsenals of free societies." But Fascell worried that civilian government agencies, particularly the State Department, failed to recognize the national security potential of social research. In 1966, he introduced legislation designed to strengthen social science by forging stronger ties between scholars and civilian agencies. He called on the White House to organize a conference on social research to set future federal policy. He suggested that the Executive Office establish an Office of Social Sciences, modeled on the influential Office of Science and Technology, to advise the president on matters of social science and social policy. And he proposed that Congress create a National Social Sciences Foundation—an independent federal agency parallel to the National Science Foundation (NSF)—which would administer grants for basic research, award scholarships for graduate education, and provide a coherent national policy for social science. Fascell's resolutions would have catapulted the social sciences into political parity with the hard sciences. But the congressman was playing politics; he sought less to restructure federal support for social knowledge and more to "begin a dialogue" on the Hill about the problem of social research sponsorship.[31] His bills died with little notice.

Oklahoma Democrat Fred Harris proved more devoted to the cause. Known as the "Senator for Science," Harris was, like Fascell, a vocal proponent of the national security state's need for social knowledge. Professing his "democratic belief that the long-range interests of our Nation will be best served by a free and independent academic community," he feared that the Pentagon's dominance over social research funding threatened free inquiry and, by extension, democracy. Like a growing number of Americans, he implicated the gray area in the growing militarization of American foreign policy. Galvanized by revelations about Project Simpatico, he argued that Pentagon research funding bore significant blame for the United States' "militaristic image" in Latin America. The military's support of policy research, he argued, indicated to foreigners that the United States preferred military organizations to emerging democracies. To dispel the perception abroad "that our foreign policy is very influenced, if not made by, military and intelligence agencies," he trained his sights on the Pentagon's social research program.[32]

For over two years, beginning in the summer of 1966, Harris convened a series of hearings. Soliciting testimony from dozens of government officials and social scientists, he sought to restructure the relationship between social science and the federal government. Every year between 1966 and 1969, he introduced a bill to establish a National Foundation for Social Sciences (NFSS). Harris's proposals received considerably more attention from Congress and the social scientific community than the Fascell bills had. When he first introduced his proposal to the Senate in 1966, he boasted cosponsorship from such congressional luminaries as Mike Mansfield, Eugene McCarthy, and J. William Fulbright. Like Fascell's proposed foundation, the NFSS would support basic social research through grants to scholars, universities, and other nonprofit research organizations. Social scientists had clamored for more federal funding for basic research since the close of World War II, with little success. In 1965, only 2 percent of the $1.7 billion the federal government allocated to basic research went to social science. Within the NSF, support of social science was meager; political science—because its political relevance might tie the NSF to politicization—received almost no funding at all.[33]

Harris hoped to contain the militarization of scholarship and policy, but his proposal revealed his own inability to come to grips with the problem. His bill contained two provisions designed to protect academic research from the perils of Defense Department sponsorship. First, all knowledge devolving from NFSS funds would be unclassified and publicly available. Under no circumstances would the foundation support classified research. But Harris believed that social research was necessary to cold warriors. After all, he explained, if the army was "getting ready to ship some people to Timbuktu," they did not have time "to wait around until somebody spontaneously decides to write a thesis about the mores and customs" there. To ensure that the national security state had access to the area knowledge it needed to accomplish its mission, he included a provision allowing military and intelligence agencies to transfer their research to the new foundation, provided that the projects were unclassified. The foundation would serve as "a sort of filter to remove any taint from military-sponsored or politically sensitive research abroad."[34]

But Harris's proposal would not civilianize the research; it would militarize the proposed foundation. Harris proclaimed that his system would ensure that projects desperately needed by the national security state would be carried out freely and openly, benefiting social science and national security policy while easing American foreign relations with the third world. Leland Haworth, director of the NSF, struggled to persuade Harris otherwise. If the Pentagon or CIA funneled money to the new foundation for research, even if that research was unclassified and politically neutral, he argued, "the new agency and all of its grantees would in all probability be 'contaminated' in foreign eyes." Such "funding subleties," he explained, were lost on foreigners. Even the Defense Department agreed that Harris's proxy clause "counteract[ed] the basic need to assure" the new foundation's "total independence."[35] It took two years for Harris to realize that the proxy clause would defeat his purpose. When he reintroduced his bill for the last time in 1969, he dropped it.

The proxy clause was far from the only issue standing between the Harris bill and a new National Foundation for Social Science. Despite expressing repeatedly their own concerns about military patronage, most social scientists were unreceptive to the proposal. Of fifty-three social scientists called to testify in front of

Congress in 1967, only fourteen unequivocally supported it. Many preferred to maintain their ties to the NSF, fearing that by creating a new institution, they were admitting that the social sciences were not, in fact, scientific. Others expressed concern that the new institution would only increase government interference in their disciplines. As psychologist James A. Bayton explained, he and his colleagues at Howard University "seriously question the professional competence of many who administer and conduct social research in the government." The NFSS could prove as dangerous to research as the State Department's new control over social research.[36]

Even if social scientists had supported the Harris bill, however, the congressional political will to create a new social science research agency in the context of mounting wartime spending was meager. In 1967, Representative Emilio Daddario introduced an amendment to the original NSF legislation that widened the foundation's mandate, allowing it to support applied social research. This modest reform succeeded. President Johnson signed the amendment into law. It did nothing, however, to address the issue of militarization in either scholarship or foreign policy.[37]

The "Empire" Strikes Back

The Pentagon took advantage of social scientists' and public officials' inability to agree on solutions to the intellectual and policy problems posed by its support for social science. In fact, it turned to its growing contingent of beneficiaries and defenders to shore up the contract state. As the Harris hearings commenced in 1966, the Department of Defense called on the Defense Science Board for guidance. Seemingly deaf to the changing political climate, the board produced a classified report that boldly endorsed continued military support for social science and staunchly defended the expanded role of the Department of Defense in the Cold War. "The DOD mission," the panel argued, "now embraces problems and responsibilities which have not previously been assigned to a military establishment. . . . The DOD must now wage not only warfare but 'peacefare' as well." Despite the political challenges posed by its research programs, the report argued, the Pentagon required studies of pacification techniques, persuasion, and social change to protect American national security. Rather than addressing the substantive concerns, shared among elected officials and some social scientists, about the impact that such projects had on scholarship and foreign affairs, the panel treated the controversy over military funding as a public relations problem. The report called upon elite social scientists working for the Department of Defense to publicize their commitment to national security work "as a way of reassuring younger scientists and improving our research image." The board also suggested that the Pentagon hire an "eminent behavioral scientist" and outfit him with a staff whose duty it would be to promote DOD-funded social research in Congress. In a stark indication of its lack of concern about militarization, the panel recommended that the Pentagon pay *foreign* social scientists to study the military establishments of U.S. allies.[38]

Even some members of the Defense Department expressed concern that the Defense Science Board committee failed to recognize the prevailing sentiment in Washington and academia. The head of counterinsurgency research for the Defense Advanced Research Projects Agency (ARPA) characterized the report's recommendations as "beyond the realm of political feasibility." For once, Horowitz and the Pentagon were in agreement. He warned that the study, which never addressed the question of the Pentagon's hold over research or foreign affairs, "can easily be read as the ominous conversion of social science into a service industry of the Pentagon."[39]

Indeed, that conversion had already occurred in scientific institutions thought to be far purer than anyone expected the Defense Science Board to be. Throughout the second half of the 1960s, the National Academy of Science's Advisory Committee on Government Programs maintained its lucrative contract with the Pentagon to provide support for and advice about its foreign area research projects. The advisory committee had been created at the behest of the Pentagon after the Camelot episode, but its leaders had so carefully managed its relationship to the Pentagon that some of its members claimed to be unaware of their contractual obligations. When the Pentagon asked the committee to review the Defense Department's entire foreign area program and advise it on the proper goals of its research in the spring of 1967, some members balked. Social psychologist Herbert Kelman offered to resign, explaining that although he had accepted research funding from the Defense Department, he could not advise the Pentagon as a matter of principle. Rather than losing its members, the NAS allowed them to recuse themselves from their advisory duties. Perhaps Senators Morse and Case were correct; the government relied on expertise only from like-minded scholars. Through both the NAS Advisory Committee on Government Programs and the Defense Science Board, elite social scientists continued to advise the Pentagon on issues including personnel psychology for pacification missions, strategies for attracting scholars to DOD work, and "how the behavioral and social sciences can relate to the missions of the Pentagon" more broadly.[40] Meanwhile, the Pentagon's critics railed from outside the halls of influence.

Although some Pentagon officials were concerned by the boosterism of the Defense Science Board report, the Pentagon remained openly defiant toward congressional and scholarly concerns about militarization. Throughout the late 1960s, John Foster Jr., the Pentagon's director of research and engineering, reiterated his belief that Pentagon sponsorship was fully compatible with academic values and objectives. DOD funds, he insisted, kept scholars at the forefront of international research and ensured the Pentagon a ready labor force equipped to protect national security. Likewise, the Pentagon's Donald MacArthur informed an audience at the 1967 annual meeting of the American Psychological Association that the Pentagon would continue to support the high-payoff field of foreign area research. He asserted boldly that there was "simply no question" about the matter. He asked psychologists to continue to push for theoretical and methodological breakthroughs relevant to social change, persuasion, and other subjects pertaining to the Cold War. The *American Psychologist*, the APA's flagship journal, reprinted MacArthur's address for the benefit of all APA members.[41]

The Pentagon's budget proved that MacArthur was sincere. In 1967, the agency increased funding for social research by 18 percent, from $34 million to $40 million. It also introduced a new funding initiative designed to enhance its support for long-range, militarily relevant academic research. Headed by ARPA and code-named Project Themis, the initiative sought to develop new centers of research excellence in the sciences and social sciences at American universities, particularly those "not already heavily involved in defense research." In its first year, Themis funded fifty projects at universities in forty-two states; fourteen of the projects involved behavioral research. The Pentagon enhanced its ties to the so-called ivory tower. Meanwhile, the State Department's share of foreign area research continued to decline.[42]

The Pentagon seemed eager to demonstrate goodwill toward academia—including academic values of openness. To that end, Foster announced in November 1967 that the Pentagon was declassifying basic research carried out on university campuses. What seemed like a sacrifice, however, was only a bureaucratic sleight of hand. Classified basic research amounted to less than 3 percent of the $154 million that the Defense Department spent on basic research at American universities. Furthermore, the Pentagon had no intention of canceling its classified basic research projects. Instead, it recategorized classified basic research studies it deemed crucial to national security as applied research. In a move that his opponents may have found insulting, Foster justified his new policy by invoking academic freedom. While critics of the DOD's research practices attacked classification as a threat to academic freedom, Foster argued the opposite: "Academic freedom is maintained not externally, but internally by the universities themselves in their autonomy to select and promote faculty." Refusing a scholar permission to work with the DOD, Foster implied, violated academic and institutional freedom. Furthermore, he reminded social scientists, the issue of freedom to publish was a moot point, at least as far as foreign area research was concerned. He reminded the public that, as a result of the Camelot episode, all government-funded social research relevant to foreign policy had to be reviewed prior to dissemination—a government-wide policy enforced by the State Department, not the DOD.[43] According to Foster, it was not the military that damaged academic freedom. Rather, those who attempted to curb the militarization of research—including the State Department—threatened it. Militarization was freedom. Demilitarization was censorial.

Such symbolic acts were not confined to the Pentagon. A month after Foster announced the new Pentagon policy, twenty-one government agencies, including the armed services, pledged to refrain from covertly supporting social research in foreign countries. This move came as part of a new set of guidelines issued by the Foreign Area Research Coordination Group, a State Department–managed, Defense Department–funded consortium of government agencies that sponsored social research abroad. Although the new guidelines attracted positive coverage from science journalists, they had almost no impact on government research practices. Most of the member agencies had never supported research clandestinely. Furthermore, the research coordination group was a voluntary organization, and the recommendations, too, were voluntary. Finally, the guidelines did nothing to reduce classified contracts. Just as some degree of militarization might be necessary to protect American democracy, the committee implied, so too was some degree of secrecy. The group simply suggested that agencies move their classified work from university campuses to nonacademic institutions.[44] Institutionally murky organizations like CRESS, which could claim to be academic or nonacademic as circumstances dictated, did not even take notice of the new guidelines.

The Foreign Area Research Coordination Group's guidelines revealed that federal government representatives, like the Harris Committee, and social scientists themselves sought a simple bureaucratic solution to the problems posed by the contract state. The group's desire to tackle the political and intellectual problems of military contract research coexisted uncomfortably with social scientists' need to sustain financial support for their work. As science journalist Daniel Greenberg remarked, the new guidelines indicated that social scientists and government officials "persist in striving for the impossible. They want the academic social sciences to partake of the presumed purity of the academic world and, at the same time, to serve as instruments of a government that quite readily acknowledges its involvement in some less than pristine activities around the world."[45] Indeed, time after time, scholars' and policymakers' efforts to rein in militarization—from the *Report from Iron Mountain*'s mockery, to social scientists' epistemological and bureaucratic debates—were ill-equipped for the challenge. Those who satirized the military-industrial-academic complex drew chuckles, but they offered no constructive solutions that would curb expert complicity in the Defense Department's growing power. Social scientists were paralyzed—whether by their financial dependence on the Defense Department, their fear of exposing the more value-laden aspects of their endeavors, or their reluctance to impose consensus on one another—and their paralysis rendered them unable to act beyond narrow professional self-interest.

No More Vietnams

Instead, opponents of the Vietnam War took control of the problem. Efforts to contain the military's impact on social research and foreign policy unfolded in tandem with Americans' growing opposition to the Vietnam War. The failure of social and psychological engineering programs, from propaganda campaigns to rural development schemes, to win Vietnamese hearts and minds tied social science to military failures that bore staggering financial and human costs. Senator J. William Fulbright, once a supporter of the peaceful and beneficent international mission of social research, became one of the most vocal critics of the military's social research program. In May 1968, he seized the opportunity offered by expanding public opposition to the war, convening the Committee on Foreign Relations for two days of hearings that would tie foreign area research to American failures in Vietnam. But Fulbright had a more ambitious goal. The Pentagon's social research program provided the Arkansas Democrat an opportunity to attack militarization itself.

Fulbright's hearings were a display of political showmanship intended to harness the military's social research program to its failures in Vietnam. He called only two men to testify—the Defense Department's Foster and navy admiral Hyman Rickover. Foster appeared first, and Fulbright commenced his attack. He challenged the witness to defend his agency's multimillion-dollar investment in social research that, though the Pentagon might call it "peacefare," in fact strayed far into territory that Rickover argued was more rightfully the province of the State Department and Congress. Foster replied with his typical defense. The State Department, he explained, had failed to perform research in areas where "national needs are clear"; the Pentagon would be happy to relieve itself of the burden of social research if only the State Department would take responsibility for more national security work. Foster also argued that far from militarizing foreign policy, social science reduced the armed services' militaristic tendencies. Contract research, he insisted, "create[s] an environment in which civilian, usually academic, analysts temper the purely military view with political, economic, and social perspectives." They would help the military pursue peacefare.[46]

Those arguments were mere prelude. Foster spent the bulk of his testimony defending the justification the Defense Department had invoked for two decades in support of its growing influence in Washington and around the globe. The Cold War had blurred the distinction between the civilian and the martial to such an extent, he argued, that the Pentagon's jurisdiction could not be clearly differentiated from that of the State Department. He explained, "We believe the Defense Department clearly shares responsibilities for international security and for preparations to ensure national security, which go beyond narrowly military considerations." This meant that research could not "be labeled categorically as 'military,' and therefore, the exclusive responsibility of the Defense Department; or 'political' or 'economic' and, therefore, the responsibility of the State Department or Agency for International Development. Serious research, responsive to actual national security problems, must cut across the board."[47]

Ten years before, Foster's statements would have elicited assent. In fact, they underpinned the justification for the Pentagon's growing research budget and its contract state. But by 1968, the politics of militarization had shifted, and Foster played right into Fulbright's hands. The leader of Pentagon research articulated precisely the mind-set that the senator intended to discredit. The Pentagon, Fulbright objected, had appropriated "responsibility for making political judgments all over the world." It usurped the power of other federal agencies, dominated the executive branch, ignored Congress, and "absorb[ed] practically all of the resources of the country" in secretive, profligate, and intellectually useless contract research institutes Fulbright also tied social research to the military's failures in Southeast Asia. When Foster tried to defend the Pentagon's social research portfolio by arguing that social science helped the military to understand events in Vietnam, Fulbright pounced. Referring to the Pentagon's repeated false claims about American success in the battle against the Vietcong, he retorted, "Well, I am sorry to hear that. It has not been very accurate, has it? We have been misled in this committee year after year."[48]

In contrast to Foster's tense and combative interaction with Fulbright and his committee, Rickover's testimony was friendly and comedic. Like Fulbright, Rickover's quarry was not merely social science, but rather the Pentagon's expanded physical, financial, and policy scope. The naval officer and the dovish senator joined forces in hopes of restoring the military to its traditional status. The Pentagon, Rickover complained, "now looks like an inverted pyramid, a huge civilian bureaucracy bearing down on the armed forces command over which it exercises almost total control." Social scientists were some of the most visible and easily targeted stones in the structure. Much to the delight of his audience, Rickover repeatedly ridiculed social science. He asserted, "there has got to be something wrong with you if you understand what they are saying."[49]

The committee's discussion of an army contract study code named Pax Americana captured well the tenor of Rickover's testimony. Also known as "Projected World Patterns, 1985," the study was a classified, $84,000 policy-planning project designed to infer the nature of international diplomatic relations for the next twenty years. Conducted under contract with Douglas Aircraft Corporation, it was intended "to stimulate long-range planners to speculate on the impact on national security policies and requirements that various alternative future world alignments would have." Armed with that information, the Pentagon could determine the best means to maintain American "world hegemony in the future." The study concluded rosily that by 1985 the world would likely move "toward a genuine Pax Americana."[50]

The project provided perfect fodder for the committee, where disdain for such research crossed party lines. While Fulbright and his fellow Democrats challenged what they saw as the Pentagon's effort to use social science to legitimize and extend its control of global events, Republicans ridiculed it as irrelevant and wasteful. Senator Karl Mundt attacked the army's choice of research contractor. He exclaimed, "I can't for the life of me see how an aircraft company is going to have a specialist in diplomacy and foreign relations and crystal ball gazing so they could project what our diplomatic posture is going to be in 1985." The fact that Pax Americana was security classified heightened the committee's suspicion that the Pentagon used secrecy as a cover for wasteful and inept contract research. Mundt wondered aloud "whether they classified this just to keep the taxpayer from knowing they were wasting the money." Indeed, experts in American foreign affairs who had seen the report told the *New York Times* that Pax Americana "reads like a freshman paper." The State Department concurred with these assessments, although not publicly. Following the media attention the study received courtesy of Fulbright's hearings, the department put its embassies on alert. It suggested that if local officials asked about it, the embassies "downplay [the] importance and value of [the] study, even to [the] point of deprecating its merit." Rickover's assessment was only slightly less generous. He told the Senate that "you get as profound and meaningful a statement from an average high school graduating class."[51]

Fulbright's hearings were a political success. They were timed to coincide with the Senate's appropriations hearings on the Pentagon's 1969 research budget. Although the Fulbright committee focused narrowly on foreign area research, which accounted for only 6 percent of the Pentagon's research budget in 1968, Rickover had managed to make it seem like the Pentagon's entire $8 billion research budget was devoted to costly, useless, and shoddy social research. And by demonstrating the Pentagon's sustained recalcitrance in the face of criticism—in his testimony Foster was singularly unapologetic about the department's expansive reach into research and policy—the hearings also seemed to prove that serious action was needed to contain the agency. In what *Science* described as a spontaneous revolt against military spending, senators on the left and the right united in the spring of 1968 to cut defense spending. And while they only managed to reduce 3 percent of the DOD's total research budget, that was no small feat. In the past, Congress had been unable to cut R&D spending even to that extent. The budget reduction may have been more symbolic than substantive, but it made a significant dent in the Pentagon's foreign area spending. The Pentagon had asked for $27 million for foreign policy–related research. In the end, it received only $13.7 million, $3.3 million of which could be used for foreign fieldwork. This was a heavy cut. Fulbright had successfully targeted what his colleague, Senator John Stennis, called "the softest spot in all the research and development program."[52]

At the same time that Fulbright and his colleagues assailed social science, a new and substantial threat to the gray area emerged. Student activists who mobilized against the Vietnam War also rallied against the Pentagon's social research program. For students as for senators, social scientists' argument that their work protected human freedom and extended democracy rang hollow in the face of the human suffering the United States inflicted on Southeast Asia. By the spring of 1968, opposition to U.S. foreign and military policy on university campuses was a part of almost daily life for students and faculty. At the University of Michigan, Cornell University, and Johns Hopkins University, students and faculty publicly debated the propriety of accepting classified and DOD-funded research. But it was Columbia University that attracted the most attention when, in April, violence erupted after over one thousand demonstrators seized five buildings on campus. Although it was the university's imperialist attitude toward Harlem, not the Pentagon's imperialist attitude toward Vietnam, that catalyzed the events, the Columbia chapter of Students for a Democratic Society (SDS) used the occasion to target the military-industrial-intellectual complex. Columbia University was a member of the Institute for Defense Analyses (IDA), the Pentagon-created, Washington-based nonprofit research corporation governed by a consortium of twelve universities. IDA was well known for its studies of counterinsurgency in Vietnam, and Columbia's affiliation with it was a concrete symbol of the university's complicity in the Vietnam War.[53]

Student activism developed more slowly at American University. But in late spring 1968, AU's student body too began to mobilize against the Vietnam War. Perhaps emboldened by the news that Hurst Anderson, AU's president since 1952 and the man whose zeal for international affairs had brought SORO to campus in 1956, was retiring, AU students went on strike. They issued a list of fifteen demands, including the total separation of the university from the national security state and full disclosure of the university's relationship with government. Nothing substantive came of the strike, but students returned to campus in the fall of 1968 emboldened by the presence of a new president open to change. At his inauguration, President George H. Williams broadcast his desire to shake things up. "Most universities have fallen into positions of defense," he explained, although he did not indicate if he intended the pun. His institution, he promised, would not be dominated by "the conservative who views change as an assault upon the bastion of stability."[54] Student activists were determined to hold him to his word.

By the fall of 1968, CRESS bore two stains. As a research institute performing classified foreign area work on university grounds, it was destined to attract attention. As a federal contract research center, it was targeted by Congress as one part of a grand system designed to expand the Pentagon's power. On AU's campus, student groups ranging from the reformist to the radical argued that CRESS made the university "a tool of government agencies."[55] Flyers announcing student strikes alleged that the university was teaching "bureaucrats to administer America's imperialistic foreign policy," accepting research funds from CIA fronts, awarding "degrees in counter-insurgency and develop[ing] techniques to repress the people of the Third World." The university, activists declared, was "part of the interlocking corporate power elite—the industrial (exploitation)-military (kill for freedom and/or money)-education (indoctrination) complex."[56] They insisted that CRESS be closed.

In the wake of the uprising at Columbia, this bombastic rhetoric generated tension among army officials and CRESS researchers. The research office hired a security guard to protect its cache of classified documents. Army officials put the local police and the U.S. attorney general on alert. But CRESS's contracting officer at the Pentagon was not convinced that these measures were enough to safeguard the research office. He was so concerned that radicals might "'march' on CRESS" that he tried to remove all classified documents from the research office, even though such a measure would dramatically slow the progress of research. He failed to persuade the army, but in true military fashion, CRESS and its sponsors created a standard operating procedure that would go into effect if students tried to occupy the CRESS offices, damage research, or steal classified materials.[57]

CRESS's planning was never put to the test. Despite its bombastic language, the AU student body was not particularly radical. No march on CRESS came to pass. In fact, when SDS members forcibly occupied President Williams's office during the 1968–69 academic year, they were ousted with equal force by a group of AU fraternity members and athletes. But the damage to the gray area done by the Fulbright hearings, appropriations debates, and conflicts at elite academic institutions meant that even moderate members of the university community insisted on change. The New AU, a non-militant campus reform group composed of students and faculty, did not insist that CRESS be closed; it did, however, request the university to cease accepting classified research contracts.[58]

For the university administration, growing student activism and congressional criticism signaled that the $270,000 in overhead funds the university reaped annually for housing CRESS no longer offset the cost to the university's public image. The New AU's attacks on the military-industrial-academic complex were only the latest in a series of public relations problems that had started with Project Camelot and had never abated. By 1968, the fact that AU was ranked ninth among universities receiving government funding for social science was cause for concern, not celebration. CRESS's board of advisers, established in the wake of Camelot to upgrade the research office's academic credentials, recommended that the research office reconsider its relationship to the university.[59]

Unlike Anderson, Williams was receptive to student and faculty concerns. Soon after his arrival on campus, he announced that an advisory board composed of university trustees, faculty members, and students would consider the future of classified research—and of CRESS—on campus. After lengthy deliberations, in April 1969, the committee released its findings. Although it did not reject Defense Department contracting on campus, it recommended that henceforth, the university only accept contracts for "projects whose primary purpose is basic research and/or the collection and release of findings in the normal matter of open research." It was clear that CRESS could not continue on at American University. The committee's findings reflected a sentiment similar to those at campuses across the nation—the urge to return to basic, unclassified research and the cessation of research activities unrelated to pedagogy. In an effort to more clearly relate the university's teaching mission to its research, the AU advisory committee insisted that the university should no longer maintain a class of research scientists who were not also active members of the teaching faculty. Research contracts could be negotiated only by full-time faculty members with regular appointments. Of course, as at other universities, AU's committee determined that temporary exemptions against classified research could be granted in times of national emergency. Its members gave no indication, however, that they considered the Vietnam War to be such an emergency. Williams announced that the university and the army would sever their ties the following fall.[60]

Williams's action was timely. In appropriations hearings for the DOD budget in the spring of 1969, Fulbright hit even harder at the social sciences than he had the previous year. He argued that the DOD's many studies of foreign nations indicated that Pentagon planners "are busily engaged in blueprinting strategies where our military will play the key role in trying to maintain order in a disordered world." "The thinking permeating much of this research is likely to lead," he argued, "to more Vietnams." With renewed congressional attacks accompanied by a year of student activism, some of it violent, the Defense Department finally bowed to public pressure. In an effort to protect the rest of its budget, it voluntarily cut foreign area research dramatically and vowed a further 70 percent reduction over the next two years. For fiscal year 1970, the Pentagon would spend only $6.9 million on foreign area research, and less than $1 million on fieldwork in foreign areas. The DOD also offered the State Department $400,000 to start its own foreign area research program, which was still only funded at $125,000, an offer they accepted.[61] And to ensure that the Pentagon ceased its incursions into nonmilitary research, Congress passed the Mansfield Amendment, which required that all Pentagon-funded research have "a direct and apparent relationship to a specific military function or operation."[62] The militarization of research and foreign policy, it seemed, was being tamed.

On October 31, 1969, American University and the army officially terminated their relationship. This assuaged AU students and faculty, and they promptly turned their attention to other issues of university reform and antiwar activism. But not all stakeholders were satisfied. Concerned that research vital to national security was being abandoned, Ithiel de Sola Pool sent a dire warning to Congress. He argued that with the reduction of DOD support for social science, "valuable and important efforts to make the defense program of this country more rational, more economical, and more humane, will be crushed between the millstones of the economy drive on the one hand and militant nihilists on the other." The Defense Department would become "the mindless doctrinaire organization that they [student activists] accuse it of being."[63] The director of his own for-profit federal contract research outfit and a member of MIT's Center for International Studies, Pool may have had a financial and professional stake in the continued largesse of the Defense Department. Even so, in a number of unexpected ways, he would prove to be right.

FADE TO BLACK

The Enduring Warfare State

The Vietnam War compelled American activists to attack the military-industrial-academic complex. But their goals were far loftier than merely ending the conflict in Southeast Asia. As Michael Klare argued emphatically in his 1970 exposé *War without End*, "only the complete dismantling of the Pentagon's intervention capability . . . will guarantee that we will not be dragged into more Vietnams." By systematically unmasking what Klare termed "the Pentagon's counterinsurgency apparatus"—its rich coffers, dense institutional network, faulty science, perverse psychology, and secretive and brutal operations—activists aspired to end militarization itself. The war, it seemed, had proven Harold Lasswell prophetic. Secrecy, national security, and third world stability trumped unfettered scientific inquiry, government accountability, and participatory democracy as the Pentagon's "specialists on violence" assumed dictatorial control of American foreign and domestic policy. The military, economist Seymour Melman warned, was becoming a "para-state"; unless stopped, it would lead the United States down the path to fascism.[1] So when CRESS and American University officially terminated their relationship in October 1969, activists rejoiced. It was a small victory in the broader battle against militarization, but they believed they had reinstated the boundary between academia and the military, at least as far as American University was concerned. The warfare state, they believed, could no longer rely on CRESS to legitimate its actions.

But they were wrong. The day after American University severed its ties to CRESS, its staff arrived at their offices as usual. Rather than reporting to American University, they checked in with a new parent organization—the large, private, nonprofit contract research agency American Institutes for Research (AIR). This development was far from unusual in the late 1960s and early 1970s. Antiwar activists' critiques were compelling enough to oust a number of the military's research outfits from campuses across the country, but divestiture proved a poor match for the tremendous scope and power of militarization. By the end of the 1970s, the number of private contract research agencies had grown exponentially. The military would come to be even more dependent on militarized expertise; but after universities severed their ties to the Pentagon, the quality of that expertise diminished and its institutions became more clandestine. The gray area faded to black in the 1970s as the curtain descended between the military's researchers and their former colleagues on academic campuses. Yet those researchers also became more powerful. Over the course of the 1970s, Sorons would come to wield unprecedented influence over counterinsurgency strategy, both abroad and at home.

From Exile to Growth

AIR began modestly in John C. Flanagan's basement. A Harvard-educated psychologist who was unable to secure an academic appointment during the Great Depression, Flanagan turned instead to military research. In 1941, after persuading the army that it needed a "practical psychologist" to tackle the personnel and human factors challenges of training a fleet of pilots, the Army Air Forces commissioned him at the rank of major and charged him with creating an aviation psychology program. By war's end, he was directing 150 commissioned psychologists and a support staff of over fourteen hundred researchers.[2]

Flanagan left his wartime experience with a finely honed sense of his client's research needs and the government's financial largesse. To capitalize on growing research budgets in the military and other federal agencies, he incorporated AIR in 1946 as an independent, nonprofit institute. Declaring that "for the Institute knowledge is not an end in itself," he approached research contracting as a client-centered business in which his company would provide research-based solutions to problems requiring "immediate practical" results. His model was a success. By 1956, AIR boasted seven research divisions devoted to studying personnel selection and evaluation, military and industrial leadership, and human factors problems. In its first decade, the institute completed over one hundred studies for clients including the Defense Department and the individual armed services, as well as the Pennsylvania Turnpike Commission and various private industries.[3]

Unendowed nonprofit institutes, which relied on a steady source of contracts for their operating funds, could be financially precarious. To shelter AIR from the vagaries of research contracting, Flanagan shrewdly insisted that research contracts also result in tools and techniques that were marketable to other users. The system was not always successful. One project—a classified Defense Department study that was designed to simplify the Manhattan Project's research and development model "so that nonscientifically-trained personnel can put on repeat performances"—never amounted to much. But by the 1950s, AIR regularly applied its military aviation selection, classification, and training tools to civilian aviation. By 1969, AIR ranked sixty-third among all nonprofit research institutes (including the largest nonprofit weapons researchers) that contracted with the federal government. Most of its contracts, which totaled $1.68 million that year, were with the Defense Department.[4]

AIR's military training research led the institute onto CRESS's turf. In the early 1960s, AIR pioneered a program that would become one of the army's most successful, or at least one of its longest-running, Cold War social science endeavors. Called "Fight the Cold War: A War of Ideas and Convictions," the training program taught American soldiers stationed abroad how they could spread goodwill and stability by displaying their cultural sensitivity. AIR pioneered the program in Korea. Using attitude surveys and interviews, researchers isolated the causes of enmity between American soldiers and Korean nationals. They found that Americans perceived Koreans as "dishonest, unsanitary, fatalistic, and immoral (due to engagement in 'rampant prostitution')." Koreans, not surprisingly, bridled at this stereotype, creating a self-perpetuating cycle of cultural misunderstanding. Having isolated the causes of this misunderstanding, AIR researchers designed a training program for Korean nationals and American troops that, they argued, successfully changed perceptions and eased relations. Army officials reported that in the wake of the training program, the number of criminal offenses Koreans committed against U.S. personnel declined by almost 50 percent. The army was so pleased with this outcome that it contracted with AIR to extend the program to Thailand in 1967.[5]

AIR's success established it as a leader in cross-cultural and counterinsurgency research at precisely the time that the United States was increasing its investment in such work in Southeast Asia. In 1968, ARPA awarded AIR $1.2 million to assess the effectiveness of the Thai government's U.S.-backed counterinsurgency programs. Researchers proposed a system to evaluate the results of economic, political, and social action programs, sorting those that most successfully united the population behind the government from those that had little effect. True to form, they expected that their measurement tools could be widely applicable to other counterinsurgency and cross-cultural contexts. Foreshadowing events of the early 1970s, they also anticipated extending the study's methodology to domestic problems in the United States. Researchers explained, "In many of our key domestic programs, especially those directed at disadvantaged sub-cultures, methodological problems are highly similar to those described in this proposal."[6] Counterinsurgency was a growth industry, and AIR was poised to benefit.

The Thai study's researchers were specialists in international educational testing and vocational training, not in counterinsurgency. But the Cold War transformed education, like so much else, into a military tool. So when former Sorons reported for work at AIR after they were severed from American University, they found themselves quite at home. The merger of the two institutions proceeded without a hitch. American University simply transferred its army contract (and CRESS's office space) to the institute. CRESS's director, psychologist Preston Abbott, remained at AIR with much of his staff. Researchers continued their investigations of revolution, counterinsurgency, and psychological warfare as they had before. By acquiring CRESS, Flanagan's outfit significantly increased its counterinsurgency expertise. It also dramatically expanded its research portfolio. AIR more than doubled its contract research income; the institute shot to thirty-sixth among nonprofit government contractors, and first among those focusing exclusively on social scientific research.[7]

The military benefited in multiple ways from CRESS's divestiture. In the 1950s and early 1960s, military research managers had argued that federal contract research centers uniquely melded scholarly objectivity to national security relevance. But CRESS's patrons had complained repeatedly throughout the 1960s that the research office was too oriented toward academic values to fulfill the army's operational needs. Uniformed officials charged that researchers failed to sufficiently understand the practical challenges confronting those battling for foreign hearts and minds. But under Flanagan's client-centered tutelage, former Sorons soon found themselves the recipients of Pentagon accolades. The Pentagon's Seymour Deitchman ranked AIR alongside RAND as one of the top "sources of first-rate talent" available to the Defense Department in the 1970s.[8]

Ironically, congressional action designed to reduce military influence over research also encouraged social researchers to intensify the military relevance and rhetoric of their work. In 1969, Congress passed the Mansfield Amendment, which required that all Pentagon-funded research have "a direct or apparent relationship to a specific military function or operation." Congress intended the amendment to put an end to the military's profligate support of projects like Camelot and Pax Americana that seemed only to allow the Pentagon to further encroach on the State Department's turf. But the tightened budgets of the Mansfield era made it crucial that the army spend its money wisely by fitting its research programs even more closely to military needs. As a result, the Pentagon asked researchers to emphasize operational, rather than scientific, aims. At AIR, former CRESS researchers ceased arguing for the scholarly relevance of their work and instead focused directly on its utility to military and national security policy. Whether investigating counterinsurgency or third world vocational training, they tied their research directly to anticommunist military goals.[9]

But all of this happened beyond the purview of the American public. CRESS's move to AIR insulated it from the penetrating gaze of intrusive antiwar activists; it also protected it from congressional meddling. As an FCRC, CRESS had suffered constant financial instability. Because FCRC budgets were allocated annually by Congress, long-term planning was difficult even in flush years. Furthermore, because the Pentagon had to line-item budget the funding for each of its research centers, CRESS and its compatriots were easy targets for cost-cutting congressmen. Once at AIR, however, CRESS quickly shed its FCRC classification, freeing itself from line-item budgeting and the constraining budget ceilings that Congress had placed on FCRCs in 1967.[10] Liberated from congressional and activist scrutiny, yet more beholden than ever to their military clients, former Sorons continued their research.

CRESS's expulsion from its university home along with its rebirth in the private sector was far from an isolated phenomenon. In the late 1960s, student activists and public intellectuals successfully ousted a number of similar institutes from university campuses. But they failed to shutter the military-industrial-academic complex itself. For example, activists forced the Institute for Defense Analyses (IDA)—the multimillion-dollar DOD-funded consortium of twelve elite universities—to sever its ties from the University of Chicago, Princeton University, and Columbia University in 1968. *Science* reported that many IDA supporters feared that student activists had "lacerated the guts of one of the Defense Establishment's most elite and intricately constructed institutions," but actually the institute only sustained a flesh wound. IDA's trustees—each of whom represented one of the twelve member universities—reconstituted the organization as a private, nonprofit contract research institute. The institute's three hundred researchers continued to serve the Defense Department from their desks at IDA's headquarters, a ten-story office building on the outskirts of the Pentagon. Similarly, the Human Resources Research Office (HumRRO)—CRESS's sister institution at George Washington University—reorganized as a private, nonprofit institute in 1969 after sustaining repeated attacks from student and antiwar activists. Its research staff of approximately 275 social scientists continued studying human factors for the army.[11]

Activists had sought to dismantle the entire military-industrial-academic complex, but they repeatedly scored only Pyrrhic victories. Private, university-affiliated institutes with close ties to the Pentagon also vanished from campuses in the wake of student protests. The Stanford Research Institute (SRI), for example, created in 1946 to house the university's growing contract research portfolio, earned three-quarters of its income, an impressive $28 million in 1968 alone, from Pentagon-funded studies of counterinsurgency, weapons development, and other defense-related technologies. When protests forced Stanford's reluctant board of trustees to divest the university of SRI, it privatized as an independent, nonprofit contract research organization. A number of Stanford faculty followed defense dollars and left academia for SRI. In 1974, with $40 million in government contracts, the facility was the second-largest nonprofit federal contractor in the country. Once separated from the university, however, it largely fell from activists' radar.[12]

Academic exile did not simply allow military contract work to continue beyond scholars' and activists' notice. It also encouraged the growth of a lucrative private research contracting sector. With government contracting largely removed from academic environments, private nonacademic institutes could compete more readily in the market. A significant contingent of contract researchers struck out on their own when their institutions were severed from universities. While twenty-five members of Stanford's staff left the university for SRI, six more left to create their own businesses.[13] The same was true of Sorons. While many joined AIR, a number added their own research agencies to the landscape of Pentagon contracting. Instead of taming the military-industrial-academic complex, divestiture fueled the growth of an insular network of think tanks and consulting agencies that would serve the national security state well into the 1980s.

Institutional proliferation was fueled by the remarkable flexibility of militarized knowledge. Social psychologist Lorand Szalay, for example, reinvented CRESS's militarized studies of communist social psychology as investigations of domestic race relations and substance abuse, which he carried out on contract for a variety of federal agencies. Szalay had come to social psychology by way of Budapest. He had served in the Hungarian army during World War II, and his harsh treatment as a Soviet POW inspired him to study systematically ideology's impact on behavior. He joined CRESS in 1962, a year after immigrating to the United States. Seeking a technique that would substitute "solid, empirically founded knowledge" for the "guesswork and intuition" that guided American interactions with communist-threatened peoples, he developed a method that, he argued, revealed the psychological meanings that peoples of different cultures attached to various words.[14] A kind of parlor-game-turned-military-research-tool, the method rested on free association. Szalay would give his subjects a word—like "freedom," "equality," or "ideology"—and for one minute, he would record all their associations. After tabulating responses from hundreds of subjects, he created "dictionaries of cultural use" that informed Americans what different cultures *really* meant by those terms. At CRESS, and later at AIR, Szalay applied the method, which he named Associative Group Analysis (AGA), to psychological operations and cross-cultural communications research on Vietnam and Korea.[15] He found, for example, that Americans and South Koreans had very different associations with the theme "food." For Americans, the term sparked associations related to generous U.S. aid packages; Koreans associated it with corruption. Perhaps less usefully, Szalay's method also revealed that many Americans correlated "respect" with Aretha Franklin, while Koreans did not.[16]

Once at AIR, Szalay diversified his research subjects, adding investigations of domestic race relations to his examinations of U.S.-Korean communication. In studies funded by the Office of Naval Research, he investigated racial divergences among whites, blacks, and Puerto Ricans in the armed services.[17] Research on race attracted funding in the late 1970s. Szalay left AIR in 1976 to open a private consulting agency, the Center for Comparative Cultural Studies; he took Jean Bryson, a colleague since his CRESS days, with him. The center performed research on race and communication for any government agency that paid. From the late 1970s through the 1990s, Szalay adapted AGA to investigations of Iranian-American communication for the Department of Education, Hispanic sailors' "psychocultural dispositions" for the navy, various groups' attitudes toward civil defense for the Federal Emergency Management Administration, and Puerto Rican drug abusers for the Department of Justice.[18]

While AGA made no discernible impact on the field of social psychology, its flexibility allowed it to travel with other former Sorons into a variety of contract research and consulting agencies, including those created by Szalay's former colleagues. The adaptability of militarized knowledge to a variety of topics and venues played an important role in the remarkable intellectual insularity of the growing contract research industry. Howard Kaufman, whose tenure at CRESS had overlapped with Szalay's, applied AGA to research he performed under the auspices of two different FCRCs and his own consulting agency. Kaufman, an anthropologist who was for a time a member of IDA's elite Jason Division, which advised the Pentagon on cutting-edge counterinsurgency strategies for Southeast Asia, left CRESS in 1967 for the Cornell Aeronautic Laboratory, another defense FCRC. The laboratory had been hired to assess a Pentagon-funded Thai government program designed to use technology to enhance rural villagers' allegiance to the central government. Officials in Bangkok hoped that by providing televisions to a number of rural Thai villages, they could win peasants' hearts and minds. To assess the technology's efficacy as a medium of attitude change, Kaufman went to Thailand armed with a battery of projective psychological tests, including the AGA. Kaufman used the technique to probe Thai villagers' changing associations with words like "progress," "government," and "sponger."[19]

AGA was not the only CRESS product Kaufman recycled in the Thai countryside. He modeled his study on Project Simpatico, SORO's effort to measure the impact of U.S.-financed Colombian civic action programs on the attitudes of rural Colombians. Although Simpatico had attracted unwanted media attention when SORO's Colombian researchers filed lawsuits against the research office, Kaufman described the project as a success. He explained, "In Colombia it had been possible, by employing relatively inexperienced field researchers with limited educational background, to gather a quantity of reliable data." He used the same technique in Thailand, hiring village headmen to administer psychological tests, including the AGA, in eight villages. Whether the study was as successful as Project Simpatico remains a mystery. Kaufman never published its results in the open literature. But it successfully applied SORO's militarized techniques to projects that adapted a domestic technology to militarized goals. And when the Cornell Aeronautic Laboratory met a fate similar to CRESS's in the late 1960s, Kaufman struck out on his own. He continued his research for USAID through his new consulting firm, Rural Research Inc.[20] Although intended to reduce the collusion of scholarship and national security, university divestiture ironically encouraged researchers to adapt their methodologies and techniques to new institutions, for new sponsors, and in ways that further enhanced the projection of militarization abroad.

Divestiture did not merely increase the contract industry's intellectual insularity; it also fostered insularity in the contracting workforce. Contract research institutes had long taken advantage of a revolving door with the Pentagon to bring military expertise into the private research sector. With the exception of C. Wright Mills, who warned in 1956 that behind the revolving door lay "the great structural shift of modern American capitalism toward a permanent war economy," most Americans took little notice. But by the late 1960s, critics argued that this phenomenon endangered democracy. As military officials moved from the Pentagon to high-paying research jobs and consulting positions, they influenced military policy as civilians. According to one congressional investigation, by 1970 over two thousand retired high-ranking military officials were employed in the top one hundred defense contracting firms—a number three times higher than it had been in 1960. And this human resources insularity, not surprisingly, intensified the intellectual narrowness of national security research and advising. Lieutenant Colonel Phillip Katz, a retired psychological operations officer who worked for both CRESS and AIR, for example, used his research studies as opportunities to persuade the U.S. military to increase its use of psychological operations in urban warfare.[21]

The growing contract research industry also created a revolving door for civilian defense intellectuals. While most former Sorons remained research contractors at AIR or other institutions, Jeanne S. Mintz used her expertise in defense contracting as a stepping-stone to the Pentagon itself. She had left SORO in 1966 to join the Center for Naval Analyses (CNA), the Defense Department's oldest FCRC. Her CNA work took her to Vietnam, where she oversaw an effort to develop electronic sensors, like urine sniffers and seismic monitors, that were designed to detect insurgents. Mintz left CNA when the Pentagon ceased renewing the institute's electronic battlefield research contract as a result of the Nixon administration's Vietnamization policy. In the early 1970s, Mintz freelanced on a variety of ARPA-funded electronic battlefield spin-off projects. That work took her to DOD's MITRE Corporation, the private consulting firm Braddock, Dunn and McDonald, General Research Corporation, and the Systems Planning Corporation. In the late 1970s, she finally joined the Defense Department itself. As a staff specialist for planning, she designed and managed the Pentagon's long-range R&D programs related to counterinsurgency; she also managed the Pentagon's relationships with its independent contractors. During the 1980s, she served as assistant deputy undersecretary of defense for Asia, Middle East, and Southern Hemisphere Affairs in the Pentagon's Economic Security Directorate. Her dedication to using her political scientific and area studies expertise in the service of American national security was perhaps best reflected by the fact that Richard Perle, President Ronald Reagan's assistant secretary of defense and a longtime member of the Defense Policy Board Advisory Committee, eulogized her at her memorial service in 1994.[22]

The proliferation and growing insularity of research contracting agencies in the 1970s were also artifacts of the revolving door. While Mintz moved from contract research to the Pentagon, other researchers moved from Pentagon strategy positions to private research institutes, where they won contracts by exploiting their personal connections to national security agencies. Soron R. D. McLaurin built a long and successful career in this manner. After earning his master's degree from the Tufts Fletcher School of international affairs in 1966, he worked for three years as a Middle Eastern specialist in the Pentagon's office of International Security Affairs (ISA), advising the Defense Department on international politico-military issues. He left the Pentagon for CRESS in 1969 and transitioned to AIR later that year. He spent six years at AIR performing contract research studies for ISA; he also continued to consult privately with the Defense Department.

McLaurin maintained very close contact with his ISA colleagues, thanking them into the 1980s in the acknowledgments of his unclassified publications.[23]

McLaurin was also a key participant in the proliferation of research contracting agencies in the 1970s. In 1975, Preston Abbott—the director of CRESS who remained with his staff when CRESS was absorbed by AIR—left AIR and established Abbott Associates, his own private, for-profit research contracting firm. Several former Sorons—political scientists William E. Hazen and Paul Jureidini, former State Department official James R. Price, and retired psychological operations expert Katz—defected with him. So did McLaurin, and his contracts with his former ISA employers formed a crucial part of Abbott Associates' contract portfolio; some of those contracts, furthermore, were subcontracted through AIR.[24]

The growing insularity of government contracting did not go unnoticed among those who left the contract research world. In the early 1970s, critics of the Pentagon's contracting system worried that researchers, invested as they were in maintaining a steady flow of income, often advised their patrons to continue, and even escalate, conflict.[25] Writing from Abbott Associates, McLaurin and his colleague Jureidini nearly admitted as much. Arguing against policymakers and scholars who hoped that the Israeli-Palestinian conflict might be drawing to a close in the wake of the Camp David Accords, they explained that it was a "protracted social conflict" that was immune to intervention; they counseled Americans to let the conflict run its course. Their argument was eerily reminiscent of the satirical *Report from Iron Mountain*. McLaurin and Jureidini explained, "It is in the nature of the dynamics of protracted social conflict that the many benefits accruing from an institutionalized conflict are clearer or more real and immediate than those devolving from peace." Peace, in fact, would be a "crisis" for "scholars whose productivity is rooted in the conflict."[26] It certainly would have been for Jureidini and McLaurin; they and their colleagues at AIR and Abbott Associates held contracts with the army's Limited Warfare Laboratory throughout the 1970s and 1980s for a series of studies of the conflict in the Middle East; and they often published sanitized versions of their research in the open literature. They were not unusual for holding such long-term contracts. A 1981 study by the General Accounting Office (GAO) found that once a research contract corporation had a contract, they fought against its termination; GAO reported that nearly 60 percent of the contracts it studied had been renewed repeatedly, some for as long as twenty-eight years.[27]

By removing CRESS and similar research institutes from universities, activists hoped to reinsert the boundary between scholarly expertise and the national security state. They were partially successful; by the late 1960s, they had evicted much of the military-industrial-academic complex from university campuses. But activists had also hoped that this boundary-drawing exercise would tame the militarization of foreign policy and American government institutions. Instead, it unwittingly intensified it. Facing the tightened R&D budgets of the Mansfield era, the military's researchers carefully articulated their military relevance. They could no longer argue that they might help create a more pacific, civilianized approach to American military and foreign policy.

Tightened military budgets, furthermore, inspired researchers to seek out nonmilitary funding. CRESS's intellectual approaches traveled from Korea and Colombia to Southeast Asia; but just as important, they also traveled to Washington as psychological warfare and counterinsurgency research methodologies were reborn in Szalay's studies of domestic racial, educational, and health issues. By the 1970s, the world of research contracting was more militarized. It was also more insular, in both its intellectual output and its personnel. Fifteen years after CRESS was exiled from American University, its researchers still moved through research contracting and advising positions, drawing upon their government connections to build their own niches in the military-industrial complex.

Yet, with the most egregious examples of Cold War scholarship driven off university campuses, and with activists exhausted by years of protest and activism against the Vietnam War, the private contract research sector largely vanished from public consciousness by the mid-1970s. The problem of militarization faded from public debate at the same time that the research contract landscape fostered by the American obsession with national security expanded in size and scope. The changing American political climate, too, helped to obscure militarization's persistence. With the polity moving decidedly to the right, policymakers endorsed the privatization of national security research as good free-market politics as well as a tool for containing government growth. According to one count, by 1984, the United States boasted between four and five hundred not-for-profit social research centers devoted to both military and civilian research. And the older divested research centers continued to prosper. Analysts of research contracting in the 1970s identified AIR and HumRRO as two of the best social research centers in the country.[28]

In an era of conservatism and opposition to the ostensible big government and antibusiness policies of the Great Society, Republicans argued that privatization delivered intellectual goods better and more efficiently than Johnson's warfare (and welfare) state had. And they did so from another set of proliferating research institutes. At the same time that the military's contract researchers established their growing, insular network, private conservative research foundations like the American Enterprise Institute (AEI), the Heritage Foundation, and the Cato Institute commanded increased influence in Washington.

These organizations had origins distinct from those of AIR and other military contracting institutes. They also had different goals. The military's contract researchers understood themselves as technical advisers, hired to provide nonpartisan, scientific research of use to their clients. Researchers at AEI, Heritage, and other institutions of the New Right were political advocates funded by private institutions; their think tanks were created to break what the Right saw as the Left's grip on political discourse. They produced reports designed to market their ideas to the public, Congress, and the media. But as they gained in power and prestige, they also drew attention away from militarization's perpetuation in the less visible institutions of the contract state; in the 1970s and 1980s, academic and journalistic exposés of the so-called "shadow government" focused largely on these think tanks.[29]

Serving Power with Impunity

Had the policymakers and commentators who endorsed AIR and its ilk as models of government-funded social research more fully examined the intellectual products of the contracting world, their assessments might have looked quite different. Expelled from universities, contract researchers became even more isolated from first-rate social scientific thought and even more dependent upon their patrons than they had been in the first twenty years of the Cold War. In the 1950s and 1960s, Sorons and others often served power; but some had also sought to challenge the policy status quo. In the 1970s, however, the Pentagon's researchers truly became servants of power; they produced knowledge that by design openly and unquestioningly affirmed the Cold War status quo. And even more consequentially, some of the knowledge they produced shaped national security policy more profoundly than SORO's hybrid military-social scientific knowledge ever did. Just as militarized research accomplished some its most significant applications, it also proved to be deeply flawed.

After absorbing CRESS, AIR revamped the research office's psychological warfare work. Led by former Soron Katz, researchers created a new and influential psychological warfare research and planning tool. Named PAMIS, it was a computerized information storage and management system that systematized the dizzying variety of information required to plan, carry out, and evaluate psychological warfare programs. Katz and his compatriots had sought a system for rationalizing psychological operations since SORO was created in 1956. But SORO's work had fallen short. Researchers had produced a series of country-specific handbooks—the fruits of Project Prosyms—that counseled psyops officials on how best to communicate with communist-threatened peoples. The handbooks included some of the same information that PAMIS would provide—descriptions of the major social, cultural, political, and ethnic groups in target countries, the types of media they consumed, and the common symbols that evoked particularly powerful psychological responses. But even some of the Sorons who had worked on the project, including Jeanne Mintz, expressed reservations about its usefulness; it stereotyped various foreign populations, its psychological appeals were untested, and its methodology was unproven.[30]

By contrast, PAMIS was a resounding success. Far more comprehensive than CRESS's communications guides, PAMIS was composed of three databases. The Foreign Area Data System stored abstracts of scholarly work, intelligence documents, and think tank research in order to provide a searchable, analytical database of the social groups, values, and media of target countries. Just as they had with the Human Relations Area Files in decades previous, psyops planners could generate descriptive summaries of and bibliographies about the populations they planned to influence. The Foreign Media Analysis System was a repository of indigenous media analysis that purported to reveal the psychological vulnerabilities of target populations. To create the database, analysts combed foreign media sources, identifying the topics that foreign populations considered important—from U.S. foreign aid to Soviet military developments—and tracked how foreigners viewed the Cold War's protagonists. The Effects Analysis System maintained records of every American psychological warfare program—past and present—as well as all known enemy programs; it was hoped such information would help psychological operations specialists assess American successes, failures, and vulnerabilities. For Katz and his colleagues, PAMIS was a fully automated, fully militarized version of the Human Relations Area Files.[31]

The army began operationalizing PAMIS in 1972. By 1976, all three databases were fully operational. When the army issued a *Field Manual for Psychological Operations* in 1979, it devoted a chapter to explaining PAMIS, which all psychological operations staff officers were required to use. With PAMIS established as a central tool for psychological warfare planning and evaluation, the Joint Chiefs of Staff took on financial responsibility for maintaining and updating the system. Its massive mainframes were housed in the Pentagon.[32]

PAMIS was well suited to the insular world of 1970s defense contracting. Its architects used their command of the system to win further Defense Department contracts over the course of the decade. McLaurin and Katz, working from both AIR and Abbott Associates, used PAMIS to analyze Arab perceptions of the United States for ISA.[33] They hoped, in fact, to demonstrate PAMIS's applicability beyond the realm of psychological warfare operations; they used the system to demonstrate its utility to long-term foreign policy and military strategists. Perhaps, they reasoned, PAMIS could accomplish something Camelot had failed to; it might render unsystematic diplomatic gamesmanship into a scientific, rational, systematic exercise. This high-reward research idea even attracted ARPA funding to Abbott Associates. In a 1977 report for what was arguably the most elite wing of Pentagon research funding, researchers explained that their goal was to develop a policymaking approach "sufficiently simple and concrete that it could, once applied, be easily employed by Defense Department analysts having little or no connection with and no knowledge of the research on which the system is based." With automated tools, bureaucrats with no other expertise than the ability to manage punch cards and a mainframe could predict foreign responses to U.S. military actions and recommend the most effective strategies for achieving American aims.[34]

Given ARPA's secrecy, it is impossible to know if PAMIS proved its merits in this regard. But its designers and users at AIR and Abbott moved into increasingly influential policy advising positions in the 1970s and 1980s. In addition to assuming the presidency of Abbott Associates in the late 1980s, McLaurin served as a private consultant for the Lebanese Ministry of Defense and the Lebanese army. A remarkably prolific researcher, he penned dozens of contract research studies and authored, coauthored, and edited at least eight books on psychological warfare, U.S.–Middle East relations, and U.S.-Korean relations between 1975 and 1988.[35] Jureidini was perhaps more influential. He participated in President Carter's Cabinet Committee to Combat Terrorism in the 1970s, briefing representatives from the CIA, the FBI, the DOD, and the State Department on the likelihood of future Palestinian terrorist attacks on Americans. In the 1990s, he was a consultant for the conservative Washington Institute for Near East Policy, which advised the George H. W. Bush administration on U.S.–Middle East policy. He earned this position by virtue of his long association with the army's Human Engineering Laboratory; he was the Washington Institute's resident expert on terrorism and urban violence.[36]

Jureidini and McLaurin did not achieve their influence by producing pathbreaking intellectual work. Quite the opposite. They owed it in part to their political affinity with presidential administrations more conservative than those of the 1960s; but their willingness to defend the Pentagon's position on the Middle East—a position that was under fire in academic circles in the late 1970s— was crucial to their continued success. Jureidini, McLaurin, and their fellow researchers at AIR and Abbott were unusual in the world of contract research for frequently issuing declassified monographs for public consumption. And in reviews of their work, the scholarly community roundly criticized their corpus as politically reactionary. In 1977, University of Manitoba anthropologist Louise E. Sweet pilloried McLaurin's colleagues William E. Hazen (a former Soron) and Mohammed Mughisuddin for their edited volume *Middle Eastern Subcultures*. A collection of writings by men connected to U.S. foreign policy research and advising, she explained, the work expressed "only pro-American viewpoints of the more reactionary varieties." Showing "more than ignorance," she continued, "the book is anti-communist and anti-socialist, and the authors fail to face the issues of poverty, oppression, colonialism, and imperialism as sources of social movements in the Middle East." Jureidini and McLaurin's *Beyond Camp David* fared equally poorly. One reviewer, who was himself a consultant for the national security state, complained that it was little more than "a cut-and-paste synopsis of the reports of their government consulting efforts." Brandeis University's Avigdor Levy was blunter. The book, he said, was "a 'science fiction' approach to complex socio-political realities."[37] But as research projects like Camelot and research systems like PAMIS indicated, simplified approaches to complicated policy problems were precisely what the Pentagon sought, and successful contractors knew how to deliver. Military agencies repeatedly relied upon these men for expert research and policy advice about the Middle East. Despite their inferior intellectual contributions—or perhaps because of them—some contract researchers inserted themselves handily into the world of national security policymaking.

Academic researchers, who by the 1970s were increasingly concerned with the complicated social and political ramifications of the projection of American power, were increasingly irrelevant to Washington policymakers. They were also increasingly irrelevant to contract researchers. Sweet's critique signaled that the intellectual and political divide between the worlds of contract research and academia continued to grow. While scholars in anthropology and area studies examined the nature of Western hegemony, contract researchers remained insulated from work on the microphysics of power and social domination. Although the activists of the 1960s could likely never have foreseen this consequence, research contractors severed from their ties to academia continued to peddle outmoded intellectual models and theories well into the 1970s.

This problem was perhaps most acute in the field of military modernization. The devastating failure of American-backed modernization efforts in South Vietnam discredited both America's military interventionism and the theories that supported it among wide swaths of the academic social science community. Yet former Sorons continued to offer new studies to their military patrons that relied on scholarly models of modernization that had been declared bankrupt by the academics who had once been their greatest defenders.[38]

In the early years of the Cold War, military planners, policymakers, and many social scientists took on faith the idea that civic action programs—American-funded development projects carried out by the indigenous military forces of a communist-threatened nation—were powerful tools in the battle against communism. In the first twenty-five years of the Cold War, the United States had supported over forty such programs, providing funding for militaries to build roads, hospitals, and schools and to provide health, education, and job-training services. Such projects were based on the conviction that they would improve the local population's welfare and, in the process, their good opinion of the government and its military. But time after time, these projects failed to achieve their intended results, and by the late 1960s a growing number of Americans, including a few military officials, questioned the idea that Pentagon support for development projects guided by foreign militaries in unstable and often undemocratic nations—from Vietnam and Korea to Guatemala and Brazil—benefited either American national security or developing peoples.[39] And without a social scientific tool kit with which to assess the success or failure of their programs, neither military policymakers nor the Pentagon's social scientists could defend their programs effectively.

AIR promised to rectify this problem. In late 1969, a team of four former Sorons began the search for scientific criteria that uniformed civic action teams could use to design and evaluate their programs. Veteran Soron Ralph Swisher led the charge. He had been enticed away from graduate studies in international relations by the offer of a slot on the Project Camelot team. When Robert McNamara canceled the study in 1965, Swisher remained at SORO; he transitioned to AIR in 1969. Swisher and his collaborators grounded their study in military and social scientific theory, combing the literature to identify all the ways that civic action was thought to encourage national development and internal stability. They then devised a set of assessment criteria, complete with data collection instruments, and applied them to American-supported civic action programs in South Korea. The study resulted in a three-volume report, published in 1972, that covered the scientific and practical sides of civic action. True to AIR's form, it yielded tools that nonspecialists could apply in any national or regional context; in AIR's work, as in much contract research about foreign areas, history and culture were either universal or irrelevant. One volume, designed for civic action personnel unversed in the social sciences, described a hypothetical, communist-threatened developing nation called "Lunaria," which was beset by an ethnic insurgency, rural underdevelopment, and illiteracy. Swisher applied his assessment techniques to prescribe and evaluate an appropriate civic action program, which included such staples as technical agricultural assistance, literacy training programs, and road construction. Lunaria was perhaps one of the most success-ful cases of American civic action efforts. In Swisher's evaluation of the hypo-thetical program, he reported that five years in, there was a "growing impression [among Lunarians] that the military are genuinely committed to the well-being of the population."[40]

Distribution of Swisher's report was limited to government agencies. But had opponents of the military's research contract industry been given the opportu-nity to see it, they would have found a troubling fact: it not only failed to ques-tion civic action as a nation-building technique; it also bore out a number of the criticisms leveled against research contracting by opponents of the industry, particularly contractors' tendency to support the policy status quo and ignore innovations in social knowledge. In this case, those tendencies were mutually reinforcing. Noting that there was little scientific evidence that could prove or disprove the assumption that civic action fostered feelings of national conscious-ness, Swisher began his investigation by simply endorsing the technique. Citing the Joint Chiefs of Staff definition of civic action, which was, in essence, an as-sertion of its anti-communist benefits, Swisher explained that such programs "contribute not only to welfare, but also to socioeconomic development" and the "strengthening [of] internal defense." His study was designed to demonstrate how, not if, civic action achieved such lofty goals.[41]

Swisher's unwillingness to challenge the policy status quo was partly due to the structural constraints of contract research. A researcher's duty was, above all, to fulfill his client agency's needs without being too critical of its policies. This was a lesson some contractors learned the hard way in the 1960s, when those who voiced political opinions or reached conclusions critical of their sponsors saw their funding threatened or terminated. In the early 1960s, the U.S. Agency for International Development canceled contracts with the Univer-sity of Oregon and Oregon State University after researchers criticized govern-ment policies in South Korea and Thailand. And in 1968, the armed services sent a clear message to scholars who accepted defense funding; when a group of academic mathematicians supported in part by military funds published an antiwar statement in the journal of the American Mathematical Society, the Army Research Office and the Office of Naval Research threatened to terminate their research contracts.[42]

Beholden to his patrons' political values, Swisher produced a report that rested on a set of outdated social scientific theories. *Military Civic Action* taught uniformed personnel to test whether their programs instilled in traditional populations two crucial modern psychological sensibilities: confidence in the possibility of economic, political, and personal progress, or, in social scientific terms, "achievement orientation"; and "scientific and empirical orientation," the belief that one can control one's own environment and destiny through technical development. Military personnel were instructed to pre- and post-test target populations by asking them to respond to statements like, "It is better to live for today and let tomorrow take care of itself," and "There is usually a way of dealing with any problem, and if you try to solve problems, you will usually obtain some successful results." By the time Swisher published his report, these ideas were under sustained assault within the very social scientific community that had nurtured them. But insulated as he was from academic social science, he produced a report that rested on discredited scholarship. Prior to the report's publication, twenty-five uniformed civil affairs officers and a handful of Swisher's colleagues at AIR reviewed his work. But neither AIR nor the army circulated the study to social scientists—or indeed, any other external experts—for review.[43]

The activists who attacked research contracting in the late 1960s were right: power and politics were deeply embedded in contract research. But that problem only intensified as contract work was removed from academic settings. Even at SORO, the army's researchers had been nominally attached to academic life; some trained students and taught courses. Many presented papers at annual meetings of social science societies. And a number published their research in academic journals. Once at AIR, researchers had little contact with their peers in academia, and academics had little knowledge of the work contract researchers produced. Like Swisher's project, most research reports took the form of "gray literature"—they were distributed in limited numbers to the agency that paid for the work and to other interested research outfits and federal agencies. They were not peer reviewed, nor were they widely available to scholars even when they were unclassified. Research emanating from contract research institutes was treated as proprietary knowledge. And its quality suffered as a result.[44]

As Swisher's work indicates, once banished from academic settings, military contract researchers continued to produce studies that rested on outdated intellectual assumptions. In fact, they had to. Researchers who questioned the policy status quo found themselves without contracts, even when their challenges were less profound than those of the contract researchers who attacked the Vietnam War. Kaufman—the Thai specialist who established the consulting agency Rural Research Associates in the late 1960s—took on a contract with USAID in 1970 to study the relationship between economic development and counterinsurgency in the Thai countryside. With financial support from the United States, the Mekong Coordinating Committee hoped to promote economic development in rural Thailand by damming various portions of the Mekong River. The committee's goal was to use economic development to contain the rural insurgency that plagued the nation. AID hoped that by lengthening the growing season, the dam would allow Thai farmers to increase their productivity and income. But AID officials and the Thai government were concerned that farmers, mired as they were in tradition, would refuse to alter their agricultural practices. Kaufman set out to investigate the problem. After seventeen months in the field, he produced a report that departed dramatically from the status quo in U.S. government-funded modernization theories. He wrote that neither fatalism nor laziness kept Thai farmers from second cropping. Farmers were sold on American ideas of progress and profit; only 3 percent of his research subjects were content with their lot in life. But they knew that there was no market available for their extra crops. "The allegedly tradition-bound farmer is prepared to innovate, to radically change his farming habits," Kaufman explained, if only these farmers could be guaranteed "a fair price for their produce."[45] That was a feat that could only be accomplished by structural economic reform. Modernization rested not on Thai farmers' achievement orientation, but on the Thai government.

Kaufman's departure from the policy status quo sounded the death knell for Rural Research Incorporated. He was not disenchanted with modernization theory so much as he was vexed by the way USAID and other government agencies used it to obscure the political causes of rural poverty. He concluded his report with an unsolicited and unorthodox section titled, "Some Post Mortem Thoughts Worthy of Consideration." In it, he excoriated American experts who continued to assume that the denizens of the third world suffered from "underdevelopment syndrome." He suggested that rather than continuing to fund social research, the United States invest in practical programs that would reduce the corruption in Bangkok and enhance rural markets. His frustration evident, he informed USAID that "the shelves are filled with excellent socio-economic research papers describing the farmers' needs, problems and aspirations. The literature is replete with recommendations. The time has come to stop all of this research, to synthesize all that has been written, and to initiate various action programs."[46] Research had become a means of evading confrontation with the Thai government, and Kaufman refused to participate further. His consulting agency folded.

AIR, by contrast, continued to prosper as it produced research that fully embraced the ideology of the Cold War. Institute researcher Robert L. Humphrey spent the early 1970s repackaging AIR's "Fight the Cold War" training materials, originally developed for U.S. soldiers stationed in Korea, for a broader audience. He renamed the program and its text *Human Values and the War of Ideas: A Set of Discussion Materials*. Funded by the Office of Naval Research, the text was the basis for an educational program designed to stimulate marines stationed at home and abroad to articulate their national ideology. Humphrey's materials guided the marines' instructor, or in AIR's terms, the "ideological warfare discussion leader," through conversations that encouraged enlisted men to "identify and activate [their] common values."[47] The benefits of the training program, of course, would ramify abroad, as marines were stationed around the world, and into American society more broadly after trainees left the service.

Humphrey's work was designed to counter the climate of ideological fatigue that marked American society in the years after the Vietnam War. His text would ensure that Americans continued to frame their common values in Cold War terms. Humphrey posited that because the Cold War was fundamentally ideological, the United States' greatest assets were "our most cherished political values . . . *freedom and equality.*" Yet, he insisted, his program was no mere exercise in patriotic jingoism. He based the training materials on his PhD thesis, in which he claimed to have scientifically proven that there is "one basic, universal, natural value in human relations"—the idea of human equality—and that value was best served by American democracy.[48] All humans valued their own lives, he reasoned; they also equally valued the existence of the species as a whole. Democracy, of course, was the system that best balanced the interests of the individual and the group.

The belief that scientific reason and democracy operated in symbiosis, and the conviction that democracy was best protected by experts—values expressed by Sorons like Earl DeLong in the early 1960s—lived on in Humphrey's work. His system, he argued, rested on a scientific ethic; it was "a rational system by which most persons will gain the confidence and ability to perceive what is scientifically right," and will act accordingly. Perhaps cognizant that his continued support for the military status quo would guarantee further contracts, he even used his "scholarly" method to justify American support for the less-than-democratic regimes the United States aided abroad. He explained that, unfortunately, freedom did not mean the same thing for all peoples. Rather, it "means *all of the freedom that is possible, consistent with freedom's purpose,* which is maximum support of . . . human life" in any given context. "In the small, poor, hard-pressed developing countries," he explained, "very little freedom or democracy is possible if freedom is to serve its life-supporting purpose." After all, the government needed to ensure that there was enough stability and order to sustain life. However, he explained, as long as those countries "generally support[ed] the side of democracy versus the dictatorial form of government as a goal," they were demonstrably democratic and deserving of American support. Humphrey's argument perhaps even exonerated American actions in Vietnam; he dedicated the publicly available version of his training materials to his brother, who had been killed in the war.[49]

Humphrey's work indicates the persistence of Cold War ideology in contract research; it also demonstrates its flexibility. He had adapted a version of his scientific ethic to a program used by the Americans in the late 1950s and early 1960s to persuade the Italians and Turkish to accede to American emplacement of Jupiter missiles. AIR used it to ease cross-cultural communication problems during the Vietnamization of the war in the late 1960s and early 1970s. And the Office of Naval Research extended it broadly to marines enlisted in the corps' Human Relations Program.[50]

By the 1970s, former Sorons could finally claim that they had influenced military and foreign policy. But at precisely the moment that research attained its greatest significance, it also became its most opaque—the military versions of Humphrey's work were as unavailable to academics and the public as were the fruits of Swisher's civic action work and Katz's PAMIS system. The activists who helped to dismantle the military-industrial-academic complex intended to protect democracy from the military's experts. Unexpectedly, in the wake of divestment, contract researchers were free to serve power with impunity.

Counterinsurgency at Home

Divestiture had yet another troubling unanticipated consequence. Militarized knowledge was so flexible that its purveyors easily adapted techniques for cross-cultural communication and counterinsurgency to domestic problems like racial unrest. By the early 1970s, Humphrey's *Human Values and the War of Ideas* training program instructed marines to turn America's foreign policy values back onto the United States. A unit devoted to race relations encouraged soldiers to approach the issue at home just as they did cross-cultural interactions abroad.[51] Instead of combating the militarization of American foreign policy, divestiture helped militarize American domestic policy.

When Congress sought to rein in the Defense Department's growing influence and financial power in the late 1960s, Pentagon research managers realized that their FCRCs—which had long been restricted solely to defense work—would have to court contracts from civilian agencies in order to survive. RAND paved the way in the mid-1960s. Its contractors increasingly chafed at air force control over their work, and when the service threatened to significantly reduce RAND's funding, researchers began to move from civil defense problems to the study of urban communications and renewal. By the end of the decade, RAND experts funded by the New York City government researched the creation of a "crisis anticipation system" for the city that would use public opinion research to predict and avert riots. The military's other FCRCs followed suit. When Congress slashed defense research funding in the spring of 1969, Secretary of Defense Melvin Laird wrote to the heads of several civilian agencies, including the Department of Housing and Urban Development and the Department of Health, Education, and Welfare, to offer the services of RAND, IDA, CRESS, and others. Concurrently, the Pentagon's director of research encouraged its FCRCs to actively pursue their "opportunities to help with domestic needs such as transportation, urban development, housing, pollution control, medical services, and other fields."[52]

Applying counterinsurgency expertise to domestic community development made intellectual sense to military-funded social scientists. As Chester L. Cooper, the head of IDA's International and Social Studies Division, explained, "I have the feeling that, when you get a group of bright guys together you have a responsibility to cope with the problems not only of Saigon and Prague, but places like Washington as well." By the end of the decade, IDA's experts moved among research projects on urban housing, natural disaster planning, and Southeast Asian counterinsurgency. As historian Jennifer S. Light has explained, with urban problems reframed as national security challenges, it seemed natural that military approaches were well suited to domestic problems. Social welfare, too, could be understood in militarized terms.[53] It only seemed natural that former defense research managers should oversee the new civilian research divisions that mushroomed at former military research institutes in the late 1960s and early 1970s. Seymour Deitchman, who had been instrumental in leading the Pentagon's counterinsurgency research program during the 1960s, helmed IDA's Office of Civil Programs in the 1970s.[54]

CRESS's domestic research was notably more militarized than much of the work done at IDA and the New York City–RAND Institute. Policymakers and the FBI had worried since the 1940s that black activists were instruments of the Communist Party. By 1967, the threat appeared significant enough to enlist the CIA; agents began gathering intelligence on civil rights activists under the cover of a project code-named Operation Chaos. The army began collecting intelligence about political dissidents the following year, and in 1969, it enlisted CRESS researchers in a study of race riots.[55] With Carl F. Rosenthal leading the way, Sorons set about containing domestic national security threats with the same techniques they had projected abroad. And they would take their domestic focus with them to AIR.

Rosenthal, who had joined SORO in 1965, was an expert on communist subversion techniques. For much of his tenure at SORO, he analyzed civil disturbances in foreign countries, evaluated psychological warfare techniques, and investigated the role of intelligence in counterinsurgency planning. He completed his master's degree at the University of Illinois in 1967 with a study of "Communist Insurgency in Theory and Practice," a thesis that emerged directly out of a SORO research study of almost the same title.[56] In 1969, he extended his expertise to a study of American race riots, funded by the army's Limited Warfare Laboratory. Like most white Americans at the time, Rosenthal found racial unrest deeply unsettling. Worried that the United States was experiencing strife that was surpassed in violence and hostility only by the Civil War, he warned, "If nothing is done to relieve the conditions that prompt hostile outbursts, it is conceivable that underground black organizations could organize widespread campaigns of violence and that white organizations could retaliate with campaigns of counterviolence." He forecast that, unless social scientists discovered and treated "the psychological and social ills" that divided the races, black unrest "could even become an underground movement" threatening the nation's survival.[57]

Rosenthal cast his project in the language of social science. But in fact it was part of a wider army effort to generate less lethal and more effective population control technologies—an effort developed after the Kerner Commission and internal army reviewers both excoriated the service for relying heavily on rifles, shotguns, and even submachine guns to restore order in cities like Detroit and Newark. Rosenthal's client, the Limited Warfare Laboratory, had been founded in 1962 to design and test counterinsurgency technologies for the third world; by the late 1960s, it sought technologies useful at home. Despite Rosenthal's lip service to the liberal argument that government should address the underlying social conditions leading to violence, he concluded his report with the suggestion that the army use chemical means, like tear gas and dyed water vapors, to cause disorientation and break up mobs. After all, he reasoned, perhaps these riots would never have occurred if the police had used better nonlethal weapons during the early phases of race disturbances.[58] Rosenthal's report had limited distribution; had black activists and intellectuals had access to it, they would have had powerful ammunition to support their claim that they confronted a militaristic colonialism within the United States.

Rosenthal's work extended military methods to domestic contexts, but it was not until they were at AIR that former Sorons found themselves able to more fully militarize population control at home. At SORO, Rosenthal and his colleagues were restricted from contracting with domestic agencies. Once at AIR, however, they were free to apply their psychological warfare and counterinsurgency expertise to problems faced by domestic agencies. In the process, they continued to redefine political dissent—whether directed against white supremacy or American foreign and military policy—as insurgency. Upon arriving at AIR, Rosenthal took on a Department of Justice contract for a study of conflict and violence on

American university campuses. Hypothesizing that student unrest was a phenomenon nearly identical to third world revolution and race riots—after all, student protesters showed their disloyalty to their university just as guerrillas and black rioters showed disloyalty to the regimes they opposed—Rosenthal used the same techniques he had applied in previous studies to investigate American student movements. Just like communists, he surmised, student ideologues could whip their fellow classmates into frenzy by playing on the faddism of youth.[59]

Not one to challenge the extension of military and paramilitary methods into civilian life, Rosenthal suggested that chemical tools like tear gas were among the best means available to contain unrest when it reached the riot stage. (Ironically, those same methods would soon be forbidden to U.S. counterinsurgency forces operating abroad when the United States banned the practice in 1975.) But he also suggested that the authorities—faculty, administrations, local police, and even the National Guard—work to proactively contain student unrest by giving it little fertile ground in which to take root. The university, with the support of trained covert police officers, should create their own in-house version of Operation Chaos to "identify revolutionaries, known troublemakers, and other antisocial elements" who were most apt to foment or join demonstrations. In addition to maintaining up-to-date biographies of suspected rabble-rousers, Rosenthal recommended that university administrations gather intelligence about social and political concerns on campus. Hopefully, he wrote, the authorities could intervene before events reached the crisis stage; but at the very least, they would be ready when protests erupted.[60]

The youth movement fractured in the early 1970s, but white Americans continued to worry about black radicalism. Rosenthal's fear that, left untreated, the "riot virus" could foment domestic revolution motivated other AIR researchers in the 1970s.[61] Citing quantitative evidence marshaled from her comparative study of forty-four revolutions, longtime Soron Doris Condit argued against the idea, nurtured by the American failure in Vietnam, that henceforth the United States should consider supporting foreign revolutionaries seeking change. She explained, "Revolution appears to be a highly infectious commodity. . . . It is thus not idle to ask whether, if the United States supports revolution abroad, this will not in turn give impetus to internal demands, for example, the newly-discovered 'nationalism' of ethnic groups within the country." Condit's report was published the same year that fears of race war made their way to Hollywood. In 1973, audiences of *The Spook Who Sat by the Door* discovered that black CIA agents might use their counterrevolutionary training to whip up black nationalist sentiment and start a race revolution at home.[62]

While Rosenthal's and Condit's work militarized violent domestic conflict and treated rioters and political dissidents as enemies of the state, other AIR research

projects militarized urban life itself by framing nonviolent minority urban populations as potentially troublesome groups requiring the expert managerial skills
of defense intellectuals. Development experts concerned with the third world
had argued since at least the early 1950s that civilian police forces abroad were
often the front line in the battle to win hearts and minds; the Eisenhower administration even included police training programs as required components
of some of its foreign aid packages.[63] In the early 1970s, AIR researchers turned
to Humphrey's highly adaptable "Fight the Cold War" approach to extend this
logic to domestic contexts. They contracted with the city of San Francisco for a
study designed to ease the relationship between the city's police department and
minority communities.

While the project drew its inspiration, in part, from foreign aid programs, it
owed its methodology to Humphrey's research in Korea, which had demonstrated
that cross-cultural misunderstandings were responsible for the problematic relationship between Korean nationals and U.S. troops. As AIR police-community
relations researchers explained, the problems of "cross cultural relations abroad"
and "subcultural relations" at home were remarkably similar. American soldiers
in Korea criticized Koreans' responses to the U.S. foreign aid program: "Americans basically felt we were giving money away to people who did not want to
work and who were lazy. The analogous critical issue in the police-community
relations context was welfare."[64]

Just as they had in Korea, AIR researchers conducted attitude surveys, interviews, and community engagement forums to determine the key sites of
rupture in this particular "cross-cultural" conversation. They investigated their
subjects' views of police brutality, racial profiling, and black political action
to create educational materials that would overcome the community-police
perceptual divide, creating goodwill by breaking down racist myths and community resentment. Researchers helped police officers to understand and sym-
pathize with the African American plight by leading them in discussions of
The Autobiography of Malcolm X. And upon discovering that police strongly
agreed with the survey prompt "There is a possibility of armed revolution from
the Black community" (a statement to which community members, both black
and white, responded neutrally), they educated community members about the
"historical consequences of internal turbulence in determining the survival of
a country."[65]

The study never resulted in a long-term police-community education program. Residents, not surprisingly, expressed concerns that by trying to adjust
public attitudes about the police rather than responding substantively to community concerns, AIR had created a domestic "pacification program." And police officers only reported to training sessions when they were made mandatory

(a requirement that the police officers quickly dispatched). But AIR researchers considered the study a qualified success. Policymakers, citizens, and police agencies in forty-five cities across the country expressed interest in the program.[66] The AIR study was part of a much wider phenomenon. Over the course of the late 1960s and 1970s, a variety of community policing programs spread across urban America. And the military continued to hold a central role in domestic policing. The army trained perhaps as many as ten thousand police administrators and officers in riot control, "civil disturbance planning," and other policing techniques through the late 1970s.[67]

With political protest reframed as revolution and riot control recast as counterinsurgency, the military's experts extended their purview to domestic contexts and, in the process, criminalized dissent. From AIR, IDA, and other contract research institutes, they imposed the logic of population control, underdevelopment, and containment on American cities, university campuses, and minority populations. And many police departments, from Washington, D.C., to Chicago to Los Angeles, were receptive to these techniques.[68] Activists had hoped to protect democracy from the dangerous side-effects of militarization; they hoped to disempower the state's experts, reduce the national security state's intellectual opacity, and reopen discussion of American foreign and domestic policy to public participation. But ironically, the implications of divestiture further threatened democracy. Researchers continued to provide their clients with classified and otherwise unavailable knowledge. Perhaps more dangerous, they and their clients cast domestic movements for enhanced political participation as military problems. By defining social movements intended to enhance democratic participation in domestic and foreign policy as subversive, contract research implicitly devalued participatory democracy.

Academic Retreat

Carl Rosenthal and his cohort never perceived their actions as antidemocratic. Quite the opposite. By invoking the language and methods of social research, contract researchers believed that they could successfully reframe contested political problems like racism, nationalism, and economic and political inequality as technical, scientific challenges. The idea that social science could render policymaking scientific, objective, and value-free was alive and well in the world of contract research during the 1970s. The scholarly argument that values could not be divorced from knowledge—an argument that motivated many critics of the military-industrial-academic complex—failed to persuade most defense intellectuals to leave contracting for more academic (or at least less politically coercive) pursuits. Fewer than a dozen of the more than two hundred men and women who worked at SORO over its fifteen-year existence left research contracting for academia.[69] As the national security state came to rely even more exclusively on second-rate research reports produced by institutions isolated from advances in academic research and insulated from outside scrutiny, policymaking and democracy suffered. Despite the best efforts of scholars, academic critiques of militarization failed to resolve the tensions between the military's expertise and participatory democracy. Militarization's bureaucratic momentum and intellectual flexibility outlasted and overpowered its opponents.

Even the few researchers who were persuaded by the events of the 1960s to leave the national security state did not do so because they objected to militarization. Like Robert Boguslaw, rural sociologist Ritchie Lowry left SORO for academia in 1966 in the wake of Project Camelot's cancellation. Far more dedicated to Cold War ideology than Boguslaw, he believed that the research office's failure to realize the lofty aims of the project was a national tragedy. In his letter of resignation, he wrote passionately, "Never in the history of our government has there been so great a need to marry effectively the diverse worlds of government and social science." But as both sides blamed the other for Camelot's failure, the two spheres were becoming "*openly* hostile to one another." Although he was leaving research contracting for Boston University's Sociology Department, he promised not to yield in the fight for scientifically informed national security policies. To his former boss Theodore Vallance he wrote, "For my small part, I will continue in any way possible from my position in academe to promote, encourage, and conduct the kind of fundamental research which is so vital to all of our interests."[70]

Lowry did not object to militarization. To the contrary, he normalized the militarization of international politics in a 1970 article in the respected journal *Social Problems*. The growth of military governments abroad and the increased power of the military-industrial complex at home were not, he argued, the consequences of "plots, cabals, or coups." Rather, they were "the result of evolutionary processes of change." As militaries became more important to the management of international peace and the political and economic development of new nations, he explained, they naturally took on more civilian and political roles. Lowry's evolutionary scheme absolved American policymakers of responsibility for supporting militarized, undemocratic regimes in the developing world. Critics who accused the United States of hypocrisy for supporting military dictatorships while denouncing communism as undemocratic failed to recognize that "the nondemocratic, nonresponsible nature of governments in many new nations may be a function of the sequence of developmental processes" of the nations themselves. Military rule was merely an evolutionary step on the path to democracy.[71]

Lowry conceded that some aspects of militarization contradicted the tenets of American democracy. In 1972, he published an article based on his experience at SORO that attacked security classification. Most opponents of secrecy worried that classification undermined democracy by limiting public access to government information and protecting decision makers from public scrutiny and accountability. Lowry offered another trenchant critique of classification: it enabled "the production and protection of relatively useless and unreliable knowledge, [and] the consequent guarantee of individual and organizational and job security." Security classification, he revealed, helped to guarantee the financial health of the contract state while protecting its intellectual deficiencies.[72]

But by the end of the 1970s, Lowry appeared to have resigned himself to the permanence of militarization and the secrecy that helped to support it. In a review of leftist critiques of CIA covert operations, he mused, "If one attacks the system with an axe, will they not simply be cut down?" All critics accomplished, he explained, was "challenging the [national security state] to become more effective at what they are doing." Lowry had a point. Critics of state-sanctioned secrecy had few successes of which to boast. The *Pentagon Papers* helped to further discredit an already unpopular war, but they certainly did not dissuade Richard Nixon from pursuing secrecy in Southeast Asia and in his own reelection campaign. Criminally secretive acts destroyed his presidency, but he escaped criminal sanction. And while the Senate Select Committee on Intelligence publicly exposed the FBI's and CIA's secretive surveillance of American citizens in the mid-1970s, it too failed to rein in secrecy. By the 1980s, Lowry gave up on the possibilities of reforming the military-industrial complex and turned instead to publishing popular guides to socially responsible investing. Disillusioned with both the government and his own ability to act with consequence against the national security state, he withdrew to the private sector.[73]

Social scientists' professional associations proved no more adept at tackling the militarization of scholarship and politics. In 1970, members of the American Anthropological Association's (AAA) fledgling ethics committee received evidence that seemed to implicate some of the association's members in Pentagon-funded counterinsurgency programs. In the spring, the Student Mobilization Committee to End the War in Vietnam forwarded a set of documents, obtained via dubious methods, to three members of the ethics committee, including its chair, Eric Wolf. The materials indicated that three anthropologists were involved in Pentagon-funded research designed to control the communist insurgency in Thailand. Wolf and his fellow committee members immediately and publicly condemned their colleagues for breaching the AAA's policies regarding clandestine research, without further investigation. The association again found itself mired in a contentious debate over the relationship between knowledge, national security, and American hegemony.[74]

Anthropologists trod a fine line. After debating the implications of government-sponsored foreign area research in the wake of Project Camelot, the AAA had approved a "Statement of Anthropological Research and Ethics" that condemned anthropologists' participation in clandestine intelligence operations. But the association was as divided over its own disciplinary police powers as it was over the appropriate boundary between scholarly research and government advising. The statement discouraged academic institutions from undertaking classified defense research projects and urged anthropologists to avoid clandestine intelligence activities, but it did not condemn private consulting carried out through nonacademic venues. It was also nonbinding. And although it urged researchers to "be especially concerned" about the impact sponsors might have on their work, it also encouraged them to lend their expertise to government.[75] By acting in the service of the government, they risked becoming accomplices of the national security state's repressive acts; but by failing to act, they might be complicit in the government's uninformed actions.

Not surprisingly, the AAA was uncomfortable with its own institutional power over its members. The ethics committee's mandate was ambiguous. First convened in 1969, it had not yet determined the extent of its jurisdiction over scholarly ethics. Senior AAA officials had only empowered it to "build up a file of anonymous cases diagnostic of ethical conflicts."[76] As Eric Wakin explains in his careful examination of the controversy, Wolf and his compatriots acted on the belief that the documents—minutes of meetings and copies of research contracts—were damning evidence of the "direct complicity of scholars in the antischolarly task of implementing counter insurgency programs." The evidence, they argued, "comprises untenable corruption of social science and scholarship."[77] The accused, however, defended their actions and questioned the ethics committee's jurisdiction. Herbert Phillips, whom Wolf revealed as a participant in USAID- and ARPA-funded studies of American intervention in Thailand, suggested that the ethics committee's actions posed a potential threat to scholarship, national security, and scholars' political freedom of expression. He asked, "Is one's primary loyalty to the truth, to one's own integrity, to the Thai people, to one's profession and colleagues, to one's nation, to one's political beliefs?"[78] The association's power might be as repressive as the state's.

The question was a serious one for a discipline that was increasingly concerned about the coercive nature of intellectual and institutional power. Opinions on the subject were divided—perhaps even more so than they had been during the days of Project Camelot. While Phillips argued that "the establishment of such priorities is essentially one's own moral business, not something to be established by some external moral authority," others argued that the anthropologists were endangering Thai freedom and American democracy. Wolf and Marshall Sahlins argued that Phillips's collusion with the state would eventually allow the Pentagon to apply "the methods of totalitarian manipulation now being perfected by our scientists abroad" to the United States itself.[79] AIR's work, of course, demonstrated that such fears were well founded. But other anthropologists viewed Wolf's actions as the greater threat. Ralph Beals, one of the principal architects of the association's ethics code, insisted that Wolf and his colleagues be removed from the ethics committee. Wolf's allies, in turn, demanded that Phillips and his fellow contractors be ousted from the association. After months of debate, a reluctant executive board established a committee, chaired by Margaret Mead, to investigate the controversy.

But the committee also failed to resolve the problem. After an investigation, it condemned Wolf and his allies for engaging in "McCarthyite tactics" by publicly attacking the Pentagon's consultants without a fair investigation. In a finding that seemed to tacitly accept the militarization of anthropology, it exonerated the Thai specialists by arguing that counterinsurgency research was not "as sinister as it sounds." It was merely a label applied by the Defense Department to a set of activities that included "construction of roads, schools, and organization of medical care, . . . much the same activities that were called 'community development' in an earlier time." But when the Mead committee presented its report to the association's voting membership, it was roundly rejected. Instead, in a midnight session, the AAA voted to "consider the issue of anthropologists in Thailand unresolved."[80] Anxious about the potentially coercive nature of power, a number of anthropologists were reluctant to exercise their own institutional power—even in the name of protecting their knowledge from what many perceived to be military corruption. The consultants found themselves in an ambiguous place; they had been exonerated by the committee, but remained suspect in the eyes of many of their colleagues. A few resigned their membership in the AAA permanently.

Some anthropologists would continue to call on their colleagues to confront what they saw as the problematic consequences of militarization throughout the 1970s, but to little effect. In his 1976 Presidential Address to the AAA, Walter Goldschmidt chided the discipline for its inability to confront power. "We fear power, we avoid the centers of power, we do not even see the uses of power within the tribes we study," he explained. Even when anthropologists attempted to counter the power of the military-industrial complex, he argued, they resorted only to political protest. Wary of exercising coercive intellectual power themselves, they failed to use their knowledge of Southeast Asia to attack American foreign policy. Although Goldschmidt appealed to anthropologists to recommit themselves to using their knowledge to solve social and political problems, his plea went largely unheeded.[81] Critics of militarization were right: it had enhanced the coercive power of the state and of knowledge. But the critique of militarization had drawn attention to the myriad, often invisible forms of intellectual and institutional power. Hyperaware of the potentially repressive power of their own knowledge, many anthropologists scorned action altogether.

Other social sciences fared little better. The Caucus for a New Political Science had struggled in the late 1960s and early 1970s to make the American Political Science Association more democratic and the discipline more politically relevant. Invoking a critique that echoed Boguslaw, the caucus's members condemned their elders for being "technicians rather than scientists" and called for their discipline to take a more critical and activist stance in American political life. But the caucus's candidates failed to penetrate the top ranks of the discipline's leadership. While the behavioralist paradigm crumbled under the weight of political instability at home and abroad, the dons of political science turned not to the radical critiques of American hegemony suggested by the caucus, but to an accommodationist literature. As Ido Oren explains, some of the most influential political science texts of the 1970s argued that the American political system, while requiring some reform to enhance economic equality and political participation, was fundamentally sound. The caucus had hoped to replace the discipline's quest for a value-free, objective science of politics with an activist and socially engaged approach. But by the end of the 1970s, many political scientists turned from behavioralism to rational choice theory as the best hope for achieving a science of politics.[82]

Fade to Black

In 1962, Harold Lasswell cautioned Americans. "The master challenge of modern politics," he wrote, "is to civilianize a garrisoning world, thereby cultivating conditions for its eventual dissolution."[83] Antiwar activists, scholars, and policymakers took on that challenge. They demonstrated that militarization damaged scholarship, encouraged secrecy, and threatened participatory democracy.

But they failed through no fault of their own to civilianize the warfare state. Their efforts proved no match for militarization's remarkable durability. Instead, American scholarship and foreign policy continued to be shaped by national security concerns as researchers continued to pursue military-funded nation-building projects and psychological warfare programs; and militarization extended to domestic contexts, as contractors managed urban unrest and political dissent with the tools of counterrevolution and counterinsurgency.

Equally troubling, the Pentagon's researchers stood at the ready as the State Department, long considered by social scientists and the Defense Department retrograde in its reluctance to use social research, at last increased its external research contracts in the 1970s. In 1971, the State Department conceded that it was no longer "the sole source of wisdom on foreign affairs," and the Bureau of Intelligence and Research tripled its research budget. By fiscal year 1972, the bureau spent almost $1 million on research; most of that money flowed to research institutes that had long served the Pentagon. Seeking advice on long-term trends in U.S.–Latin American relations, political dissent in China, and NATO's role in preserving European security, the State Department turned to military-created think tanks, including RAND, the Center for Naval Analyses, and the Institute for Defense Analyses. It also relied on private for-profit corporations like American Management Systems, which was founded in 1970 by five former Defense Department officials. The bureau even contracted with former SORO contractor Ted Gurr for a study of the relationship between population growth and violent unrest.[84]

Yet, divorced from academia and buried in gray literature, militarization became more hidden from the public. By retreating from government research and advising, academic social scientists unwittingly ceded more territory to the Pentagon's increasingly insular network of contract research agencies. They retreated from power itself; but as Goldschmidt charged, they also "redefined politics in cultural terms." As a result, Daniel Rodgers explains, the workings of power "grew less tangible, less material, more pervasive, more elusive."[85] Ensconced in private agencies, the national security state's researchers were no longer forced to wrestle with the political and ethical implications of their expertise. They evaded activists' and scholars' trenchant critique of militarized expertise as antidemocratic and technocratic As the Vietnam War finally drew to a close, the unified political movement opposing militarization fractured as academics, activists, and politicians turned their attentions elsewhere. By the end of the 1970s, the once widespread fear that militarization threatened scholarship and democracy had almost disappeared from intellectual and public debate. The gray area faded to black.

MILITARIZATION WITHOUT END?

The American public betrayed little concern about the persistence of both the contract state and militarization after the gray area's demise. But when four American contractors were burned alive by insurgents in Fallujah, Iraq, in 2004, Americans once again expressed concern. With American military forces stretched thin in the Middle East, federal contracting mushroomed beyond the realm of ideas and doctrine; to many Americans, it seemed that the government was contracting for war-fighting itself. In the mid-2000s, the national security state's relationship with private firms became the subject of vigorous concern. With an estimated one contractor in the field for every soldier deployed, journalists and pundits remarked snidely that President George W. Bush's "coalition of the willing" was in fact a "coalition of the billing." Scholars, too, renewed their efforts to shine a bright light on the murky world of national security research and policymaking.[1]

The heavy reliance on contractors in the years after 9/11 is, of course, not new. It is an intensification of a system that had hummed along in Washington since the early 1970s. Driven by the conservative conviction that private enterprise was cheaper and more efficient than the public sector, the Nixon and Ford administrations repeatedly urged federal agencies to outsource more of their functions. For decades, scholars and commentators had worried that the line between the public and private sectors was eroding, but by the late 1970s, experts on contracting pronounced the line obsolete. Harold Orlans predicted that the "muddled hybrid sector" would continue to expand in the decades to come.[2]

As they had in the late 1960s, policymakers in the 1970s made some efforts to contain contracting. In 1977, President Jimmy Carter declared a nine-month moratorium on new defense contracts, citing congressional concerns that they sabotaged the democratic policy process by moving decision making into private hands. But as the Cold War heated up at the end of Carter's presidency, the Pentagon's reliance on universities and private firms for classified research and development rose again. Between 1979 and 1982, military spending on university campuses increased 70 percent. At Princeton, where classified research had been banned from campus in the late 1960s, 160 staff members held security clearances; even Princeton's president had one. The Reagan administration continued the trend, with private defense firms like Rockwell International reaping tens of billions of dollars for research and development related to the B-1 bomber, the MX missile, and the Strategic Defense Initiative.[3] Little is known about the impact of the renewed Cold War on research budgets at social science institutes and consulting agencies such as AIR and Abbott Associates; that information is closely held. But the publication record indicates that former Sorons continued to find ample sources of funding from the Defense Department.

The end of the Cold War did little to rein in defense spending or contracting. Ann R. Markusen estimates that by 2000, private contractors were responsible for half of all defense-related work, up from 36 percent in 1972. While that figure includes contracting for services as well as expertise, the numbers for military research show similar growth. The navy, for example, increased its reliance on outside research contractors by 20 percent between 1970 and 1996; by the end of the 1990s, it outsourced 50 percent of its research.[4] Ironically, the end of the Cold War also encouraged growth in a new sector. As Peter Singer explains, the shrunken defense budgets of the post–Cold War world left former soldiers searching for new jobs. They found them in privatized military firms, which contracted with U.S. and foreign governments in the 1990s for services directly related to combat. Companies like Military Professional Resource Services Inc. advised militaries on strategic planning, intelligence collection, military training, and even combat operations.[5]

It is no surprise that private contracting further intensified after 9/11. On September 20, 2001, George W. Bush announced a new era of national vigilance and a new expression of global power. He promised Congress, "We will direct every resource at our command—every means of diplomacy, every tool of intelligence, every instrument of law enforcement, every financial influence, and every necessary weapon of war—to the disruption and to the defeat of the global terror network."[6] A decade after the end of the Cold War, the nation was on a permanent war footing. Private research agencies and scholars were once again in demand as weapons of war.

The social sciences adapted easily, for the intellectual and ideological similarities between the Cold War and the War on Terror are striking. As they did in the Cold War, Americans again view the United States as threatened by a diffuse, often invisible enemy that operates both within and beyond national boundaries. And they again are waging combat in ideological and political terms, battling for the hearts and minds of populations long regarded as peripheral to American interests. As in the Cold War, insurgency and counterinsurgency play a crucial role. And social science once again seems necessary for victory.

The military quickly resurrected SORO's old investigations of insurgency. The fruits of three SORO projects, including one that was a precursor to Project Camelot—Paul A. Jureidini's *Casebook on Insurgency and Revolutionary Warfare*—appear on a list of motivational reading released by the navy SEALs that is designed to attract potential recruits. AIR's *Art and Science of Psychological Operations*, which recycled a number of old SORO reports and was used in the 1970s as a psychological warfare primer, is also endorsed by the SEALs. These books, navy recruiters explain, will help readers "understand regional and cultural sensitivities that Navy SEALs must be capable of dealing with deftly."[7]

The War on Terror has required new research as well, and that work bears striking similarity to SORO's intellectual approach. RAND researchers seeking a science of Islamist insurgency have produced a "conceptual model" of terrorism that purports to reveal its complex causes. The RAND study is, in essence, a Camelot for the War on Terror, although RAND analysts did not include fieldwork in the project. By collecting and collating social scientific studies of terrorism, insurgency, and radicalism, they created a factor tree that purports to answer the question: "When and why does terrorism arise?" Their answer incorporates international systemic causes such as globalization and cultural imperialism, political and economic causes such as discontent and disenfranchisement, and cultural causes such as religious ideology and the presence of "a cultural propensity for violence." The model leads RAND analysts to a simple conclusion: the likelihood that terrorism will occur increases when terrorists believe that violence is legitimate, and when social structures exist that permit terrorists to act. Researchers admit that their work is in its infancy, but hope it will help frame future scholarship and policy.[8]

Camelot researchers aspired to create a computerized system to predict revolution and insurgency. Bolstered by the revolution in information technology, researchers fighting terror promise to do the same. Seeking to understand how terrorists think, University of Pennsylvania engineer Barry Silverman has created computer models of Afghan villages that *Boston Globe* journalist Farah Stockman describes as "complete with virtual people based on actual inhabitants."

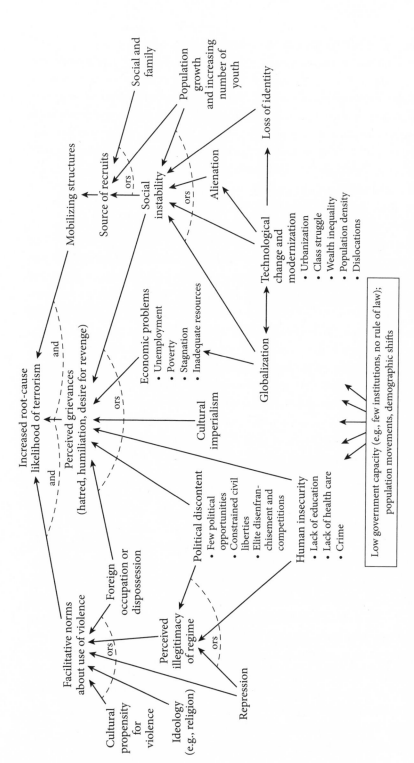

FIGURE 3. "A Factor Tree for Root Causes of Terrorism." In Paul K. Davis and Kim Cragin, eds., *Social Science for Counterterrorism: Putting the Pieces Together* (Santa Monica, Calif.: RAND, 2009), figure S.1. Courtesy RAND.

Silverman's computer programs are designed for intelligence analysis, not for training; his goal is for the avatars to indicate how Afghans might react to U.S. military action or to humanitarian aid. The programming for each avatar is based on a combination of over one hundred social scientific theories; it is supplemented by empirical data, including profiles of suicide bombers. Silverman has not revealed who is bankrolling his current effort, but similar work has been funded by the CIA and the Defense Intelligence Agency. Like Camelot researchers, Silverman understands his work as peacefare. He explains that "war is the worst-case scenario. . . . The goal is to resolve things long before that."[9]

Predictive models of terrorist thought and action require significant intelligence inputs. Silverman and other terror researchers hope that the Human Terrain System, which embeds social scientists in military brigades, can help provide that information. To that end, the Pentagon has funded the creation of a new software system called MAP-HT. The system is designed to store, organize, and analyze the vast quantities of "human terrain" data that the military's social scientists encounter in the field. Defense officials envision MAP-HT as the first step in the technological management of the War on Terror. Ultimately, contractors hope to produce a "database augmented with specific sociocultural objects and an entity extraction capability for tagging narrative and freetext documents."[10] Like Silverman's avatar programs, the system would mechanize counterterror efforts. Armed with databases, supported by state-of-the-art computer software, analysts would be able to decode the sociopolitical environment of insurgency—including the actions of specific individuals—predict flare-ups, and suggest appropriate responses. Beginning in 2007, the Pentagon negotiated contracts worth tens of millions of dollars with researchers who promised to "forecast changes in the human terrain."[11] Just as they did during the Cold War, Pentagon officials continue to seek technical methods for managing the complex problems of foreign and military policy.

Since 2008, some members of the armed forces have condemned the Pentagon's enchantment with counterinsurgency strategy. While some soldiers object that it threatens the military's ability to wage conventional war, others argue that it reaches far beyond the bounds of military capabilities and concerns. Placing the onus of nation-building on military operations, one soldier explains, "requires the military to be both destroyer and creator"; soldiers are responsible for vanquishing the enemy while creating democratic institutions.[12] This criticism has spread beyond the armed services. Boston University's Andrew Bacevich argues that, at its most basic, counterinsurgency "is a call for Western-engineered nation building on a stupendous scale."[13]

The Pentagon, unmoved by these arguments, has continued to invest in counterinsurgency research. In 2008, Secretary of Defense Robert Gates resurrected the ghost of Project Themis, the Defense Department's late-1960s effort to mobilize academic institutions in support of the Cold War. He created the Minerva Initiative, a program that funds university researchers pursuing social research relevant to the War on Terror. Minerva looks to Cold War successes for its inspiration; the initiative is designed to "leverage and focus the resources of the Nation's top universities, analogous to the Cold War development of Kremlinology and game theory."[14] Minerva funds research in specific priority areas such as "Strategic Impact of Religious and Cultural Changes" and "Terrorism and Terrorist Ideologies."[15] Its portfolio includes an effort by researchers at Arizona State University to identify and amplify the voices of Muslims who reject violence in order to contain the spread of extremism. Similar to SORO's psychological research, the project promises to provide the government with information about how moderate and extremist messages travel and who consumes them, knowledge that researchers promise "will enhance irregular warfare capability with respect to radical Islam."[16] In a similar effort, researchers at the Virginia Military Institute and Virginia Commonwealth University are investigating the cohesion of rebel groups in order to identify the kinds of strategies and tactics that could fragment them. They suggest that in addition to informing U.S. "grand strategy" in Africa and the Middle East, their work will "provide practical guidelines to strategic field officers."[17]

The Minerva Initiative has sought to pull academic social scientists into the Defense Department's orbit. Seeking even tighter connections, the program diversified in 2010, adding a set of endowed faculty chairs designed to entice academic social scientists to join the Pentagon's academic institutions for three-year terms. Intended to build bridges "between civilian and defense research enterprises and foster new defense connections in the academic world," "ideal" candidates for the chairs, Minerva program officers explained, would "have little to no previous experience working with the Department of Defense." By 2012, such ideal candidates had yet to materialize. Minerva chairs have included Norman Cigar, a retired member of the Marine Corps Command and Staff College and former senior Pentagon analyst, and Human Terrain System architect Montgomery McFate.[18] Rather than bringing academics into the military's educational institutes, Minerva seems to have provided yet another home for Pentagon analysts and research contractors. As a result, the national security state continues to contract for knowledge that preserves the policy status quo.

These social science efforts are just one part of an enormous contracting system that provides the research, intelligence, services, and equipment that help the government wage the War on Terror. After a two-year investigation, *Washington Post* journalists reported that they had uncovered "an alternative geography of the United States, a Top Secret America created since 9/11 that is hidden from public view." Focusing only on contractors performing top secret work—including those working on projects with the lower classification level of "secret" yielded too many results to manage—they found 1,931 security firms, consulting agencies, and other organizations with government contracts devoted to counterterrorism and intelligence.[19] At least thirty-seven of these companies hold contracts supporting the federal government's psychological operations programs. For example, for $10 million, General Dynamics, a defense behemoth with revenues in excess of $30 billion, creates psychological operations websites for the U.S. Special Operations Forces Command that are designed to favorably influence foreigners' views of the United States.[20] A staggering 164 companies hold contracts supporting special operations. Among them is CACI International, a for-profit contract firm created in 1962 to develop software and other high-technology services for various government agencies. In the 1970s, CACI helped design the computer software system that drove PAMIS, the Defense Department's automated psychological warfare system created by former Sorons. Today, it is among the ten largest defense contractors, but it is perhaps most famous for allegations that its contractors were involved in the torture of prisoners at Abu Ghraib.[21]

The contract research, development, and services sectors have grown remarkably in the years since 9/11. According to Martha Minow, the Defense Department's contracting budget more than doubled between 2000 and 2005.[22] But these numbers are estimates. Despite a few attempts since the 1970s, the federal government never created a system for overseeing and managing its contracts. There are no regulations requiring the Defense Department to disclose how many contractors it has.[23] Given the lack of information, it has been difficult for analysts to tease out the distinctions between contracts for research, like those that fund efforts to simulate Afghan villages, and contracts for services, like General Dynamics' management of psychological warfare websites. Most investigations lump them together.[24]

When it comes to counterinsurgency and counterterrorism, the lines between research and services are as blurry as those between the government and the growing private sector. Since the 1990s, the scope of functions that private national security contractors perform has broadened to include national security activities long considered to be the province of the government; these include conducting intelligence operations, carrying out strategic and tactical planning, training domestic and foreign soldiers and law enforcement, and interrogating prisoners of war.[25] While there are important differences between the privatization of war fighting and the privatization of expertise and policy advising, the consequences of their existence are similar. Heavy reliance on the private sector threatens to undermine democratic norms of transparency and accountability. As Deborah Avant explains, contractors are hired by the executive branch, leaving Congress largely unable to access information about contracts. The White House and the Department of Defense "can use this advantage to evade restrictions on U.S. actions, effectively limiting congressional checks on foreign policy."[26] The problem that J. William Fulbright sought to correct in the late 1960s remains. Analysts continue to worry, too, that by contracting for research and policy, the government might be creating a "hollowed-out state" by "outsourcing its brain."[27]

Scholarly and journalistic analyses of the post-9/11 contract state seem to indicate that forty years after antiwar activists ousted classified research from university campuses, the American public and the American government have even less of a grasp of the enormity of the contracting sector than they did in the Vietnam years. Like activists in the late 1960s, some Americans are trying to rein in the growth of the Pentagon's private contractors. Most recommend that the Pentagon develop better oversight capabilities in order to ensure that contracts are independently evaluated; they also insist that Congress pass legislation enhancing the transparency and accountability of contractors.[28]

Interestingly, much of the critical focus on contracting for national security in the post-9/11 environment focuses on the dangers of privatization, not on those of militarization. Analysts forecast that national security contracting might threaten the state's monopoly on violence, but they do not typically link the privatization of national security to an unhealthy American obsession with national security itself. That private firms who create and sell drones are diversifying their contracts from intelligence agencies to domestic law enforcement, for example, attracts attention for invading privacy, but not for militarizing the home front. Efforts by Defense Department intelligence agencies and the National Security Agency to mine domestic communications for evidence of terror networks have elicited similar concerns. But very few activists or scholars have linked such surveillance programs to an intensification of militarization in an age of counterterror.[29] Perhaps, after decades of increased American investment in national security, most Americans have assimilated militarization into their daily lives to the point that it is practically invisible. In a counterinsurgent war that many military officials argue is as political as it is military, it seems that the elision from military to civilian seems appropriate to many Americans. Instead of threatening a garrison state, militarization seems to offer many Americans a sense of security.

Militarization continues to have a remarkable momentum. The national security state's patronage has proven so lucrative, and the intellectual and technological manifestations of militarized knowledge are so flexible, that militarization remains difficult for Americans to contain or reverse. It also remains highly seductive. Michael Sherry has argued that Americans were reluctant to give up militarization in the years after Vietnam because they were devoted to their image of the nation as a global superpower. This suggests that militarization would last as long as Americans continued to measure their national greatness by their global might.[30] The Defense Department's rationale for attacking Iraq in 2003 seems to bear out this hypothesis. When asked by a journalist why the United States would invade a nation with no responsibility for the 9/11 attacks, one of Defense Secretary Donald Rumsfeld's advisers responded, "How do you send the message . . . that we don't allow these things—you inflict damage."[31] Of course, the War on Terror, like all American wars preceding it, has been fought in the name of more than inflicting damage. It is also driven by the long-standing conviction that the United States is a beneficent global power. This faith allows Americans like historian Paul Johnson to argue that in Iraq, Americans were carrying on the Jeffersonian torch; quoting the nation's second president, he insisted that the United States remained "an Empire of Liberty." "America's search for security against terrorism and rogue states," he elaborated, "goes hand in hand with liberating their oppressed peoples."[32] As long as Americans remain convinced that their investment in national security is both inflicted by external aggressors and part of a program of global uplift, militarization will persist. It may not lead to Lasswell's garrison state, for Americans by and large have not been the targets of the national security state's programs. But for the nations targeted by the War on Terror—for the men and women who live with the effects of American policy—militarization looms large. It is overseas where militarization seems to be reaching its saturation point, where policies designed to export freedom in fact foster the opposite.

Notes

INTRODUCTION

1. Jacob Kipp, Lester Grau, Karl Prinslow, and Captain Don Smith, "The Human Terrain System: A CORDS for the 21st Century," *Military Review* (September–October 2006): 8–15; Nathan Finney, *Human Terrain Team Handbook* (Fort Leavenworth, Kans.: Human Terrain System, October 2008), 26, http://www.box.net/shared/a256bdhlg4 (accessed September 30, 2011).

2. Cf. Montgomery McFate, "The Military Utility of Understanding Adversarial Culture," *Joint Force Quarterly* no. 38 (2005): 42–48; Montgomery McFate and Andrea Jackson, "An Organizational Solution for the DoD's Cultural Needs," *Military Review* 85, no. 4 (July–August 2005): 18–21; Roberto J. González, "'Human Terrain': Past, Present, and Future Applications," *Anthropology Today* 24, no. 1 (February 2008): 21.

3. Cf. González, "'Human Terrain'"; Network of Concerned Anthropologists, *The Counter-Counterinsurgency Manual: Or, Notes on Demilitarizing American Society* (Chicago: Prickly Paradigm Press, 2009); American Anthropological Association Commission on the Engagement of Anthropology with the US Security and Intelligence Communities, *Final Report on the Army's Human Terrain System Proof of Concept Program*, October 14, 2009.

4. Richard H. Wagner, "Profile: Dr. Montgomery McFate," *The 104th Anniversary Dinner Program*, Navy League of the United States, New York Council, March 2007, in author's possession. The website of Montgomery McFate, http://montgomerymcfate.com/ (accessed October 4, 2011).

5. Yvette Clinton et al., *Congressionally Directed Assessment of the Human Terrain System* (Alexandria, Va.: Center for Naval Analyses, November 2010), 86.

6. Maximilian C. Forte, "Mapping the Human Terrain of War Corporatism: The Human Terrain System within the Military-Industrial-Academic Complex," *Zero Anthropology* (blog), http://zeroanthropology.net/all-posts/mapping-the-terrain-of-war-corpo ratism-the-human-terrain-system-within-the-military-industrial-academic-complex/, updated September 30, 2011.

7. Clinton et al., *Congressionally Directed Assessment of the Human Terrain System*, 42, 48.

8. Jesse Ellman et al., *Defense Contract Trends: U.S. Department of Defense Contract Spending and the Supporting Industrial Base* (Washington, D.C.: Center for Strategic and International Studies, May 2011).

9. Cf. Martha Minow, "Outsourcing Power: Privatizing Military Efforts and the Risks to Accountability, Professionalism, and Democracy," and Jody Freeman and Minow, "Reframing the Outsourcing Debates," in *Government by Contract: Outsourcing and American Democracy*, ed. Jody Freeman and Martha Minow (Cambridge, Mass.: Harvard University Press, 2009); P. W. Singer, *Corporate Warriors: The Rise of the Privatized Military Industry* (Ithaca, N.Y.: Cornell University Press, 2003), 65.

10. T. N. Greene, introduction in *The Guerrilla—and How to Fight Him: Selections from the Marine Corps Gazette*, ed. T. N. Greene (New York: Frederick A. Praeger, 1962), v.

11. Laura McEnaney, *Civil Defense Begins at Home: Militarization Meets Everyday Life in the Fifties* (Princeton, N.J.: Princeton University Press, 2000), 6. See also Michael Geyer, "The Militarization of Europe, 1914–1945," in *The Militarization of the Western World*, ed. John R. Gillis (New Brunswick, N.J.: Rutgers University Press, 1989), 65–102. The most comprehensive treatment of American militarization remains Michael S. Sherry, *In the Shadow of War: The United States since the 1930s* (New Haven, Conn.: Yale University Press, 1995).

12. Harold D. Lasswell, "The Garrison State and Specialists on Violence," *American Journal of Sociology* 46 (January 1941): 455–68.

13. E. K. Karcher, "Army Social Science Programs and Plans," in *Proceedings of the Symposium "The Limited-War Mission and Social Science Research,"* ed. William A. Lybrand (Washington, D.C.: SORO, 1962), 344–59.

14. Harold K. Johnson, "The Army's Role in Nation Building and Preserving Stability," *Army Information Digest* 20 (November 1965): 13.

15. On the American tendency to mask militarization behind expertise see Sherry, *Shadow of War*, 81.

16. Stuart W. Leslie, *The Cold War and American Science: The Military-Industrial-Academic Complex at MIT and Stanford* (New York: Columbia University Press, 1993).

17. U.S. Congress, Office of Technology Assessment, *History of the Department of Defense Federally Funded Research and Development Centers* (Washington, D.C.: Government Printing Office, 1995); Gene M. Lyons and Louis Morton, *Schools for Strategy: Education and Research in National Security Affairs* (New York: Frederick A. Praeger, 1965).

18. Lyons and Morton, *Schools for Strategy*, 5; Paul Dickson, *Think Tanks* (New York: Atheneum, 1971), 14.

19. Cf. Brian Balogh, "Reorganizing the Organizational Synthesis: Federal-Professional Relations in Modern America," *Studies in American Political Development* 5, no. 1 (1991), 119–72; Donald T. Critchlow, "Think Tanks, Antistatism, and Democracy: The Nonpartisan Ideal and Policy Research in the United States, 1913–1987," in *The State and Social Investigation in Britain and the United States*, ed. Michael J. Lacey and Mary O. Furner (Cambridge: Woodrow Wilson Center Press and the Press Syndicate of the University of Cambridge, 1993), 279–332.

20. Quoted in Sherry, *Shadow of War*, 234.

21. See, for example, Noam Chomsky, *American Power and the New Mandarins* (New York: Pantheon, 1969); J. William Fulbright, "The War and Its Effects: The Military-Academic Industrial Complex," in *Super-State: Readings in the Military-Industrial Complex*, ed. Herbert I. Schiller and Joseph D. Phillips (Urbana: University of Illinois Press, 1970), 173–78; Michael T. Klare, *War without End: Planning for the Next Vietnams* (New York: Vintage Books, 1972); and Seymour Melman, *Pentagon Capitalism* (New York: McGraw-Hill, 1970).

CHAPTER 1

1. Philip M. Hauser, "Are the Social Sciences Ready?" *American Sociological Review* 11 (1946): 380.

2. Ad Hoc Advisory Group on Psychology and Social Sciences, "Defense Needs for Long-Range Research in Psychology and Social Sciences," December 19, 1957, p. 1, HSR Briefing folder, box 3, Record Unit 179, Smithsonian Institution Research Group in Psychology and the Social Sciences, Records (Smithsonian Institution Archives, Washington, D.C.); Charles Bray, untitled speech, undated, HSR briefing folder, box 3, Smithsonian Institution Research Group in Psychology and the Social Sciences; Paul Linebarger, *Psychological Warfare* (Washington, D.C.: Infantry Journal Press, 1948), 29.

3. Alvarez quoted in Jesse Orlansky to Ithiel de Sola Pool, September 8, 1961, IDA-Misc. folder, box 72, Ithiel de Sola Pool Papers, Massachusetts Institute of Technology, Institute Archives and Special Collections (Cambridge, Mass.).

4. Andrew J. Birtle, *U.S. Counterinsurgency and Contingency Operations Doctrine, 1942–1976* (Washington, D.C.: Center of Military History, United States Army, 2006), 25; Lt. Col. T. N. Greene, *The Guerrilla—and How to Fight Him* (New York: Praeger, 1962), v.

5. A classic interrogation of the relationship between patronage and scholarship in Cold War science is Paul Forman, "Behind Quantum Electronics: National Security as a Basis for Physical Research in the United States, 1940–1960," *Historical Studies in the Physical Sciences* 18 (1988): 149–229. On militarization and American national identity see Sherry, *Shadow of War*.

6. Aaron L. Friedberg, *In the Shadow of the Garrison State: America's Anti-Statism and Its Cold War Grand Strategy* (Princeton, N.J.: Princeton University Press, 2000); Odd Arne Westad, *The Global Cold War: Third World Interventions and the Making of Our Times* (Cambridge: Cambridge University Press, 2005), chap. 1; Marilyn B. Young, "The Age of Global Power," in *Rethinking American History in a Global Age*, ed. Thomas Bender (Berkeley: University of California Press, 2002), 274–94.

7. Ellen Herman, *The Romance of American Psychology: Political Culture in the Age of Experts* (Berkeley: University of California Press, 1995), 81, chaps. 2–3; Eugene M. Lyons, *The Uneasy Partnership: Social Science and the Federal Government in the Twentieth Century* (New York: Russell Sage Foundation, 1969), chap. 4.

8. Friedberg, *Shadow of the Garrison State*, 327–30; Larry Owens, "The Counterproductive Management of Science in the Second World War: Vannevar Bush and the Office of Scientific Research and Development," *Business History Review* 68 (1994): 515–76.

9. Quoted in Virginia Yans-McLaughlin, "Science, Democracy, and Ethics: Mobilizing Culture and Personality for World War II," in *Malinowski, Rivers, Benedict and Others: Essays on Culture and Personality*, ed. George W. Stocking Jr. (Madison: University of Wisconsin Press, 1986), 184–217, 214. The literature on the physical sciences in the Cold War is immense. Useful overviews include Roger L. Geiger, *Research and Relevant Knowledge: American Research Universities since World War II* (New York: Oxford University Press, 1993), and Stuart W. Leslie, *Cold War and American Science: The Military-Industrial Complex at MIT and Stanford* (New York: Columbia University Press, 1993). On the challenges of uniting the physical sciences and the military after the war see Amy Sue Bix, "Backing into Sponsored Research: Physics and Engineering at Princeton University, 1945–1970," *History of Higher Education Annual* 13 (1993): 9–52; and Michael A. Dennis, "'Our First Line of Defense': Two University Labs in the Postwar American State," *Isis* 85 (1994): 427–55.

10. Ron Theodore Robin, *The Making of the Cold War Enemy: Culture and Politics in the Military-Intellectual Complex* (Princeton, N.J.: Princeton University Press, 2001), 47, 50–51. On the exclusion of the social sciences from the NSF see Daniel Lee Kleinman and Mark Solovey, "Hot Science / Cold War: The National Science Foundation after World War II," *Radical History Review* 63 (1995): 110–39.

11. Quoted in Michael McClintock, *Instruments of Statecraft* (New York: Pantheon Books, 1992), 36. On the history of psychological warfare in the U.S. military see also Stanley Sandler, *Cease Resistance: It's Good for You! A History of U.S. Army Combat Psychological Operations* (Fort Bragg, N.C.: United States Army Special Operations Command, 1999); and Christopher Simpson, *Science of Coercion: Communication Research and Psychological Warfare, 1945–1960* (New York: Oxford University Press, 1994).

12. Herman, *Romance of American Psychology*, 124.

13. Quoted in Robin, *Making of the Cold War Enemy*, 120.

14. Quoted in McClintock, *Instruments of Statecraft*, 230.

15. "Progress Report 1954–1955," typescript, p. 9, Special Warfare: HRAF Progress RPTS, 2/55–4/57 (U) folder, box 3, entry 156, Records of the Office of the Chief of Special Warfare, Security-Classified Correspondence Relating to Special Warfare Area Handbooks, 1954–58, RG 319: Records of the Army Staff (National Archives 2, College Park, Md.); McClintock, *Instruments of Statecraft*, 37–39.

16. Human Relations Area Files, "Quarterly Progress Report, 1954–1955," typescript, p. 33, Special Warfare: HRAF Progress RPTS, 2/55–4/27 (U) folder, box 1, entry 156, Records of the Office of the Chief of Special Warfare, Security-Classified Correspondence Relating to Special Warfare Area Handbooks, 1954–58, RG 319. On concerns about classified research contracts see Harold W. Dodds, "The Dangers of Project Research," *Social Problems* 1 (1954): 90–93; and J. L. Morrill, "Higher Education and the Federal Government," *Annals of the American Academy of Political and Social Science* 301 (1955): 41–45.

17. David C. Engerman, "The Rise and Fall of Wartime Social Science: Harvard's Refugee Interview Project, 1950–1954," in *Cold War Social Science: Knowledge Production, Liberal Democracy, and Human Nature*, ed. Mark Solovey and Hamilton Cravens (New York: Palgrave Macmillan, 2012), 29, 35.

18. Kluckhohn quoted in Engerman, "Rise and Fall of Wartime Social Science," 37; Harvard University, *The Behavioral Sciences at Harvard: Report by a Faculty Committee, June 1954* (Cambridge, Mass.: Harvard University Press, 1954), 289–93.

19. Matthew Farish, *The Contours of America's Cold War* (Minneapolis: University of Minnesota Press, 2010), 64–66; Clellan Ford, "Human Relations Area Files: 1945–1969," *Behavior Science Notes* 5 (1970): 1–27; Rebecca M. Lemov, *World as Laboratory: Experiments with Mice, Mazes, and Men* (New York: Hill & Wang, 2005), chaps. 8–9.

20. Milton D. Graham to C. D. Leatherman, January 18, 1955, Special Warfare: HRAF Correspondence, 54–58 (U) folder, box 1, entry 156, Records of the Office of the Chief of Special Warfare, Security-Classified Correspondence Relating to Special Warfare Area Handbooks, 1954–58, RG 319.

21. Ibid.

22. Clellan Ford to Gen. William C. Bullock, February 4, 1955, Special Warfare: HRAF Correspondence, 54–58 (U) folder, box 1, entry 156, Records of the Office of the Chief of Special Warfare, Security-Classified Correspondence Relating to Special Warfare Area Handbooks, 1954–58, RG 319.

23. "FY 59 M&O Funds to Be Programmed—$160,000—Contract No. DA-49–083–973," n.d. [c. December 1956], Special Warfare (RAC) 1956 (U) folder, box 2, entry 156, Records of the Office of the Chief of Special Warfare, Security-Classified Correspondence Relating to Special Warfare Area Handbooks, 1954–58, RG 319.

24. Description drawn from Foreign Area Studies Division, *Special Warfare Area Handbook for Ethiopia* (Washington, D.C.: SORO, October 1960), American University Archives and Special Collections (Washington, D.C.). For the template see Office of the Chief of Psychological Warfare, Department of the Army, "Format for a Psychological Warfare Country Plan," September 9, 1955, Special Warfare: HRAF Correspondence, 54–58 (U) folder, box 1, entry 156, Records of the Office of the Chief of Special Warfare, Security-Classified Correspondence Relating to Special Warfare Area Handbooks, 1954–58, RG 319.

25. HRAF, "Quarterly Progress Report," p. 28, 30–2, Special Warfare: HRAF Progress RPTS, 2/55–4/27 (U) folder, box 3; Office of the Chief of Psychological Warfare to Clellan Ford, April 17, 1957, Special Warfare: HRAF Correspondence, 54–58 (U) folder, box 1, entry 156, Records of the Office of the Chief of Special Warfare, Security-Classified Correspondence Relating to Special Warfare Area Handbooks, 1954–58, RG 319.

26. Dr. E. K. Karcher Jr., "Army Social Science Programs and Plans," in *Proceedings of the Symposium "The U.S. Army's Limited-War Mission and Social Science Research,"* ed. William A. Lybrand, 344–59 (Washington, D.C.: SORO, 1962), 349; Hurst R. Anderson to Col. C. B. Hutchinson, March 31, 1964, SORO/1964 folder, box 1, Papers of the Special Operations Research Office (American University Archives and Special Collections).

27. "Remarks of Leonard W. Doob," in Lybrand, *Proceedings of the Symposium*, 236. On Bandung see Westad, *Global Cold War*, 99–103.

28. Catherine Lutz, *Homefront: A Military City and the American Twentieth Century* (Boston: Beacon Press, 2002); Robin, *Making of the Cold War Enemy*, 24–25; Michael E. Latham, *Modernization as Ideology: American Social Science and "Nation Building" in the Kennedy Era* (Chapel Hill: University of North Carolina Press, 2000), chap. 1.

29. Friedberg, *Shadow of the Garrison State*, 130–33; Eisenhower quoted at 133.

30. Andrew J. Bacevich, *The Pentomic Era: The U.S. Army between Korea and Vietnam* (Washington, D.C.: National Defense University Press, 1986), 49–53. See also James M. Gavin, *War and Peace in the Space Age* (New York: Harper, 1958); and Maxwell D. Taylor, *The Uncertain Trumpet* (New York: Harper, 1960).

31. U.S. Army, Official Contract DA-49–083 OSA-973, typescript, April 17, 1956, p. 1, SORO-973 file, box 10, entry 1393, Accession 73-A-2008, OCRD [Office of the Chief of Research and Development], DAR [Director of Army Research], Transaction Files, 1967–69, RG 319; Ritchie P. Lowry, "Toward a Sociology of Secrecy and Security Systems," *Social Problems* 19 (1972): 439.

32. Quoted in McClintock, *Instruments of Statecraft*, 170. For SORO's early budget see U.S. Army, Official Contract DA-49–083 OSA-973, typescript, April 17, 1956, SORO-973 file, box 10, entry 1393, Accession 73-A-2008, OCRD [Office of the Chief of Research and Development], DAR [Director of Army Research], Transaction Files, 1967–69, RG 319.

33. On the growth of the Special Forces and third world trouble spots see McClintock, *Instruments of Statecraft*, 163–66, 180. On SORO staffing and budgets see Walter Pincus, "Pentagon Plans to Clear 'Camelot Studies,'" *Washington Star* [c. July 1965], Camelot (Publicity)/1965 file, box 1, Special Operations Research Office Papers. On SORO's relationship to Fort Bragg see Col. William H. Kinard, "The New Dimensions of Special Warfare," in Lybrand, *Proceedings of the Symposium*, 60.

34. Harold Orlans, *Contracting for Knowledge* (San Francisco: Jossey-Bass, 1973); and U.S. Office of Technology Assessment, *A History of the Department of Defense Federally Funded Research and Development Centers*, OTA-BP-ISS-157 (Washington, D.C.: Government Printing Office, June 1995), 7–20.

35. Orlans, *Contracting for Knowledge*; U.S. Office of Technology Assessment, *History of the Department of Defense Federally Funded Research and Development Centers*, 7–20; McClintock, *Instruments of Statecraft*, 44.

36. Orlans, *Contracting for Knowledge*; U.S. Office of Technology Assessment, *History of the Department of Defense Federally Funded Research and Development Centers*, 20.

37. On the presence of military officers on SORO's staff see Joy Elizabeth Rohde, "'The Social Scientists' War': Expertise in a Cold War Nation" (PhD diss., University of Pennsylvania, 2007), 108–14. On Dame's career see Walter G. Hermes, *Truce Tent and Fighting Front: The Last Two Years* (Washington, D.C.: Center of Military History, U.S. Army, 1990), chap. 11; and Kate Montressor, "Dame-Conary-Hanson-Fuller Genealogy," Person Card for Hartley Fuller Dame, http://www.aviatrix.com/genealogy/ps01/ps01_222.htm (accessed November 10, 2005). Dame's SORO reports include Hartley Dame and Aubrey Lippincott, *Selected Aspects of the San Blas Cuna Indians* (Washington, D.C.: SORO/CINFAC, 1964); and Margaret P. Hays, Christy Ann Hoffman and Hartley Dame, *The Political Influence of University Students in Latin America* (Washington, D.C.: SORO/CINFAC,

1965); Hartley Fuller Dame, "The Causes and Effects of Military Intervention in Politics in Hispanic America: Argentina, a Case Study" (MA thesis, American University, 1969).

38. Rohde, "'Social Scientists' War,'" 114–15; "Jacobs, Norman," *American Men and Women of Science: The Social and Behavioral Sciences*, 12th ed. (New York: Bowker, 1973), 1117–18. On Daugherty see R. D. McLaurin, ed., *Military Propaganda: Psychological Warfare and Operations* (New York: Praeger, 1982), 376.

39. U.S. Office of Technology Assessment, *History of the Department of Defense Federally Funded Research and Development Centers*, 20–27.

40. On these institutions see Sharon Ghamari-Tabrizi, *The Worlds of Herman Kahn: The Intuitive Science of Thermonuclear War* (Cambridge, Mass.: Harvard University Press, 2005); Gene M. Lyons and Louis Morton, *Schools for Strategy* (New York: Praeger, 1965); and Bruce L. R. Smith, *The RAND Corporation: Case Study of a Nonprofit Advisory Corporation* (Cambridge, Mass.: Harvard University Press, 1966). On Simulmatics see Joy Rohde, "The Last Stand of the Psychocultural Cold Warriors: Military Contract Research in Vietnam," *Journal of the History of the Behavioral Sciences* 47 (2011): 232–50.

41. Sherry, *Shadow of War*, 138; Friedberg, *Shadow of the Garrison State*.

42. Friedberg, *Shadow of the Garrison State*, 332–34. On the explosion of contracting see Harold Orlans, *The Non-Profit Research Institute: Its Origin, Operation, Problems, and Prospects* (New York: McGraw-Hill, 1972), 5, 11.

43. Quoted in Friedberg, *Shadow of the Garrison State*, 334.

44. Annex A to Contract No. DAHC-19–67-C-0046, DAHC19–67-C-0046, CRESS Employee Benefits (Insurance, Travel, Salaries and Wages) file, box 10, entry 1393, OCRD, DAR, Transaction Files, 1967–69, RG 319; William J. Baumol, "On the Financial Prospects for Higher Education: The Annual Report on the Economic Status of the Profession," *AAUP Bulletin* 54 (1968): 194.

45. On overhead costs see "Budget, Fiscal Year 1958," Special Warfare: RAC, 1957 (U) file, box 2, entry 156, Records of the Office of the Chief of Special Warfare, Security-Classified Correspondence Relating to the Special Warfare Area Handbooks, RG 319; and "Contract No. DAHC-19–67-C-0046," typescript, July 1, 1967, p. 6, DAHC19–67-C-0046 American University (CRESS) Basic Contract and Modifications file, box 10, entry 1393, Accession 73-A-2008, OCRD [Office of the Chief of Research and Development], DAR [Director of Army Research], Transaction Files, 1967–69, RG 319. On the history of the social sciences at American University see John R. Reynolds and Joanne E. King, *Highlights in the History of American University, 1889–1976* (Washington, D.C.: Hennage Creative Printers, 1976), 61. On AU's ranking see U.S. Congress, House, Committee on Government Operations, Subcommittee on Research and Technical Programs, *Use of Social Research in Federal Domestic Programs*, pt. 1, Federally Financed Social Research: Expenditures, Status, and Objectives (Washington, D.C.: Government Printing Office, 1967), 65. For a case of the impact of government funding on university status see Rebecca Lowen, *Creating the Cold War University: The Transformation of Stanford* (Berkeley: University of California Press, 1997).

46. Reynolds and King, *Highlights in the History of American University*, 25, 57. When the First World War ended, the army buried its large cache of weapons on and around AU's campus. Some long-term residents in the neighborhood have since complained of rare illnesses. Cf. Carol D. Leonnig, "Residents' Federal Lawsuits Blocked; Weapons Tested in Spring Valley," *Washington Post*, September 17, 2003, B8; John Ward, "Spring Valley Sick Blame Chemicals in WWI Dumping: A Survey Finds a Disquieting Number of Serious Illnesses," *Washington Times*, November 14, 2004, A1.

47. Hurst R. Anderson, *An Educational Journey: Trivia and More Important Things in the Life of a Teacher and College and University President* (Lakeside, Ohio: privately printed,

1977), 65–66; Eisenhower quoted in Reynolds and King, *Highlights in the History of American University*, 71.

48. Anderson, *Educational Journey*, 10, 15.

49. Cf. Donald Derby to Hurst Anderson, March 20, 1964, SORO/1964 file, box 1, Papers of the Special Operations Research Office.

50. Raymond V. Bowers, "The Military Establishment," in *The Uses of Sociology*, ed. Paul F. Lazarsfeld, William H. Sewell, and Harold Wilensky (New York: Basic Books, 1967), 234–74; Lyons, *Uneasy Partnership*, 143–45; Robin, *Making of the Cold War Enemy*, 50.

51. Senate Committee on Post Office and Civil Service, Subcommittee on Federal Manpower Policies, *Report on Manpower Utilization by the Federal Government through the Use of Private Contract Labor*, 83rd Cong., 1st sess. (Washington, D.C.: Government Printing Office, 1953), 5–6. See also U.S. Senate Committee on Foreign Relations, *Defense Department Sponsored Foreign Affairs Research: Hearings before the Senate Committee on Foreign Relations*, 90th Cong., 2nd sess., May 1968, 32–33.

52. Leonard S. Cottrell Jr., "Social Research and Psychological Warfare," *Sociometry* 23 (1960): 105–6. On PSYGRO and the name change see "Scope of Contract PSYGRO," March 6, 1956; C.D. Leatherman to Research Advisory Committee Members, April 18, 1956; and Minutes of RAC meeting, April 26, 1956, Special Warfare: RAC, 1956 (U) file, box 2, entry 156, Records of the Office of the Chief of Special Warfare, Security-Classified Correspondence Relating to the Special Warfare Area Handbooks, RG 319.

53. Robin, *Making the Cold War Enemy*, 54–55; House Select Committee to Investigate Foundations, *Final Report of the Select Committee to Investigate Foundations and Other Organizations*, 82nd Cong., 2nd sess. (Washington, D.C.: Government Printing Office, 1953), 6. On security clearances at SORO see HRAF/WAHRAF Clearances—Special Orders, folder 16, box 5, entry 156, Records of the Office of the Chief of Special Warfare, Security-Classified Correspondence Relating to the Special Warfare Area Handbooks, RG 319. On secrecy practices see Janet Farrell Brodie, "Learning Secrecy in the Early Cold War: The RAND Corporation," *Diplomatic History* 35 (2011): 643–70.

54. *Congressional Record* 104, pt. 14, August 14, 1958, 17516–17; Paul Kecskemeti, *Strategic Surrender: The Politics of Victory and Defeat* (Stanford, Calif.: Stanford University Press, 1958).

55. *Congressional Record* 104, pt. 14, August 14, 1958, 17520–21, 17743.

56. Karcher, "Army Social Science Programs and Plans," in Lybrand, *Proceedings of the Conference*, 359.

57. On the dragnet process see Booz, Allen, and Hamilton Inc., "Study of Organization Structure and Administrative Practices," July 1965, pp. 17–20, box 1, Papers of the Special Operations Research Office. For examples of dragnets see 1301–01 RDAF Dragnet FY 69 1968 Requirements Submitted file, box 5, entry 1295D, OCRD [Office of the Chief of Research and Development] Social Science Branch RD Administration Files, RG 319.

58. On Task Target see "Army Human Factors Research Advisory Committee Meeting," May 3, 1961, AHFRAC Meeting Minutes file, box 1, Acc 79–0068, RG 319. For SUPO see SORO, "Task Statement, 20 June 1957," and Maj. Gen. O.C. Troxel to Col. Kai Rasmussen, July 5, 1957, Special Warfare: RAC, 1957 (U) file, box 2, entry 156, Records of the Office of the Chief of Special Warfare, Security-Classified Correspondence Relating to the Special Warfare Area Handbooks, RG 319.

59. Lucien Pye, "The Role of the Military in Political Development," in Lybrand, *Proceedings of the Conference*, 164; Harry Eckstein, "Internal Wars," ibid., 250–62.

60. Harvard University, *Behavioral Sciences at Harvard*, 224–26.

61. Irwin Altman, "Mainstreams of Research in Small Groups," *Public Administration Review* 23 (1963): 203–8; Ray C. Hackman, "Purity, Body, and Flavor: The Applied Scientist," *Scientific Monthly* 81 (1955): 213–14.

62. Paul A. Jureidini and John M. Lord, *An Ethnographic Summary of the Ethiopian Provinces of Harar and Sidamo* (Washington, D.C.: SORO, October 1964); D.M. Condit, *A Counterinsurgency Bibliography* (Washington, D.C.: SORO, 1963); Elihu Katz and Paul Lazarsfeld, *Personal Influence: The Part Played by People in the Flow of Mass Communications* (New York: Free Press, 1960); Milton Jacobs, Charles E. Rice, and Lorand Szalay, *The Study of Communication in Thailand with an Emphasis on Word-of-Mouth Communication* (Washington, D.C.: SORO, July 1964); Milton Jacobs, Farhad Farzanegan, and Alexander Askenasy, "A Study of Key Communicators in Thailand," *Social Forces* 45 (1966): 192–99.

63. N.A. LaCharite and E.W. Gude, "Project Revolt," *Army Information Digest* 20 (February 1965): 39–41; Ritchie P. Lowry, "Changing Military Roles: Neglected Challenge to Rural Sociologists," *Rural Sociology* 30 (1965): 222.

64. William A. Lybrand, foreword in Lybrand, *Proceedings of the Symposium*, vii; Kennedy quoted in Seymour Dietchman, *The Best-Laid Schemes: A Tale of Social Research and Bureaucracy* (Cambridge, Mass.: MIT Press, 1976), 6.

65. Robert Endicott Osgood, *Limited War: The Challenge to American Strategy* (Chicago: University of Chicago Press, 1957), 27.

66. Ad Hoc Advisory Group on Psychology and Social Sciences, "Defense Needs for Long-Range Research in Psychology and Social Sciences," 12.

67. Dwight D. Eisenhower, "Farewell Address to the Nation," *Public Papers of the Presidents of the United States: Dwight D. Eisenhower, 1960–61* (Washington, D.C.: National Archives and Records Administration, 1961), 1038–39.

68. Department of the Army, *Psychological Operations*, Field Manual 33–5, quoted in Herman, *Romance of American Psychology*, 124.

CHAPTER 2

1. Harold D. Lasswell, "The Garrison State and Specialists on Violence," *American Journal of Sociology* 46 (January 1941): 455–68; C. Wright Mills, *The Power Elite* (New York: Oxford University Press, 1956).

2. On scientific authority see Thomas F. Gieryn, *Cultural Boundaries of Science: Credibility on the Line* (Chicago: University of Chicago Press, 1999); Theodore M. Porter, *Trust in Numbers: The Pursuit of Objectivity in Science and Public Life* (Princeton, N.J.: Princeton University Press, 1995); and Robert N. Proctor, *Value-Free Science? Purity and Power in Modern Knowledge* (Cambridge, Mass.: Harvard University Press, 1991). On social science and reform see Robert Bannister, *Sociology and Scientism: The American Quest for Objectivity, 1880–1940* (Chapel Hill: University of North Carolina Press, 1987); Mary O. Furner, *Advocacy and Objectivity: A Crisis in the Professionalization of American Social Science, 1865–1905* (Lexington: University Press of Kentucky, 1975); Thomas L. Haskell, *The Emergence of Professional Social Science: The American Social Science Association and the Nineteenth-Century Crisis of Authority* (Urbana: University of Illinois Press, 1977); Ellen Herman, *The Romance of American Psychology: Political Culture in the Age of Experts* (Berkeley: University of California Press, 1995); Dorothy Ross, *The Origins of American Social Science* (Cambridge: Cambridge University Press, 1991); and Mark C. Smith, *Social Science in the Crucible: The American Debate over Objectivity and Purpose, 1918–1941* (Durham, N.C.: Duke University Press, 1994).

3. Proctor, *Value-Free Science?* 10. On totalitarianism and democracy see David Ciepley, *Liberalism in the Shadow of Totalitarianism* (Cambridge, Mass.: Harvard University Press, 2006), 183–93; Edward A. Purcell Jr., *The Crisis of Democratic Theory: Scientific*

Naturalism and the Problem of Value (Lexington: University Press of Kentucky, 1973); and David M. Ricci, *The Tragedy of Political Science: Politics, Scholarship, and Democracy* (New Haven, Conn.: Yale University Press, 1984), 99–132. On social knowledge and American national security see, for example, Gabriel Almond, "Remarks," *Background* 9 (November 1965): 173–76; Daniel Lerner and Harold D. Lasswell, eds., *The Policy Sciences* (Stanford, Calif.: Stanford University Press, 1951); and Ithiel de Sola Pool, *Social Science Research and National Security* (Washington, D.C.: Smithsonian Institution, 1963). On the distinction between objectivity and value neutrality see Proctor, *Value-Free Science?* 175–77; and Thomas Haskell, *Objectivity Is Not Neutrality: Explanatory Schemes in History* (Baltimore: Johns Hopkins University Press, 1998), 145–74.

4. Robert Boguslaw, "Social Action and Social Change," in *Handbook on the Study of Social Problems*, ed. Erwin O. Smigel (Chicago: Rand McNally, 1971), 423.

5. Smith, *Social Science in the Crucible*, 13, 18.

6. Quoted ibid., 48, 47, 27. See also Bannister, *Sociology and Scientism*; and Ross, *Origins of American Social Science*, 390–470.

7. Richard V. Damms, "James Killian, the Technological Capabilities Panel, and the Emergence of President Eisenhower's "Scientific-Technological Elite," *Diplomatic History* 24 (2000): 58.

8. For examples of the lack of concern about military patronage see Hadley Cantril, *The Human Dimension: Experiences in Policy Research* (New Brunswick, N.J.: Rutgers University Press, 1967); W. Phillips Davison, "Foreign Policy," in *The Uses of Sociology*, ed. Paul F. Lazarsfeld, William H. Sewell, and Harold L. Wilensky (New York: Basic Books, 1967), 391–417; and Charles Y. Glock, "Applied Social Research: Some Conditions Affecting Its Utilization," in *Case Studies in Bringing Behavioral Science into Use*, ed. Charles Y. Glock (Stanford, Calif.: Stanford University Institute for Communication Research, 1961), 1–19. On anticommunism see Richard H. Pells, *The Liberal Mind in a Conservative Age: American Intellectuals in the 1940s and 1950s* (New York: Harper & Row, 1985).

9. Max F. Millikan, "Inquiry and Policy: The Relation of Knowledge to Action," in *Human Meaning of the Social Sciences*, ed. Daniel Lerner (New York: Meridian Books, 1959), 158–80, esp. 161.

10. Cf. John L. Houk et al., *Psychological Operations: Laos; Project PROSYMS* (Washington, D.C.: SORO, 1959), p. iii. On Smith see Gustav Niebuhr, "Wilfred C. Smith Dies at 83; Scholar of Religious Pluralism," *New York Times*, February 11, 2000, p. B10.

11. Wilfred Cantwell Smith to President, American University, February 8, 1960, Special Operations Research Office / Origins File, box 1, Special Operations Research Office Papers.

12. On DeLong's early research see Earl H. DeLong, "Powers and Duties of the State Attorney-General in Criminal Prosecution," *Journal of Criminal Law and Criminology* 25 (1934): 358–400; Earl H. DeLong, "Which Man for the Job?" *State Government* 8 (1935): 64–68; and Newman F. Baker and Earl H. DeLong, "The Prosecuting Attorney and Reform in Criminal Justice," *Journal of Criminal Law and Criminology* 26 (1936): 821–46.

13. Research Committee, American Political Science Association, "Instruction and Research: War-Time Priorities in Research," *American Political Science Review* 37 (June 1943): 505; Lerner and Lasswell, *Policy Sciences*; Earl H. DeLong, "Who Are the Career Executives?" *Public Administration Review* 19 (1959): 108–13.

14. Earl DeLong to Wilfred Cantwell Smith, n.d., Special Operations Research Office / Origins File, box 1, Special Operations Research Office Papers; Imogene E. Okes, "Effective Communication by Americans with Thai" (MA thesis, American University, 1960).

15. DeLong, "Who Are the Career Executives?" 108; Proctor, *Value-Free Science?*

16. DeLong to Smith, n.d., Special Operations Research Office / Origins File, box 1, Special Operations Research Office Papers.

17. David A. Hollinger, "The Defense of Democracy and Robert K. Merton's Formulation of the Scientific Ethos," *Knowledge and Society* 4 (1983): 1–15; David A. Hollinger, "Science as a Weapon in *Kulturkämpfe* in the United States during and after World War II," *Isis* 86 (1995): 440–54; Everett Mendelsohn, "Robert K. Merton: The Celebration and Defense of Science," *Science in Context* 3 (1989): 269–89; Purcell, *Crisis of Democratic Theory*; Ricci, *Tragedy of Political Science*, 99–132; and Jessica Wang, "Merton's Shadow: Perspectives on Science and Democracy since 1940," *Historical Studies in the Physical and Biological Sciences* 30 (1999): 279–306.

18. Smith to President, American University, February 8, 1960, Special Operations Research Office / Origins File, box 1, Special Operations Research Office Papers; DeLong to Smith, n.d., Special Operations Research Office / Origins File, box 1, Special Operations Research Office Papers. On absolutism and totalitarianism see Ciepley, *Liberalism in the Shadow of Totalitarianism*, 183–212; Purcell, *Crisis of Democratic Theory*, 203; and Ricci, *Tragedy of Political Science*, 155–56.

19. Ciepley, *Liberalism in the Shadow of Totalitarianism*, 196, 212–16. John G. Gunnell, *The Descent of Political Theory: The Genealogy of an American Vocation* (Chicago: University of Chicago Press, 1993), 133.

20. Gabriel Almond quoted in Nils Gilman, *Mandarins of the Future: Modernization Theory in Cold War America* (Baltimore: Johns Hopkins University Press, 2003), 47; Gabriel A. Almond and Sidney Verba, *The Civic Culture: Political Attitudes and Democracy in Five Nations* (Princeton, N.J.: Princeton University Press, 1963), 478; DeLong, "Who Are the Career Executives?" 110.

21. Ithiel de Sola Pool, "The Necessity for Social Scientists Doing Research for Government," *Background* 10, no. 2 (1966): 112. See also Gilman, *Mandarins of the Future*, 47–62.

22. Sherry, *Shadow of War*, ix, 167.

23. Jeanne S. Mintz, "My Work at the Board for the Netherlands Indies," typescript, n.d., folder 3, box 9, Jeanne S. Mintz Papers (Library of Congress Manuscripts Division, Washington, D.C.); "Indonesian Aide Going to Harvard," *New York Times*, September 30, 1951, p. 11; Jeanne S. Mintz, "Attachment A, Standard Form 57," typescript, n.d., folder 2, box 4, Mintz Papers.

24. "Indonesian Aide Going to Harvard," 11. On Emerson see Gilman, *Mandarins of the Future*, 120–21.

25. Jeanne S. Mintz, "Curriculum Vita," typescript, April 3, 1956, folder 3, box 9, Mintz Papers; Frank N. Trager, ed., *Marxism in Southeast Asia: A Study of Four Countries* (Stanford, Calif.: Stanford University Press, 1959); Jeanne S. Mintz, *Indonesia: A Profile* (Princeton, N.J.: Van Nostrand, 1961); Harry J. Benda, review of *Marxism in Southeast Asia* by Frank N. Trager, *Far Eastern Survey* 29 (1960): 141–42; Harry J. Benda, "Democracy in Indonesia," *Journal of Asian Studies* 23 (1964): 449–56.

26. Jeanne S. Mintz to Kai E. Rasmussen, May 22, 1960, folder 8, box 15, Mintz Papers; Jeanne S. Mintz, "Injunctions—Indonesia, Military: Enlisted Men," and "Injunctions—Indonesia, Military: Officers," typescript, n.d., folder 8, box 15, Mintz Papers; Jeanne S. Mintz to John Houk, November 12, 1960, folder 8, box 15, Mintz Papers.

27. Jeanne S. Mintz to Mary R. Wason, June 4, 1961, folder 8, box 15, Mintz Papers. The appeals Mintz assessed are not included in her records. See handwritten notes and draft of letter [Mintz to Rasmussen], n.d., folder 8, box 15, Mintz Papers; Laurence C. McQuade to Jeanne S. Mintz, August 23, 1961, folder 8, box 15, Mintz Papers. Nothing came of her meeting with the Defense Department, and Project Prosyms continued, evolving into a series of "Intercultural Communications Guides," covering nations from Afghanistan to Venezuela.

28. For Mintz's Prosyms appeals see Jeanne S. Mintz, "SORO: Assignment Three," typescript, October 22, 1960, folder 8, box 15, Mintz Papers. For U.S. psychological warfare

policy see Stanley Sandler, *Cease Resistance: It's Good for You! A History of U.S. Army Combat Psychological Operations* (Fort Bragg, N.C.: United States Army Special Operations Command, 1996).

29. John Houk to Jeanne S. Mintz, June 12, 1961, folder 8, box 15, Mintz Papers.

30. Jeanne S. Mintz to Rupert Emerson, April 26, 1964, folder 2, box 4, Mintz Papers; Emerson to Mintz, May 4, 1964, folder 2, box 4, Mintz Papers.

31. Special Operations Research Office, "Proposed R&D Work Program, FY 65," typescript, March 1, 1964, pp. 38–39, file 1302–01 Project Amelot [*sic*] Design and Phasing 65, entry UD-WW B-1, Accession 79–0067, RG 319, Records of the Army Staff.

32. Mintz's study was never published as a SORO report. She called her draft "The War That Was" to signify that it had been outdated by Johnson's escalation of the war shortly after she concluded her research. A declassified draft of the report can be found in Jeanne S. Mintz to Seymour Deitchman, March 1, 1965, folder 2, box 61, Mintz Papers, esp. 3.

33. George A. Carroll to Phillip I. Sperling, April 14, 1965, folder 3, box 4, Mintz Papers; George A. Carroll to Jeanne S. Mintz, May 5, 1965, folder 3, box 4, Mintz Papers; Edward Landsale to Jeanne S. Mintz, May 26, 1965, folder 3, box 4, Mintz Papers. Mintz's findings mirrored those of civilian government advisers who felt by the spring of 1965 that the military's direction of the conflict was dangerously wrongheaded. David E. Kaiser, *American Tragedy: Kennedy, Johnson, and the Origins of the Vietnam War* (Cambridge, Mass.: Belknap Press of Harvard University Press, 2000), 412–42.

34. Jeanne S. Mintz, *Mohammed, Marx, and Marhaen: The Roots of Indonesian Socialism* (London: Pall Mall Press, 1965).

35. Harold D. Lasswell, "The Policy Orientation," in Lerner and Lasswell, *Policy Sciences*, 14.

36. Robert Boguslaw, "Ethics and the Social Scientist," in *The Rise and Fall of Project Camelot: Studies in the Relationship between Social Science and Practical Politics*, ed. Irving Louis Horowitz (Cambridge, Mass.: MIT Press, 1967), 107–8, 109.

37. Robert Boguslaw, *The New Utopians: A Study of System Design and Social Change* (Englewood Cliffs, N.J.: Prentice-Hall, 1965), 47–49.

38. On Camelot see Herman, *Romance of American Psychology*, 153–207; Horowitz, *Rise and Fall of Project Camelot*; and Mark Solovey, "Project Camelot and the 1960s Epistemological Revolution: Rethinking the Politics–Patronage–Social Science Nexus," *Social Studies of Science* 31 (2001): 171–206.

39. Boguslaw, "Ethics and the Social Scientist," 109–10, 115; Robert Boguslaw, *Systems Analysis and Social Planning: Human Problems of Post-Industrial Society* (New York: Irvington Publishers, 1982), 33, 205.

40. On the intellectual traditions of Beard, Dewey, and Lynd see Alice O'Connor, *Social Science for What? Philanthropy and the Social Question in a World Turned Rightside Up* (New York: Russell Sage Foundation, 2007), 59–65; and Smith, *Social Science in the Crucible*; Alvin W. Gouldner, "Anti-Minotaur: The Myth of a Value-Free Sociology," *Social Problems* 9 (1962): 199–213; Irving L. Horowitz, "Social Science Objectivity and Value Neutrality: Historical Problems and Projections," *Diogenes* 39 (1962): 17–44; C. Wright Mills, *The Sociological Imagination* (New York: Oxford University Press 1959); Boguslaw, "Ethics and the Social Scientist," 126, 115.

41. Boguslaw, *New Utopians*, 198; Boguslaw, *Systems Analysis and Social Planning*, 211, 2; Jacques Ellul, *The Technological Society* (New York: Vintage Books, 1964).

42. Boguslaw, *Systems Analysis and Social Planning*, 2; Boguslaw, "Social Action and Social Change," 423, 433. On Dewey see Bruce Kuklick, *Blind Oracles: Intellectuals and War from Kennan to Kissinger* (Princeton, N.J.: Princeton University Press, 2006), 8–12. On Mills see Daniel Geary, *Radical Ambition: C. Wright Mills, the Left, and American Social Thought* (Berkeley: University of California Press, 2009), 143–78.

43. Boguslaw, "Social Action and Social Change," 433; Boguslaw, "Ethics and the Social Scientist," 111, 125.

44. Theodore A. Vallance to Special Operations Research Office Personnel, January 4, 1966, Robert Boguslaw File, Special Operations Research Office Personnel Records (American University Archives and Special Collections); Special Operations Research Office, "The Bystander," interoffice publication, vol. 2, no. 1, mimeo, January 1966, p. 2, Special Operations Research Office / 1966 file, box 2, Special Operations Research Office Papers.

45. Boguslaw, *Systems Analysis and Social Planning*, 206.

46. On Boguslaw's departure see Theodore R. Vallance, "Special Operations Research Office Administrative Memorandum No. 8–66, May 3, 1966," SORO/1966 file, box 2, Special Operations Research Office Papers; Robert Boguslaw, *Systems Analysis and Social Planning*; Thomas R. Ford, Review of *Systems Analysis and Social Planning*, *Contemporary Sociology* 13 (1984): 65.

47. Boguslaw, *New Utopians*, 198. On the inability of science to justify values see Proctor, *Value-Free Science?* 7–8.

48. Catherine Lutz, *Homefront: A Military City and the American 20th Century* (Boston: Beacon Press, 2001), 3.

49. Sharon Ghamari-Tabrizi, *The Worlds of Herman Kahn: The Intuitive Science of Thermonuclear War* (Cambridge, Mass.: Harvard University Press, 2005), 10; Doris M. Condit, "The Relationship of Certain Strategic Characteristics to Military Outcome in Internal Conflict Situations," *Proceedings of the Fifteenth Annual Human Factors Research and Development Conference* (Washington, D.C.: U.S. Army, 1969), 117–23; Theodore R. Vallance, "Methodology in Propaganda Research," *Psychological Bulletin* 48 (1951): 32–61; Albert Frances, "Structural and Anticipatory Dimensions of Violent Social Conflict" (PhD thesis, University of Pittsburgh, 1967).

50. Daniel Lerner, *The Passing of Traditional Society: Modernizing the Middle East* (Glencoe, Ill.: Free Press, 1958); Seymour Martin Lipset, *Political Man: The Social Bases of Politics* (Garden City, N.Y.: Anchor Books, 1960); Ted Gurr, "A Causal Model of Civil Strife: A Comparative Analysis Using New Indices," *American Political Science Review* 62 (1968): 1105. On Project Leader see Department of the Army, Office of the Chief of Research and Development, *Report of the Eleventh Annual Human Factors Research and Development Conference* (Washington, D.C.: Department of the Army, 1965), 349.

51. Harry Eckstein, *A Theory of Stable Democracy* (Princeton, N.J.: Woodrow Wilson School of Public and International Affairs, Center of International Studies Research Monograph 10, 1961), 47.

52. Marilyn B. Young, "The Age of Global Power," in *Rethinking American History in a Global Age*, ed. Thomas Bender (Berkeley: University of California Press, 2002), 274; Eckstein, *Theory of Stable Democracy*.

CHAPTER 3

1. "Project Camelot: A Research Concept Paper," August 1964, p. 20, "Project Camelot"—Theodore R. Vallance 1966 file, box 1, Special Operations Research Office Papers, American University Archives and Special Collections (Washington, D.C.).

2. Robert Boguslaw, "Ethics and the Social Scientist," in *The Rise and Fall of Project Camelot: Studies in the Relationship between Social Science and Practical Politics*, ed. I.L. Horowitz (Cambridge, Mass.: MIT Press, 1967), 120. Testimony of Theodore Vallance to the Subcommittee on International Organizations and Movements of the House Committee on Foreign Affairs, *Behavioral Sciences and the National Security*, Report No. 4, July–August 1965, 89th Cong., 2nd sess., 20.

3. On the global spread of the Camelot story see Correspondence Camelot file, box 13, Ralph A. Dungan Papers, John F. Kennedy Library, Boston.

4. Ron Robin, *The Making of the Cold War Enemy: Culture and Politics in the Military-Intellectual Complex* (Princeton, N.J.: Princeton University Press, 2003), 224. See also Mark Solovey, "Project Camelot and the 1960s Epistemological Revolution," *Social Studies of Science* 31 (2001): 171–206. Ellen Herman provides a more nuanced interpretation of the academic response to Camelot in *The Romance of American Psychology: Political Culture in the Age of Experts* (Berkeley: University of California Press, 1995).

5. On Camelot's design see SORO, "Project Camelot: Report on Research Design," April 1, 1965, box 195, Ithiel de Sola Pool Papers, Massachusetts Institute of Technology, Institute Archives and Special Collections (Cambridge, Mass.); and SORO, "Project Camelot: Design and Phasing," February 1, 1965, 1302–01 Project Amelot [*sic*] Design and Phasing 65 file, Accession 79–0067, UD-WW entry B-1, RG 319: Records of the Army Staff, National Archives II (College Park, Md.). On the popularity of modernization theory see Nils Gilman, *Mandarins of the Future: Modernization Theory in Cold War America* (Baltimore: Johns Hopkins University Press, 2003); and Michael Latham, *Modernization as Ideology: American Social Science and "Nation-Building" in the Kennedy Era* (Chapel Hill: University of North Carolina Press, 2000). For "let the experimenter" see Robert L. Sproull to Simulmatics Corporation et al., October 6, 1964, Simulmatics Urban Insurgency file, box 67, Pool Papers.

6. "Project Camelot: A Research Concept Paper," 4–7, and SORO, "Project Camelot: Report on Research Design," 18; Harry Eckstein, "Internal War: The Problem of Anticipation," in Ithiel de Sola Pool et al., *Social Science Research and National Security*, Report Prepared by the Research Group in Psychology and the Social Sciences (Washington, D.C.: Smithsonian Institution, 1963), 112.

7. SORO, "Project Camelot: Report on Research Design," 1; SORO, "Project Camelot: Design and Phasing," 9, 29–39; Sproull to Simulmatics Corporation et al., October 6, 1964, Pool Papers.

8. For "quantum jump" see SORO, "Project Camelot: Report on Research Design," 1. For "undercut," Theodore Vallance, staff memo, October 9, 1964, SORO/1964 file, box 1, SORO Papers; Pio Uliassi to Evans, May 5, 1965, Correspondence Camelot file, box 13, Dungan Papers.

9. Vallance, staff memo, October 9, 1964.

10. On SORO's intellectual content and consultants see "Project Camelot: A Research Concept Paper," 4–7, and SORO, "Project Camelot: Report on Research Design," 18.

11. S. D. Cornell to Director, Army Research Office, September 30, 1964, Behavioral Sciences General 1964 file, Division of Behavioral Sciences records, National Academy of Sciences Archives, Washington, D.C. (Division of Behavioral Sciences records hereafter cited as NAS Papers).

12. Theodore Vallance, "Conflict: A New Departure," *Conflict: A Quarterly Journal of Revolution and Social Change* 1 (1965): 5, box 1, SORO Papers.

13. Vallance to Donald Derby and William O. Nichols, December 22, 1964, SORO (Reorganization) / 1965 files, box 2, SORO Papers.

14. Gino Germani, "In Memoriam: Rex D. Hopper, 1898–1966," *American Sociologist* 1 (1965–66): 259.

15. On Hopper joining SORO see Theodore Vallance to Harold L. Hutson, January 13, 1965, SORO (Personnel) / 1965–66 file, Special Operations Research Office Personnel Records, American University Archives and Special Collections; Rex D. Hopper, "Cybernation, Marginality, and Revolution," in *The New Sociology: Essays in Social Science and Social Theory, in Honor of C. Wright Mills*, ed. Irving L. Horowitz (New York: Oxford University Press, 1964), 313.

16. Jessie Bernard, letter to the editor, *American Sociologist* 1 (1965–6): 24.

17. On Nutini's activities in Chile see Department of State to Ralph Dungan, U.S. Embassy, Lima, July 7, 1965, Correspondence Camelot file, box 13, Dungan Papers; and Subcommittee on Science, Research, and Development of the House of Representatives Committee on Science and Astronautics, *Technical Information for Congress* (Washington, D.C.: Government Printing Office, April 25, 1969, rev. May 15, 1971), 132; Gyarmati quoted in Ralph A. Dungan to Thomas L. Hughes, August 6, 1965, Correspondence Camelot file, box 13, Dungan Papers.

18. On Galtung's exposure of Nutini see Johan Galtung, "Scientific Colonialism," *Transition* 30 (April–May 1967): 10–15; and Irving L. Horowitz, "The Rise and Fall of Project Camelot," in Horowitz, *Rise and Fall of Project Camelot*, 11–14; *El Siglo* quoted in Dungan to Washington, June 14, 1965, DEF 11 US 1/1/65 file, box 1711, Subject-Numeric Files 1964–66, RG 59, Records of the State Department (file hereafter cited as State Department Telegrams 1965). Frei quoted in Embassy, Santiago, to Department of State, June 19, 1965, Correspondence Camelot file, box 13, Dungan Papers; "Politically undesirable" at Santiago to Washington, August 30, 1965, Correspondence Camelot file, box 13, Dungan Papers; "Politically dangerous" at Dungan to Department of State, June 14, 1965, DEF 11 US 1/1/65 file, State Department Telegrams 1965.

19. Joseph A. Califano Jr. to Gordon Chase, June 16, 1965, State Department Telegrams 1965. For evidence that SORO funded Nutini see Washington to Lima for Dungan, July 7, 1965, Correspondence Camelot file, box 13, Dungan Papers.

20. Richard H. Davis to Willis M. Hawkins, May 20, 1965, State Department Telegrams 1965; Hawkins to Davis, June 8, 1965, State Department Telegrams 1965.

21. Ralph A. Dungan to Washington, June 19, 1965, State Department Telegrams 1965.

22. Califano to Chase, June 16, 1965, State Department Telegrams 1965.

23. On the State Department leak see Seymour Deitchman, *The Best-Laid Schemes: A Tale of Social Research and Bureaucracy* (Cambridge, Mass.: MIT Press, 1976), 173; and David C. Geyer and David H. Herschler, eds., *Foreign Relations of the United States, 1964–1968*, vol. 31, *South and Central America; Mexico* (Washington, D.C.: Government Printing Office, 2004), entry 280, note 2. Anonymous State Department official quoted in Walter Pincus, "Army-State Department Feud Bared by Chile Incident," *Washington Star*, n.d.; McCarthy quoted in Walter Pincus, "McCarthy Calls for Probe of Army's Project Camelot," *Washington Star*, June 27, 1965, p. A-1, CAMELOT (Publicity) / 1965 (2) file, box 1, SORO Papers. For Johnson's response see "Recording of a telephone conversation between President Johnson and Thomas Mann, June 30, 1965," in Geyer and Herschler, *Foreign Relations of the United States*, vol. 31, entry 280. For McNamara's announcement see Department of Defense news release, July 8, 1965, CAMELOT (Publicity) / 1965 (2) file, box 1, SORO Papers.

24. On the State Department's declining authority see Chester Bowles, "Toward a New Diplomacy," *Foreign Affairs* 40 (January 1962): 246; and Dean Acheson, "The Eclipse of the State Department," *Foreign Affairs* 49 (July 1971): 593–606; Clark A. Miller, "An Effective Instrument of U.S. Foreign Policy, 1938–1950," in *Global Power Knowledge: Science and Technology in International Relations*, ed. John Krige and Kai-Henrik Barth, Osiris 21 (Chicago: University of Chicago Press, 2006), 153.

25. Senate report quoted in C.W. Borklund, *The Department of Defense* (New York: Frederick A. Praeger, 1968), 219; Kennedy quoted in Andrew Preston, *The War Council: McGeorge Bundy, the NSC, and Vietnam* (Cambridge, Mass.: Harvard University Press, 2006), 44. On DOD foreign policy expertise see Gene M. Lyons, *The Uneasy Partnership: Social Science and the Federal Government in the Twentieth Century* (New York: Russell Sage Foundation, 1969), 179–80. For "Defense, not State," see Borklund, *Department of Defense*, 223.

26. On funding see Walter Pincus, "Senate to Air Camelot Issue," *Washington Star*, July 6, 1965, CAMELOT (Publicity) / 1965 (2) file, box 1, SORO Papers; Uliassi to Evans, May 5, 1965, Correspondence Camelot file, box 13, Dungan Papers; Washington to Santiago, June 28, 1965, Correspondence Camelot file, box 13, Dungan Papers; Ralph Dungan to Cyrus Vance, July 27, 1965, Chronological File July 1965, box 21, Dungan Papers.

27. Dungan to Harold Brown, July 30, 1965, Chronological File July 1965, box 21, Dungan Papers; Brown to Dungan, August 31, 1965, Correspondence Camelot file, box 13, Dungan Papers.

28. Horowitz, "Rise and Fall of Project Camelot," 20; Dungan to Harold Brown, June 15, 1965, Correspondence Camelot file, box 13, Dungan Papers; Dungan to Department of State, June 21, 1965, Correspondence Camelot file, box 13, Dungan Papers; Thomas L. Hughes to Llewellyn Thompson, June 29, 1965, Correspondence Camelot file, box 13, Dungan Papers.

29. Almond quoted in Senate Committee on Government Operations, Subcommittee on Government Research, *Federal Support of International Social Science and Behavioral Research,* Hearings, 89th Congress, 2nd sess., June 27–28, July 19–20, 1966, 114; House Subcommittee on International Organizations and Movements, *Behavioral Sciences and the National Security*, 2R.

30. National Academy of Sciences, Division of Behavioral Sciences, Minutes of the Second Meeting, Advisory Committee on Government Programs in the Behavioral Sciences, December 10, 1965, p. 2, Behavioral Sciences Com on Govt Programs in Behavioral Sc: Adv Meetings: Minutes: December 1965 file, NAS Papers; Deitchman, *Best-Laid Schemes*, 209, 173. For Frelinghuysen's comments see House Subcommittee on International Organizations and Movements, *Behavioral Sciences and the National Security*, 48.

31. H. M. Ball to Dungan, July 7, 1965, Correspondence Camelot file, box 13, Dungan Papers.

32. "Pentagon: Project Camelot," *Newsweek*, July 5, 1965, in CAMELOT (Publicity) / 1965 (2) file, box 1, SORO Papers; cf. Caracas to Washington, August 10, 1965; Belgrade to Washington, August 13, 1965; Montevideo to Washington, August 19, 1965, State Department Telegrams 1965.

33. Walter Pincus, "Rusk Called to Testify in Camelot Inquiry," *Washington Star*, July 19, 1965, in CAMELOT (Publicity) / 1965 (2) file, box 1, SORO Papers; "Cancel All Camelots!" *Washington Daily News*, August 7, 1965, p. 10, CAMELOT (Publicity) / 1965 (2) file, box 1, SORO Papers.

34. Johnson quoted in Geyer and Herschler, *Foreign Relations of the United States,* vol. 31, entry 280, note 4; Dungan to Thomas L. Hughes, August 6, 1965, Correspondence Camelot file, box 13, Dungan Papers; "Burying Camelot," *New York Times*, August 12, 1965, p. 24.

35. Alfred De Grazia, "Government and Science: An Editorial," *American Behavioral Scientist* 9 (September 1965): 40.

36. Leonard E. Schwartz, "Social Science and the Furtherance of Peace Research," *American Behavioral Scientist* 9 (March 1966): 25; William Goode, letter to the editor, *American Sociologist* 1 (1965–66): 255. Goode maintained that he declined to join Camelot not out of concern for its propriety, but because he would have liked to direct it rather than serve on the staff. Almond quoted in Senate Subcommittee on Government Research, *Federal Support of International Social Science*, 112.

37. Rex D. Hopper, "Indicators of Revolutionary Potential," Presentation to the Operations Research Symposium (Washington, D.C.: SORO, May 1964), 3; Pitirim Sorokin, *The Sociology of Revolution* (Philadelphia: J. B. Lippincott Co., 1925), 12. Similar sentiments were expressed in other classics of the genre on which Camelot relied, including Lyford P. Edwards, *The Natural History of Revolution* (Chicago: University of Chicago Press, 1927),

and George Sawyer Pettee, *The Process of Revolution* (New York: Harper & Brothers, 1938). Horowitz, "Rise and Fall of Project Camelot," 7, 8.

38. For examples blaming Nutini see the comments by William J. Nagle and unidentified participants, "Discussion: The New Intelligence Requirements," *Background* 9 (1965): 195; and William Marvel, "Remarks," *Background* 9 (1965): 177–83. On the National Academy of Sciences see George P. Murdock to Frederick Seitz, June 16, 1965; and Peter B. Hammond to Maj. John H. Johns, October 6, 1965, Behavioral Sciences, Com on Non-Materiel Research: Adv Ad hoc, 1965 file, NAS Papers.

39. Dale L. Johnson, letter to the editor, *American Sociologist* 1 (1965–66): 206; and Dale L. Johnson, "Ethics of the Nature, Procedures, and Funding of Research in Other Countries," *American Anthropologist* 68 (1966): 1016–17; Marshall Sahlins, "The Established Order: Do Not Fold, Spindle, or Mutilate," in Horowitz, *Rise and Fall of Project Camelot*, 72. See also Kalman H. Silvert, "American Academic Ethics and Social Research Abroad: The Lesson of Project Camelot," *Background* 9 (1965): 215–36; and Galtung, "Scientific Colonialism."

40. Horowitz, "Rise and Fall of Project Camelot," 7, 4.

41. Silvert, "American Academic Ethics," 223; Horowitz, "Rise and Fall of Project Camelot," 40, 33.

42. Horowitz, "Rise and Fall of Project Camelot," 40, 41; Goode, letter to the editor, 256. For similar sentiments see Jessie Bernard, letter to the editor; George I. Blanksten, letter to the editor, *American Behavioral Scientist* 9 (October 1965): NS-12; Ithiel de Sola Pool, "The Necessity for Social Scientists Doing Research for Governments," *Background* 10 (1966): 120; and Dael Wolfle, "Social Science Research and International Relations," *Science* 151 (January 14, 1966): 155.

43. Brayfield quoted in Senate Subcommittee on Government Research, *Federal Support of International Social Science*, 67; Horowitz, "Rise and Fall of Project Camelot," 40. For "through some" see Luther J. Carter, "Social Sciences: Problems Examined by Senate Panel," *Science* 153 (July 8, 1966): 155. Galtung, "Scientific Colonialism," 12.

44. Harold Brown to Frederick Seitz, July 28, 1965, Behavioral Sciences Com on Govt Programs in Behavioral Sc: Adv General 1965 file, NAS Papers. On the committee membership see Minutes of the First Meeting of the Advisory Committee on Government Programs in the Behavioral Sciences, November 9, 1965, Advisory Meetings: General 1965 file, NAS Papers; On Murdock see David H. Price, *Threatening Anthropology: McCarthyism and the FBI's Surveillance of Activist Anthropologists* (Durham, N.C.: Duke University Press, 2004), 71–75. On Pool see Joy Rohde, "Last Stand of the Psychocultural Cold Warriors: Military Contract Research in Vietnam," *Journal of the History of the Behavioral Sciences* 47 (2011): 232–50.

45. Murdock quoted in Division of the Behavioral Sciences, "Advisory Committee on Government Programs in the Behavioral Sciences," December 5, 1965, p. 2, Behavioral Sciences Com on Govt Programs in Behavioral Sc: Adv General 1965 file, NAS Papers; Seitz quoted in Minutes of the Council Meeting, Appendix 2, Division of Behavioral Sciences, February 6, 1966, Behavioral Sciences Com on Govt Programs in Behavioral Sc: Adv General 1966 file, NAS Papers.

46. Brown to Seitz, July 28, 1965, Behavioral Sciences Com on Govt Programs in Behavioral Sc: Adv General 1965 file, NAS Papers. Seitz quoted in Council Meeting minutes, September 25, 1965, Behavioral Sciences Com on Govt Programs in Behavioral Sc: Adv General 1965 file, NAS Papers.

47. For the State Department's attempt to exclude the Pentagon see C. E. Sunderlin, Diary Note, October 13, 1965, Behavioral Sciences Com on Govt Programs in Behavioral Sc: Adv General 1965 file, NAS Papers. For the advisory committee's efforts on behalf of the Pentagon see C. E. Sunderlin, Diary Note, November 2, 1965; Minutes of the Council

Meeting, Division of Behavioral Sciences, Appendix 2, December 5, 1965; and C. E. Sunderlin, Diary Note, November 23, 1965, Behavioral Sciences Com on Govt Programs in Behavioral Sc: Adv General 1965 file, NAS Papers; Thomas L. Hughes, "Public Notice 242: Government-Sponsored Foreign Affairs Research, Procedures for Review," December 21, 1965, reprinted in Senate Subcommittee on Government Research, *Federal Support of International Social Science*, 45–48.

48. Hughes, "Public Notice 242," 45–48. For "clearance" see George C. Denney Jr., "State Department Procedures for Reviewing Government Sponsored Foreign Area Research," *Background* 10 (1966): 100.

49. "Research Council Activities: A Summary," *FAR Horizons* 1 no. 2 (May 1968): 6–8.

50. For embassy reactions to the study of communist subversion see Department of State to Rio, July 15, 1965; Bogotá to Department of State, July 21, 1965; Caracas to Department of State, July 22, 1965, State Department Telegrams 1965; Lincoln Gordon to Washington, July 14, 1965, State Department Telegrams 1965. For "reluctant" see Department of State to Caracas and Bogotá, August 25, 1965, State Department Telegrams 1965.

51. John Gagne, "The New Intelligence Requirements: Introduction," *Background* 9 (1965): 171. For "responsibility to government" see Ralph L. Beals, *The Politics of Social Research: An Inquiry into the Ethics and Responsibilities of Social Scientists* (Chicago: Aldine Publishing Co., 1969), 4. Gabriel Almond, "Remarks," *Background* 9 (1965): 173.

52. On the Camelot forum see Charles Windle, "SID Holds Joint Meeting on Overseas Research," in "The Bystander," interoffice publication, vol. 1 (December 1965): 3, CRESS file, box 2, SORO Papers. On the failure to censure the study see Munro S. Edmonson et al., letter to the editor, *American Sociologist* 1 (1965–6): 207–8.

53. Almond quoted in "Discussion: The New Intelligence Requirements," 196. For the document Hopper circulated see SORO, "Project Camelot," December 4, 1964, State Department Telegrams 1965.

54. Beals, *Politics of Social Research*, 10; Horowitz, "Rise and Fall of Project Camelot," 10.

55. Fellows of the American Anthropological Association, "Statement on Problems of Anthropological Research and Ethics," reprinted in Beals, *Politics of Social Research*, 192–96.

56. Sahlins, "Established Order," 79.

57. Robert A. Dahl et al., "Report of the Executive Committee," *American Political Science Review* 61 (1967): 566; Bernstein Committee, "Bernstein Committee Interim Report: Ethical Problems of Social Scientists," *PS* 1 (1968): 5–16.

58. Galtung, "Scientific Colonialism," 12; Silvert, "American Academic Ethics," 217.

59. Herbert Blumer, "Threats from Agency-Determined Research," in Horowitz, *Rise and Fall of Project Camelot*, 167, 174.

60. Klaus Knorr, "Social Science Research Abroad: Problems and Remedies," *World Politics* 19 (1967): 482; Beals quoted in House Committee on Government Operations Research and Technical Programs Subcommittee, *The Use of Social Research in Federal Domestic Programs* (Washington, D.C.: Government Printing Office, 1967), 3:20.

61. Unidentified to Vallance, July 20, 1965, SORO/AU box 1, folder: (1) Camelot 1965.

62. Eugene Stubbs to Theodore Vallance, July 9, 1965, Camelot 1965 (1) file, box 1, SORO Papers.

63. Task Statement, "Measurement of Predisposing Factors for Communist Inspired Insurgency," July 9, 1965, SORO Contracts-Legal file, box 2, SORO Papers.

64. "The Bystander," vol. 2, no. 1 (January 1966), SORO 1966 file, box 2, SORO Papers.

65. Stubbs to Vallance, July 9, 1965, Camelot 1965 (1) file, box 1, SORO Papers.

66. Stubbs to Vallance, September 29, 1965, Research Analysis Corporation: Correspondence, 1961–66 file, box 2, OCRD, DAR Transaction Files 1967–69, entry 1393, RG

319. On renaming Psyguide see "The Bystander," vol. 2, no. 1 (January 1966), p. 1, SORO 1966 file, box 2, SORO Papers.

67. On Johns see "The Bystander," vol. 2., no. 1 (January 1966), SORO 1966 file, box 2, SORO Papers. For "the substance" see draft letter, Brig. Gen. Lotz to Vallance [draft composed by Vallance for Lotz's signature], n.d. [August 1965], SORO (Personnel) / 1965–66 file, Special Operations Research Office Personnel Records; Contract DAHC 19–67-C-0046, June 30, 1967, p. 12, DAHC19–67-C-0046 the American University (CRESS) Basic Contract and Modifications file, box 10, OCRD, DAR Transaction Files 1967–69, entry 1393, RG 319.

68. Hilbert E. Friend to Vallance, August 2, 1965, Camelot 1965 (1) file, box 1, SORO Papers.

69. Harold Brown to Assistant Secretaries of the Army, Navy, and Air Force, and Director, Advanced Research Projects Agency, August 18, 1965, Com on Govt Programs in Behavioral Sc: Adv General 1965 file, NAS Papers.

70. On Sperling see Vallance to SORO Staff, September 2, 1965, SORO (Contracts/Legal) / 1965–66 file, box 2, SORO Papers; Lybrand to Vallance, May 31, 1966, SORO/1966 file, box 2, SORO Papers.

71. Delaney Dobbins, "Some Considerations in Future Behavioral Science Programs in Canal Zone and Latin America," July 28, 1967, pp. 3–4, 1303–01 CRESS Contract 67 file, box 3, entry 1295D, RG 319.

CHAPTER 4

1. For "interesting and horrifying" see Eliot Fremont-Smith, "Peace—It Could Be Horrible," *New York Times*, November 20, 1967, p. 45; best-seller list at *New York Times*, February 4, 1968, p. BR45; report quoted in "Comment: Social Science Fiction," *Transaction* 5, no. 3 (1968): 7. At the time, suspected authors included Kenneth Boulding, John Kenneth Galbraith, Irving Louis Horowitz, and Anatol Rapoport, men "whose wit, competence, and devotion to peace make them suspect" ("Comment: Social Science Fiction," 16). Of these, only Galbraith has been confirmed as a collaborator. See Victor Navasky, introduction in Leonard C. Lewin, *Report from Iron Mountain on the Possibility and Desirability of Peace* (1967; repr., New York: Free Press, 1996), v–xvi.

2. "Comment: Social Science Fiction," 19.

3. John Ernst, *Forging a Fateful Alliance: Michigan State University and the Vietnam War* (East Lansing: Michigan State University Press, 1998), 81–83, 114–15; Donald L. M. Blackmer, *The MIT Center for International Studies: The Founding Years, 1951–1969* (Cambridge, Mass.: MITCIS, 2002), chap. 6; Stanley Sheinbaum, quoted in Wayne Morse, "Dangers in Government Sponsorship of Research on Foreign Policy and Foreign Areas," *Background* 10 (1966): 125–26.

4. Rickover quoted in Senate, Committee on Foreign Relations, *Defense Department Sponsored Foreign Affairs Research*, 90th Cong., 2nd sess., pt. 1, May 9, 1968, 11; H. L. Nieburg, *In the Name of Science* (Chicago: Quadrangle Books, 1966); Clark R. Mollenhoff, *The Pentagon* (New York: G. P. Putnam's Sons, 1967).

5. Walter Pincus, "'Operation Simpatico': Pentagon in New Latin Row," *Washington Star*, January 31, 1966, SORO/1966 file, box 2, SORO Papers. On Simpatico's design see SORO, Memorandum for the Record, September 10, 1965, and SORO, Memorandum for the Record, January 28, 1966, SORO/1966 file, box 2, SORO Papers. On Andrade see "Colombian Scores U.S. over Survey," *New York Times*, February 4, 1966, p. 12; Dan Kurzman, "Hey Senor! Do You Beat Your Wives Often?" *Washington Post*, February 13, 1966, p. E2.

6. Montreal Consulate to Washington, March 1, 1966, Def 11 US 1/1/66 file, box 1711, Subject-Numeric Files 1964–66, RG 59, Records of the Department of State, Archives 2;

"Ottawa Is Upset over a U.S. Study," *New York Times*, March 3, 1966, p. 8; AU official quoted in SORO, draft press release, March 3, 1966, SORO/1966 file, box 2, SORO Papers; Theodore R. Vallance to Lester B. Pearson, March 4, 1966, SORO/1966 file, box 2, SORO Papers.

7. On institutional funds see "The Bystander," interoffice publication, vol. 2, no. 1 (January 1966): 1, SORO/1966 file, box 2, SORO Papers. On the board see CRESS, "Annual Report of the CRESS Board of Advisors," October 1968, Center for Research in Social Systems File, Office of the President, Dr. Anderson, American University Archives and Special Collections (Washington, D.C.).

8. For "less threatening" see Vallance to Anderson, July 30, 1965, SORO (Reorganization)/1965 file, box 2, SORO Papers. On the name change see CRESS, *Center for Research in Social Systems Work Program, Fiscal Year 1967* (Washington, D.C.: CRESS, August 1, 1966), p. i. For "theory-oriented research" see Theodore Vallance, "Reorientation of Present Organization," Enclosure 5, July 30, 1965, SORO/Reorganization file, box 2, SORO Papers. Vallance, Memorandum to staff, January 4, 1966, SORO (Personnel)/1965–66 file, Special Operations Research Office Personnel Records.

9. American University News Bureau, Press Release SORO 222, May 1966, CRESS file, box 2, SORO Papers; Richard Eder, "School Limits Tie to Army Project," *New York Times*, May 8, 1966, p. 30; Merrill Ewing to Eugene Stubbs, December 28, 1967, and Preston S. Abbott to George H. Williams, August 13, 1968, file Cress, Papers of the Office of the President, Dr. Anderson.

10. Col. William Moore, [Briefing on CRESS work program to semiannual meeting of the army Human Factors Research Advisory Committee], November 17, 1966, p. 12, AHFRAC Meeting Minutes 66 file, box 1, Accession 79–0068, UD-WW entry B-2, RG 319, Archives 2. On divulging results see Contract DAHC 19–67-C-0046, July 1, 1967, American University (CRESS) Basic Contract and Modifications file, box 10, OCRD, DAR Transaction Files, RG 319.

11. For CRESS's work program see Col. William Moore, [Briefing army Human Factors Research Advisory Committee], November 17, 1966, chart 17, p. 4; "Center for Research in Social Systems 1967 Annual Report," Center for Research in Social Systems file, Papers of the Office of the President, Dr. Anderson, p. 2.

12. Lt. Col. Charles E. Ramsburg to Col. Taylor, April 30, 1968; Lt. Col. A. S. Allen, U.S. Strike Command, to the Chief of Research and Development, March 8, 1968; and Charles E. Ramsburg to Director, Center for Research in Social Systems, March 12, 1968, 1303–01 Approval of CRESS Reports (68) file, box 3, entry 1295D, RG 319.

13. William John Hanna and Judith Lynne Hanna, *Urban Dynamics in Black Africa: An Interdisciplinary Approach* (Chicago: Aldine Atherton, 1971); W. Arens, "Urban Dynamics in Black Africa," *American Anthropologist* 75 (1973): 1828–29; Richard Stren, "Urban Dynamics in Black Africa," *American Political Science Review* 67 (1973): 1400–1401.

14. Luther J. Carter, "Social Sciences: Where Do They Fit in the Politics of Science?" *Science* 154 (October 28, 1966): 488. "U.S. Government Agency Obligations for Social and Behavioral Research on Foreign Areas and International Affairs, FY 1966," National Academy of Sciences Advisory Committee on Government Programs, 1966–1 file, box 98, Ithiel de Sola Pool Papers, Massachusetts Institute of Technology, Institute Archives and Special Collections (Cambridge, Mass.). For 1967 spending see National Academy of Sciences Advisory Committee on Government Programs in the Behavioral Sciences, *The Behavioral Sciences and the Federal Government* (Washington, D.C.: National Academy of Sciences, 1968), 62–63.

15. Harold Orlans, *Contracting for Knowledge: Values and Limitations of Social Science Research* (San Francisco: Jossey-Bass, 1973), 143; Leonard Reissman and Kalman H. Silvert, "Ethics and the Third Culture," *American Behavioral Scientist* 10, no. 10 (1967): 2.

16. Irving L. Horowitz and Lee Rainwater, "Comment: Our CIA Problem and Theirs," *Transaction* 4, no. 7 (June 1967): 2.

17. Richard N. Adams, "Ethics and the Social Anthropologist in Latin America," *American Behavioral Scientist* 10, no. 10 (1967): 16.

18. Irving Louis Horowitz, "Social Science and Public Policy: An Examination of the Political Foundations of Modern Research," *International Studies Quarterly* 11 (1967): 32–62, esp. 41, 56, 60; Lerner and Lasswell, *Policy Sciences.*

19. Pierre L. van den Berghe, letter to the editor, *American Sociologist* 2 (1967): 99.

20. Klaus Knorr, "Social Science Research Abroad: Problems and Remedies," *World Politics* 19 (1967): 482; Horowitz, "Social Science and Public Policy," 47, 61.

21. Morgenthau quoted in Ido Oren, *Our Enemies and Us: America's Rivalries and the Making of Political Science* (Ithaca, N.Y.: Cornell University Press, 2003), 153.

22. Kathleen Gough, "World Revolution and the Science of Man," in *The Dissenting Academy*, ed. Theodore Roszak (New York: Pantheon Books, 1968), 149.

23. Silvert testimony in Congress, Senate Committee on Government Operations, Subcommittee on Government Research, *Federal Support of International Social Science and Behavioral Research*, Hearings, 89th Cong., 2nd sess., June 27–28, July 19–20, 1966 (Washington, D.C.: Government Printing Office), 226–27, 230.

24. Theodore Roszak, "On Academic Delinquency," in Roszak, *Dissenting Academy*, 21.

25. Robert Boguslaw, *Systems Analysis and Social Planning: Problems of Post-Industrial Society* (New York: Irvington Publishers, 1982), 2.

26. The above opinions are recorded in House Committee on Government Operations Research and Technical Programs Subcommittee, *The Use of Social Research in Federal Domestic Programs*, vol. 3: for Abt, p. 9; Beals, p. 25; de Grazia, p. 74; Lyons, p. 137; and Orlansky, p. 145.

27. Ibid., for Volkart, p. 207; Gouldner, p. 103.

28. Ibid., for Coleman, p. 57; Darley, p. 40; Reicken, p. 176; Brayfield quoted on p. 41.

29. Wayne Morse, "Dangers in Government Sponsorship of Research on Foreign Policy and Foreign Areas," *Background* 10 (1966): 130; Case quoted in *Congressional Record* 115, pt. 17 (August 11, 1969), 23283.

30. U.S. Congress, House Committee on Foreign Affairs Subcommittee on International Organizations and Movements, *Behavioral Sciences and the National Security, Report No. 4, Together with Part IX of the Hearings on Winning the Cold War: The U.S. Ideological Offensive*, 89th Cong., 2nd sess., July–August 1965 (Washington, D.C.: Government Printing Office, 1965); U.S. Congress, Senate Committee on Government Operations, Subcommittee on Government Research, *National Foundation for Social Sciences, Hearings on S. 836, a Bill to Provide for the Establishment of the National Foundation for the Social Sciences*, 90th Cong., 1st sess., February, June, July 1967 (Washington, D.C.: Government Printing Office, 1967); U.S. Congress, House, Committee on Government Operations, Subcommittee on Research and Technical Programs, *Use of Social Research in Federal Domestic Programs*, pt. 1, Federally Financed Social Research: Expenditures, Status, and Objectives (Washington, D.C.: Government Printing Office, 1967).

31. For "one of the vital tools" see House Committee on Foreign Affairs Subcommittee on International Organizations and Movements, *Behavioral Sciences and the National Security*, 5R. For Fascell's proposed bill, see *Congressional Record* 112, pt. 9 (June 6, 1966), 12277–82. See also Luther J. Carter, "Social Sciences: Where Do They Fit in the Politics of Science?" *Science* 154 (October 28, 1966): 488–91.

32. For "democratic belief" see Senate Committee on Government Operations, Subcommittee on Government Research, *National Foundation for Social Sciences, Hearings*, 2. For "militaristic image" see Kurzman, "Hey Senor." For "that our foreign policy" see Senate Committee on Government Operations, Subcommittee on Government Research,

National Foundation for Social Sciences, Hearings, 84. See also Harris's remarks on the Senate floor in *Congressional Record* 112, pt. 2 (February 7, 1966), 2281–83.

33. On the NFSS episode see Mark Solovey, "Senator Fred Harris's Effort to Create a National Social Science Foundation: Challenge to the U.S. National Science Establishment," *Isis* 103 (2012): 54–82. On basic research funding see Mark Solovey, "The Politics of Intellectual Identity and American Social Science, 1945–1970" (PhD thesis, University of Wisconsin–Madison, 1996), 357.

34. Daniel S. Greenberg, "Social Sciences: Harris Bill Evokes Limited Support," *Science* 155 (February 17, 1967): 812. Harris quoted in Senate Subcommittee on Government Research, *National Foundation for Social Sciences,* 86.

35. Haworth quoted in Senate Subcommittee on Government Research, *National Foundation for Social Sciences,* 101. Foster quoted in Senate Subcommittee on Government Research, *National Foundation for Social Sciences,* 230.

36. Thomas F. Geiryn, *The Cultural Boundaries of Science: Credibility on the Line* (Chicago: University of Chicago Press, 1999), 73, n. 11. See also House Committee on Government Operations Research and Technical Programs Subcommittee, *The Use of Social Research in Federal Domestic Programs,* 3:1–214. Bayton quoted in House Committee on Government Operations Research and Technical Programs Subcommittee, *The Use of Social Research in Federal Domestic Programs,* 3:17.

37. Dennis W. Brezina, "The Congressional Debate on the Social Sciences in 1968," Staff Discussion Paper 400, Program of Policy Studies in Science and Technology, George Washington University (Washington D.C.: December 1968), 19.

38. Daniel Greenberg, "Social Sciences: Expanded Role Urged for Defense Department," *Science* 158 (November 17, 1967): 886.

39. Seymour Deitchman, *The Best-Laid Schemes: A Tale of Social Research and Bureaucracy* (Cambridge, Mass.: MIT Press, 1976), 416; Irving L. Horowitz, "Social Science Yogis and Military Commissars," *Trans-action* 5, no. 6 (1968): 30.

40. For Kelman and others' discomfort with the DOD relationship see NAS Advisory Committee on Government Program, "Minutes of the Seventh Meeting, May 19–20, 1967," p. 7, National Academy of Sciences Advisory Committee on Government Programs 1962–2 file, box 71, Pool Papers. For "how the behavioral" see Albert H. Cantril to Committee Members of Advisory Committee on the Management of Behavioral Sciences Research in the Department of Defense, October 23, 1969, file 6, box 71, Pool Papers. For the committee's continued advising role see Pool to Lincoln Bloomfield, July 23, 1969, Pool: Outgoing Correspondence June, July, and August, 1969 file, box 64, Pool Papers; and Pool to Defense Science Board, "Proposed Task Statement—DSB Summer Study—Panel on Training for Pacification Advisors, June 17, 1968, Election Research Cor, 1968 file, box 65, Pool Papers.

41. "Academic Research: Foster Defends DoD Support in Universities," *Science* 158 (November 24, 1967): 1032–34; Donald M. MacArthur, "Current Emphasis on the Department of Defense's Social and Behavioral Sciences Program," *American Psychologist* 23, no. 2 (1968): 104.

42. On 1967 budget see MacArthur, "Current Emphasis on the Department of Defense's Social and Behavioral Sciences Program," 104; Luther J. Carter, "Project Themis: More Research Dollars for the Have-Nots," *Science* 155 (February 3, 1967): 548. On the State Department's relative decline see U.S. Congress, House Committee on Science and Astronautics, Subcommittee on Science, Research and Development, *Technical Information for Congress* (Washington, D.C.: Government Printing Office, 1969), 153.

43. "News in Brief," *Science* 158 (November 10, 1967): 749; "Campuses and Conscience," *Science News,* May 4, 1968, 423–24. For "academic freedom" see "Academic Research: Foster Defends DoD Support in Universities," 1034.

44. "Academic Research: Foster Defends DoD Support in Universities," 1034. FAR membership included the U.S. Agency for International Development; the Arms Control and Disarmament Agency; the CIA; the DOD; the Department of Health, Education, and Welfare; the Department of Labor; the Department of State; NASA; the National Endowment for the Humanities; the NSF; the Peace Corps; the Smithsonian Institution; and the U.S. Information Agency.

45. Daniel S. Greenberg, "Social Science: Federal Agencies Agree to End Covert Support," *Science* 159 (January 5, 1968): 66.

46. Senate Committee on Foreign Relations, *Defense Department Sponsored Foreign Affairs Research*, pt. 1, 1, 5.

47. Ibid., 11, 4.

48. Ibid., 18, 16, 19. On the budget see *Congressional Record* 115, pt. 17 (August 11, 1969), 23281.

49. Senate Committee on Foreign Relations, *Defense Department Sponsored Foreign Affairs Research*, pt. 2, pp. 3, 30–31.

50. Pax Americana documents quoted in E.W. Kenworthy, "Pentagon Refuses to Release Secret Study on U.S. Hegemony," *New York Times*, February 16, 1968, p. 2.

51. Mundt quoted in Senate Committee on Foreign Relations, *Defense Department Sponsored Foreign Affairs Research*, 32. For "reads like" see Kenworthy, "Pentagon Refuses to Release Secret Study on U.S. Hegemony," 2. Washington to All Diplomatic Posts, March 9, 1968, DEF 11 US 1/1/68 file, box 1671, Subject-Numeric Files 1967–69, RG 59, General Records of the Department of State. Rickover quoted in Senate Committee on Foreign Relations, *Defense Department Sponsored Foreign Affairs Research*, pt. 2, pp. 33, 45.

52. "Research Absorbs the Cuts," *Science News*, May 18, 1968, p. 472; Bryce Nelson, "Military Funds: Senate Whets the Ax for ABM, Research, 'Think Tanks,'" *Science* 160 (May 24, 1968): 860–64. Previous fiscal year budget in Senate Committee on Foreign Relations, *Defense Department Sponsored Foreign Affairs Research*, pt. 1, p. 7. Stennis quoted in Philip Boffey, "Defense Research: Pressure on Social Sciences," *Science* 164 (May 30, 1969): 1037.

53. Daniel S. Greenberg, "IDA: University-Sponsored Center Hit Hard by Assaults on Campus," *Science* 17 (May 1968): 744–48; Elinor Langer, "Uprising on Morningside Heights: Background," *Science* 22 (November 1968): 879.

54. On the student movements at AU see Student Unrest files, boxes 1–3, Papers of President George H. Williams (1968–71); and House Committee on Internal Security, *Investigation of Students for a Democratic Society*, pt. 4 (American University), Hearings, 91st Cong., 2nd sess., July 24, 1969. Williams quoted in "Williams Calls for AU's 'New Era,'" American University *Eagle*, October 18, 1968, p. 6.

55. "Reform Committee Diagnoses AU's Ills," American University *Eagle*, October 4, 1968, p. 1.

56. "Blessed Be the Peacemakers," n.d. (c. Fall 1969), Student Unrest News Flyer re: Student takeover of the Administration Building file, box 1, Williams Papers.

57. On security concerns see Merrill Ewing to Frederick S. Jones, January 2, 1969, and Merrill Ewing to Frederick Jones, April 28, 1969, DAHC 19–67-C-0046 CRESS Approval of Costs file, box 10, OCRD, DAR Transaction Files, RG 319. For "a 'march'" see Frederick S. Jones to Chief, Behavioral Sciences Division, May 5, 1969; Garth B. Oswald to Frederick Jones, August 25, 1969, CRESS Security file, box 10, OCRD, DAR Transaction Files; Appendix C, "Protection of Classified Information in Case of Fire, National Disaster, or Civil Disturbance," CRESS Security file, box 10, OCRD, DAR Transaction Files.

58. "Student Demands," n.d., Student Unrest, News Flyer re: Student takeover of the Administration Building file, box 1, Williams Papers.

59. For overhead see Contract DAHC 19–67-C-0046, July 1, 1967, American University (CRESS) Basic Contract and Modifications file, box 10, OCRD, DAR Transaction Files. For AU administrative concern about CRESS's impact on the university's image see Unidentified [Ewing?] to Williams, January 29, 1969, CRESS file, Anderson Papers; Harold H. Hutson, "Annual report of CRESS Board of Advisors," October 23, 1968, p. 3, CRESS file, Anderson Papers.

60. House Committee on Internal Security, *Investigation of Students for a Democratic Society*, pt. 4, p. 1056; "Extra No. 5," American University *Eagle*, April 29, 1969; "AU, CRESS Begin Break," ibid., April 29, 1969, p. 1; "Quit Classified Research, Policy Unit Recommends," ibid., March 28, 1969, p. 1.

61. Fulbright quoted in Boffey, "Defense Research," 1037, and *Congressional Record* 115, pt. 17 (August 11, 1969), 23281. For budget details see Boffey, "Defense Research."

62. Quoted in Deitchman, *Best-Laid Schemes*, 421.

63. Ithiel de Sola Pool to Edward W. Brooke, May 16, 1969, Pool: Outgoing Correspondence, March, April, and May, 1969 file, box 64, Pool Papers.

CHAPTER 5

1. Michael T. Klare, *War without End: American Planning for the Next Vietnams* (New York: Vintage Books, 1972 [orig. 1970]), 4; Lasswell quoted in Aaron L. Friedberg, *In the Shadow of the Garrison State: America's Anti-Statism and Cold War Grand Strategy* (Princeton, N.J.: Princeton University Press, 2000), 57; Seymour Melman, *Pentagon Capitalism: The Political Economy of War* (New York: McGraw-Hill, 1970), 2.

2. "Distinguished Professional Contribution Award for 1976," *American Psychologist* 32 (1977): 72–79; Roger Pearson, "John C. Flanagan and the Development of Psychological Surveys: The U.S. Aviation Psychology Program," *Mankind Quarterly* 38 (1997): 85–97; and James H. Capshew, *Psychologists on the March: Science, Practice, and Professional Identity in America, 1929–1969* (Cambridge: Cambridge University Press), 107–10.

3. John C. Flanagan, "The American Institute for Research: A New Type of Resource Organization," in American Institute for Research, *Planning for Progress* (Pittsburgh, March 22, 1956), pp. 5–12, esp. 5. For a sanitized version of AIR's history that does not mention its Cold War research see John C. Flanagan, "The American Institutes for Research," *American Psychologist* 39 (1984): 1272–76.

4. Flanagan, "American Institute for Research," 7; Harley O. Preston, "Research Planning for AIR Programs: V. Operations and Systems Analysis," in *Planning for Progress*, 35. For AIR's ranking see Harold Orlans, *The Non-Profit Research Institute: Its Origin, Operation, Problems, and Prospects* (New York: McGraw-Hill, 1972), Appendix B.

5. "HFORD Quarterly Report for Period Ending 31 March 1965, Robert L. Humphrey, Research Scientist, Troop Community Relations Research" [attachment to letter, Casper to Sullivan, March 31, 1965] 1303–01: Korean Research Unit (65) file (folder 2) box 2, OCRD, BSD, RG 319 (National Archives 2, College Park, Md.).

6. AIR research proposal quoted in Allen Myers, "Scholars Join with US Government for Purposes of Counterinsurgency," *Student Mobilizer*, April 2, 1970, p. 14. See also Eric Wakin, *Anthropology Goes to War: Professional Ethics and Counterinsurgency in Thailand* (Madison: University of Wisconsin Center for Southeast Asian Studies, 1992), 79–116.

7. Orlans, *Non-Profit Research Institutes*, appendix B.

8. For complaints about CRESS see Memorandum for the Record, Minutes of the Semiannual Meeting of the Army Human Factors Research Advisory Committee, 9, n.d., AHFRAC Meeting Minutes 66 file, UD-WW entry B-2, Accession 79–0068, RG 319; Seymour Deitchman, *The Best-Laid Schemes: A Tale of Social Research and Bureaucracy* (Cambridge, Mass.: MIT Press, 1976), 320.

9. Amendment quoted in Deitchman, *Best-Laid Schemes*, 421. On its implications see Col. Lynch, Assistant Director of Army Research, Opening Address to Army Human Factors Research Advisory Council, February 16, 1970, AHFRAC 7 file, UD-WW entry B-5, Accession 79–0312, RG 319; Department of the Army, AR 70–8, "Research and Development: Behavioral and Social Sciences Research and Development," April 28, 1969, AR 70–4 to AR 70–8AR file, box 85, RG 287, Publications of the U.S. Government, U.S. Army 1941 (National Archives 2, College Park, Md.).

10. Donald W. Pulsifer to Commanding General, U.S. Army Materiel Command, n.d., folder DAHC 19–67–0046 CRESS Correspondence file, box 10, OCRD, DAR Transaction Files, RG 319.

11. Daniel S. Greenberg, "IDA: University-Sponsored Center Hit Hard by Assaults on Campus," *Science* 160 (May 17, 1968): 744; Judith Coburn, "University Contractors Cut Ties with CRESS, HumRRO, Army's Two Main Centers of Social, Behavioral Research," *Science* 164 (May 30, 1969): 1039–41.

12. Stuart W. Leslie, *The Cold War and American Science: The Military-Industrial Academic Complex at MIT and Stanford* (New York: Columbia University Press, 1993), 241–51.

13. Ibid., 247.

14. Lorand B. Szalay, Won T. Moon, and Jean A. Bryson, *Communication Lexicon on Three South Korean Audiences* (Domains: Family, Education, International Relations) (Kensington, Md.: AIR, May 1973), p. iv.

15. Lorand B. Szalay, with Robert Walker et al., *Persuasion Overseas (Republic of Vietnam Emphasis)* (Washington, D.C.: SORO, June 1965); Lorand B. Szalay and Jack E. Brent, "The Analysis of Cultural Meanings through Free Verbal Associations," *Journal of Social Psychology* 72 (1967): 161–87.

16. Szalay et al., *Communication Lexicon on Three South Korean Audiences* (AIR, May 1973), pp. 7–28, 7–4.

17. Lorand B. Szalay and Jean Bryson, "Measurement of Psychocultural Distance: A Comparison of American Blacks and Whites," *Journal of Personality and Social Psychology* 26 (1973): 166–77; Lorand Szalay, Jean Bryson, and Garmon West, *Ethnic-Racial Perceptions and Attitudes by Word and Picture Stimulated Associations* (Kensington, Md.: AIR, October 1974); Lorand Szalay and Jean Bryson, *Subjective Culture and Communication: A Puerto Rican–U.S. Comparison* (Kensington, Md.: AIR, 1975); Lorand Szalay and Jean A. Bryson, *Measurement of Ethnic-Racial and Cultural Perceptions and Attitudes through Word Associations* (Kensington, Md.: AIR, March 1976).

18. Lorand Szalay, *The Hispanic American Cultural Frame of Reference: A Communication Guide for Use in Mental Health, Education, and Training* (Washington, D.C.: Institute of Comparative Social and Cultural Studies, 1978); Lorand B. Szalay, *Iranian and American Perceptions and Cultural Frames of Reference: A Communication Lexicon for Cultural Understanding* (Washington, D.C.: Institute of Comparative Social and Cultural Studies, 1979); Lorand B. Szalay, *Hispanic American Psychocultural Dispositions Relevant to Personnel Management* (Institute of Comparative Social and Cultural Studies, 1984); Lorand B. Szalay, *Regional and Demographic Variations in Public Perceptions Related to Emergency Preparedness* (Silver Spring, Md.: Institute of Comparative Social and Cultural Studies, 1986); Lorand B. Szalay, *Cultural Influences and Drug Abuse Psychological Vulnerabilities of Puerto Ricans in the United States* (Chevy Chase, Md.: Institute of Comparative Social and Cultural Studies, 1991).

19. On the Jason Division see Wakin, *Anthropology Goes to War*, 51–63; "Kaufman, Howard Keva," in *American Men and Women of Science: Social and Behavioral Sciences*, 12th ed., ed. Jacques Cattell Press (New York: R. R. Bowker, 1973), 1:1196; Jasper Ingersoll, "Howard Keva Kaufman (1922–2000)," *Journal of Asian Studies* 60 (2001): 247; Howard Kaufman, "Attitude Research: The Theoretical Basis and Some Problems of Application

in Rural Thailand," in *Linguistics and Anthropology: In Honor of C. F. Voegelin,* ed. M. Dale Kinkade, Kenneth L. Hale, and Oswald Werner (Lisse, Netherlands: Peter de Ridder Press, 1975), 379.

20. Kaufman, "Attitude Research," 370; Howard K. Kaufman, *Socio-economic Factors in Farmer Response to Irrigation in Northeast Thailand* (Bangkok: U.S. Operating Mission, September 1971).

21. Mills quoted in John D. Hanrahan, *Government by Contract* (New York: W. W. Norton, 1983), 150; William Proxmire, *Report from Wasteland* (New York: Praeger, 1970), x; Phillip P. Katz and R. D. McLaurin, *Psychological Operations in Urban Warfare: Lessons from the 1982 Middle East War* (Aberdeen Proving Ground, Md.: U.S. Army Human Engineering Laboratory, 1987).

22. On CNA see U.S. Office of Technology Assessment, *A History of the Department of Defense Federally Funded Research and Development Centers* (Washington, D.C.: Government Printing Office, June 1995), 39. On Mintz's contracting and freelance work see "Standard Form 171, Personal Qualifications Statement," March 20, 1972, folder 5, box 8, Mintz Papers. On Perle see biographical clipping, folder 6, box 9, Mintz Papers.

23. On McLaurin's career see "McLaurin, R. D.," in *American Men and Women of Science: Social and Behavioral Sciences,* 13th ed., ed. Jacques Cattell Press (New York: R. R. Bowker, 1978), 806. For ISA-funded research see R. D. McLaurin and Mohammed Mughisuddin, *The Soviet Union and the Middle East: Final Report* (Washington, D.C.: AIR, October 1974); and Jon Cozean, Suheila Haddad, Phillip P. Katz, R. D. McLaurin, and Charles H. Wagner, *The Arab Elite Worldview: A Report on a Study of Arab Perceptions of Regional Security Issues* (Washington, D.C.: AIR, July 1975). For evidence of his close relationship with his benefactors at ISA see the acknowledgments in R. D. McLaurin, Mohammed Mughisuddin, and Abraham R. Wagner, *Foreign Policymaking in the Middle East: Domestic Influences on Policy in Egypt, Iraq, Israel, and Syria* (New York: Praeger, 1977); and R. D. McLaurin, Don Peretz, and Lewis W. Snider, *Middle East Foreign Policy: Issues and Processes* (New York: Praeger, 1982).

24. See, for example, R. D. McLaurin and James R. Price, *Soviet Middle East Policy since the October War* (Alexandria, Va.: Abbott Associates, 1976); and R. D. McLaurin and Suhaila Haddad, *The Political Impact of U.S. Military Force in the Middle East* (Washington, D.C.: AIR, 1977).

25. Cf. Ritchie P. Lowry, "Toward a Sociology of Secrecy and Security Systems," *Social Problems* 19 (1972): 442.

26. Edward E. Azar, Paul A. Jureidini, and R. D. McLaurin, "Protracted Social Conflict: Theory and Practice in the Middle East," *Journal of Palestine Studies* 8 (1978): 57.

27. For AIR and Abbott contract work with the Limited Warfare Laboratory see William Hazen and Abraham R. Wagner, *Israeli Perceptions of American Security Policy: Current Trends and Future Alternatives* (Alexandria, Va.: Abbott Associates, October 1976); Paul A. Jureidini, R. D. McLaurin, and James Price, *Military Operations in Selected Lebanese Built-Up Areas, 1975–1978* (Aberdeen Proving Ground, Md.: U.S. Army Human Engineering Laboratory, 1979); R. D. McLaurin and Lewis W. Snider, *Recent Military Operations on Urban Terrain* (Alexandria, Va.: Abbott Associates, July 1982); and Phillip Katz and R. D. McLaurin, *Psychological Operations in Urban Warfare: Lessons from the 1982 Middle East War* (Springfield, Va.: Abbott Associates, July 1987). Their open publications include Paul A. Jureidini and William Hazen, *The Palestinian Movement in Politics* (Lexington, Mass.: Lexington Books, 1976); and Paul A. Jureidini and R. D. McLaurin, *Beyond Camp David: Emerging Alignments and Leaders in the Middle East* (Syracuse, N.Y.: Syracuse University Press, 1981). On contract renewals see Hanrahan, *Government by Contract,* 167.

28. On the perception that privatization enhanced the private sector see Friedberg, *Shadow of the Garrison State*; W. J. McKeachie and Orville G. Brim Jr., "Lessons to Be

Learned from Large Behavioral Research Organizations," *American Psychologist* 39 (1984): 1254–55.

29. On the rise of these institutions see Alice O'Connor, "Financing the Counterrevolution," in *Rightward Bound: Making America Conservative in the 1970s*, ed. Bruce J. Schulman and Julian E. Zelizer (Cambridge, Mass.: Harvard University Press, 2008), 148–68. Exposés and academic studies include Daniel Guttman and Barry Willner, *The Shadow Government* (New York: Pantheon Books, 1976); Joseph G. Pescheck, *Policy-Planning Organizations: Elite Agendas and America's Rightward Turn* (Philadelphia: Temple University Press, 1987); David M. Ricci, *The Transformation of American Politics: The New Washington and the Rise of the Think Tanks* (New Haven, Conn.: Yale University Press, 1993); Andrew Rich, *Think Tanks, Public Policy, and the Politics of Expertise* (Cambridge: Cambridge University Press, 2004); and James Allen Smith, *The Idea Brokers: Think Tanks and the Rise of the New Policy Elite* (New York: Free Press, 1991).

30. On Prosyms see Chapter 2.

31. Phillip P. Katz, R. D. McLaurin, and Preston S. Abbott, "Persuasive Communications: A Critical Analysis of US Psychological Operations in War and Peace," *Interdisciplinary Science Reviews* 4 (1979): 71–85.

32. William Gardner Bell, compiler, *Department of the Army Historical Summary: Fiscal Year 1972* (Washington, D.C.: Center of Military History, 1974), 17; Karl E. Cocke, compiler, *Department of the Army Historical Summary: Fiscal Year 1974* (Washington, D.C.: Center of Military History, 1978), 11; Karl E. Cocke, compiler, *Department of the Army Historical Summary: Fiscal Year 1975* (Washington, D.C.: 2000), 13; U.S. Department of the Army, *Psychological Operations, FM 33–1* (Washington, D.C.: Department of the Army, August 1979), chap. 15.

33. Cozean et al., *Arab Elite Worldview*.

34. McLaurin, *Political Impact of U.S. Military Force in the Middle East*, 4.

35. R. D. McLaurin, "From Professional to Political: The Redecline of the Lebanese Army," *Armed Forces and Society* 17 (1991): 545; McLaurin, Mughisuddin, and Wagner, *Foreign Policymaking in the Middle East*; Jureidini and McLaurin, *Beyond Camp David*; R. D. McLaurin, *The Middle East in Soviet Policy* (Lexington, Mass.: Lexington Books, 1975); McLaurin, Peretz, and Snider, *Middle East Foreign Policy*; Manwoo Lee, R. D. McLaurin, and Chung-in Moon, *Alliance under Tension: The Evolution of South Korean–U.S. Relations* (Boulder, Colo.: Westview Press, 1988); R. D. McLaurin, *The Political Role of Minority Groups in the Middle East* (New York: Praeger, 1979); R. D. McLaurin, ed., *Military Propaganda: Psychological Warfare and Operations* (New York: Praeger, 1982).

36. Minutes of the 86th Meeting of the Working Group / Cabinet Committee to Combat Terrorism, June 30, 1975 (Declassified Documents Reference System 263835-i1–5); and Minutes of the 101st Meeting of the Working Group / Cabinet Committee to Combat Terrorism, February 17, 1976 (Declassified Documents Reference System 255437-i1–5); Joel Beinin, "Media and Policy Analysis: The Washington Institute for Near East Policy," *Middle East Report* 180 (January–February 1993): 10–15.

37. L. E. Sweet, review of *Middle Eastern Subcultures*, *Middle East Journal* 31 (1977): 501; Les Janka, review of *Beyond Camp David*, *Middle East Journal* 35 (1981): 642; Avigdor Levy, review of *Beyond Camp David*, *Modern Judaism* 4 (1984): 346.

38. On the decline of modernization theory see Nils Gilman, *Mandarins of the Future: Modernization Theory in Cold War America* (Baltimore: Johns Hopkins University Press, 2003).

39. Col. Irving Heymont, "The U.S. Army and Foreign National Development," *Military Review* 51, no. 11 (November 1971): 17–23.

40. On Swisher's training, career, and research interests see Ralph B. Swisher, *Military Civic Action*, vol. 1, *The Role of Military Civic Action in Internal Defense and Development: Criteria Formulation* (Kensington, Md.: American Institutes for Research, June 1972), ii. On South Korea see Ralph B. Swisher, *Military Civic Action*, vol. 3, *Testing the Relevance of Proposed Criteria and Methods of Assessment: ROK Army Civic Action in Rural South Korea* (Kensington, Md.: American Institutes for Research, June 1972). On Lunaria see Ralph B. Swisher, *Military Civic Action*, vol. 2, *Assessing Military Civic Action Programs: Applying Proposed Criteria* (Kensington, Md.: American Institutes for Research, June 1972); Swisher, *Military Civic Action*, 2:43.

41. Swisher, *Military Civic Action*, 1:6, 2.

42. Wayne Morse, "Dangers in Government Sponsorship of Research on Foreign Policy and Foreign Areas," *Background* 10 (1966): 123–30; John Walsh, "Defense Research: Questions for Vietnam Dissenters," *Science* 161(September 20, 1968): 1225–26.

43. Swisher, *Military Civic Action*, 3:54; Swisher, *Military Civic Action*, 1:iv.

44. Lisa Anderson, *Pursuing Truth, Exercising Power: Social Science and Public Policy in the Twenty-First Century* (New York: Columbia University Press, 2003), 61–63, 86.

45. Kaufman, *Socio-economic Factors in Farmer Response to Irrigation in Northeast Thailand*, 13–14.

46. Ibid., 163, 19.

47. AIR, *Human Values and the War of Ideas: A Set of Discussion Materials*, 1971 [with updated sections from January 1972, obtained through Library of the Marine Corps], ii, iii.

48. Ibid., I-3, V-60, V-17.

49. Robert L. Humphrey, *Scientific Ethic Dual Life Value: Theory and Ramifications* (San Diego: Grossmont Press, 1974), 42, 44–45, 3. Italics in original.

50. Humphrey, *Scientific Ethic Dual Life Value*, 8; AIR, *Human Values and the War of Ideas*.

51. AIR, *Human Values and the War of Ideas*, pt. A: Race Relations.

52. Jennifer S. Light, *From Warfare to Welfare: Defense Intellectuals and Urban Problems in Cold War America* (Baltimore: Johns Hopkins University Press, 2003), 69–72. See also David R. Jardini, "Out of the Blue Yonder: The RAND Corporation's Diversification into Social Welfare Research, 1946–1968" (PhD thesis, Carnegie Mellon University, 1996). Laird quoted in Orlans, *Non-Profit Research Institute*, 111.

53. Cooper quoted in Orr Kelly, "DOD: Solving the Double-Barreled Dilemma," *Armed Forces Journal*, September 28, 1968: 10; Light, *From Warfare to Welfare*.

54. Institute for Defense Analyses, *Five Year Report: Activities of the Institute for Defense Analyses, FY 71–75* (Arlington, Va.: IDA, 1975), 21.

55. Anthony M. Platt and Lynn Cooper, eds., *Policing America* (Englewood Cliffs, N.J.: Prentice-Hall, 1974), 95.

56. Rosenthal's SORO research includes Carl F. Rosenthal, *Economic, Social, and Political Factors in Counterinsurgency Intelligence Planning* (Washington, D.C.: CRESS, 1966); Carl F. Rosenthal and Curtis B. Brooks, *Effects of Military Assistance Programs on Developing Countries: A Bibliography* (Washington, D.C.: SORO, 1966); and Carl F. Rosenthal, James Dodson, and Elaine Murphy, "Some Theoretical Observations on the Assessment of Psychological Operations Effectiveness" (Washington, D.C.: CRESS, 1967); Carl F. Rosenthal, "Communist Insurgency in Theory and Practice" (MA thesis, University of Illinois at Urbana-Champaign, 1967); John M. Lord, Carl F. Rosenthal, and James M. Dodson, *Communist Theory and Practice in Subversive Insurgencies* (Washington, D.C.: SORO, 1965).

57. Carl F. Rosenthal, *Phases of Civil Disturbances: Characteristics and Problems* (Kensington, Md.: AIR, June 1971, orig. 1969), 17, iv, 5. On the Limited Warfare Laboratory

see Tracy Tullis, "A Vietnam at Home: Policing the Ghettos in the Counterinsurgency Era" (PhD thesis, New York University, 1999), 32; Rosenthal, *Phases of Civil Disturbances*, 20.

58. On the army's role in riot control see Paul J. Scheips, *The Role of Federal Military Forces in Domestic Disorders, 1945–1992* (Washington, D.C.: Center of Military History, U.S. Army, 2005). On the Limited Warfare Laboratory see Tullis, "Vietnam at Home," 32; Rosenthal, *Phases of Civil Disturbances*, 20.

59. Carl F. Rosenthal, *Social Conflict and Collective Violence in American Institutions of Higher Learning*, vol. 1, *Dynamics of Student Protest* (Kensington, Md.: AIR, 1971).

60. Ibid., 1:90.

61. Rosenthal, *Phases of Civil Disturbance*, 8.

62. D. M. Condit, *Modern Revolutionary Warfare: An Analytical Overview* (Kensington, Md.: AIR, 1973), 49; *The Spook Who Sat by the Door* (Bokan/United Artists, 1973), dir. Ivan Dixon.

63. Tullis, "Vietnam at Home," 44, 168–69.

64. Terry Eisenberg, Robert H. Frosen, and Albert S. Glickman, *Project PACE: Police and Community Enterprise; a Program for Change in Police-Community Behaviors, Final Report* (Washington, D.C.: AIR, August 1971), 2.

65. Ibid., 25–26, appendix D-8, 38.

66. Ibid., 53–54, iii.

67. Clark McPhail, David Schweingruber, and John McCarthy, "Policing Protest in the United States: 1960–1995," in *Policing Protest: The Control of Mass Movements in Western Democracies*, ed. Donatella della Porta and Herbert Reiter (Minneapolis: University of Minnesota Press, 1998), 62–64.

68. Michael T. Klare, "Bringing It Back: Planning for the City," and David P. Riley, "Should Communities Control Their Police?" in Platt and Cooper, *Policing America*, 97–104 and 190–97.

69. Figures derived from prosopographical study in Joy Elizabeth Rohde, "'The Social Scientists' War': Expertise in a Cold War Nation" (PhD thesis, University of Pennsylvania, 2007), 284–93.

70. Ritchie P. Lowry to Theodore R. Vallance, May 6, 1966, SORO/1996 file, box 2, Papers of the Special Operations Research Office.

71. Ritchie P. Lowry, "To Arms: Changing Military Roles and the Military-Industrial Complex," *Social Problems* 18 (1970): 3, 11.

72. Ritchie P. Lowry, "Toward a Sociology of Secrecy and Security Systems," *Social Problems* 19 (1972): 440. On secrecy and democracy see Stephen Aftergood, "National Security Secrecy: How the Limits Change," *Social Research* 77 (2010): 839–52.

73. Ritchie P. Lowry, Feature Review, *Sociological Quarterly* 19 (1978): 156; Carole Shelbourne George, Peter Lowry, Ritchie P. Lowry, and Susan Meeker-Lowry, *Tracking Responsible Investments: A Stock Average for Responsive Corporations* (Worcester, Vt.: Catalyst Press, 1983); Ritchie P. Lowry, *Good Money: A Guide to Profitable Social Investing in the '90s* (New York: W. W. Norton, 1991). On secrecy in the 1970s and 1980s see Christopher Capozzola, "Afterburn: Knowledge and Wartime," *Social Research* 77 (2010): 811–26.

74. The following account is derived from Wakin, *Anthropology Goes to War*, 155–238.

75. Quoted ibid., 247.

76. Ibid., 155.

77. Ibid., 159.

78. Ibid., 153.

79. Ibid., 153, 159.

80. "McCarthyite tactics" and Mead Committee quoted ibid., 205; resolution quoted at 211.

81. Walter Goldschmidt, "Anthropology and the Coming Crisis: An Autoethnographic Appraisal," *American Anthropologist* n.s. 79 (1977): 297.

82. Bryce Nelson, "Political Scientists: More Concern about Political Involvement, Ethics," *Science* 161, no. 3846 (1968): 1117–18; Ido Oren, *Our Enemies and Us: America's Rivalries and the Making of Political Science* (Ithaca, N.Y.: Cornell University Press, 2003), 162–65. See also Rogers M. Smith, "Still Blowing in the Wind: The American Quest for a Democratic, Scientific Political Science," in *American Academic Culture in Transformation*, ed. Thomas Bender and Carl E. Schorske (Princeton, N.J.: Princeton University Press, 1998), 271–305.

83. Harold Lasswell, "The Garrison State Hypothesis Today," reprinted in *Essays on the Garrison State*, ed. Jay Stanley (New Brunswick, N.J.: Transaction Publishers, 1997), 112.

84. "State's External Research Program: End-of-the-Fiscal-Year Report," *FAR Horizons* 4, no. 4 (July 1971): 1; "External Research in the Department of State," *FAR Horizons* 5, no. 3 (Summer 1972): 1–4, 7.

85. Daniel T. Rodgers, *Age of Fracture* (Cambridge, Mass.: Belknap Press of Harvard University Press, 2011), 91; Thomas Bender, "Politics, Intellect, and the American University, 1945–1995," in Bender and Schorske, *American Academic Culture in Transformation*, 39.

EPILOGUE

1. John W. Whitehead, "Privatizing the War on Terror: America's Military Contractors," Antiwar.com, January 18, 2012, http://original.antiwar.com/jwhitehead/2012/01/17/privatizing-the-war-on-terror-americas-military-contractors/ (accessed June 11, 2012). For scholarly investigations see Deborah Denise Avant, *The Market for Force: The Consequences of Privatizing Security* (Cambridge: Cambridge University Press, 2005); Laura A. Dickinson, *Outsourcing War and Peace* (New Haven, Conn.: Yale University Press, 2011); Jody Freeman and Martha Minow, eds., *Government by Contract: Outsourcing and American Democracy* (Cambridge, Mass.: Harvard University Press, 2009); and P. W. Singer, *Corporate Warriors: The Rise of the Privatized Military Industry* (Ithaca, N.Y.: Cornell University Press, 2003).

2. John Hanrahan, *Government by Contract* (New York: W. W. Norton, 1983), 89–91; Harold Orlans, "The Contract State—or Is It the Welfare State of the Professional Classes?" in *Government-Sponsored Nonprofits*, ed. Harold Orlans (Washington, D.C.: National Academy of Public Administration, November 1978), 183.

3. Hanrahan, *Government by Contract*, 92, 123–24.

4. Ann R. Markusen, "The Case against Privatizing National Security," *Governance* 16 (2003): 474–76.

5. Singer, *Corporate Warriors*, chap. 8. See also Markusen, "Case against Privatizing National Security," 489–90.

6. Quoted in Richard H. Kohn, "The Danger of Militarization in an Endless 'War' on Terrorism," *Journal of Military History* 73 (2009): 196.

7. Navy SEAL Recommended Reading List, http://www.sealswcc.com/navy-seals-motivational-reading.aspx (accessed October 10, 2011); Paul A. Jureidini, *Casebook on Insurgency and Revolutionary Warfare: 23 Summary Accounts* (Washington, D.C.: SORO, 1962); Ronald D. McLaurin, Carl F. Rosenthal, Sarah A. Skillings and others, eds., *The Art and Science of Psychological Operations: Case Studies in Military Application* (Washington, D.C.: Department of the Army, 1976). The list also includes Andrew R. Molnar, William A. Lybrand, Lorna Hahn, James L. Kirkman, and Peter B. Riddleberger, *Undergrounds in Insurgent, Revolutionary, and Resistance Warfare* (Washington, D.C.: SORO, 1963); and

Andrew R. Molnar, Jerry M. Tinker, and John D. Lenoir, *Human Factors Considerations of Undergrounds in Insurgencies* (Washington, D.C.: SORO, 1966).

8. Paul K. Davis and Kim Cragin, eds., *Social Science for Counterterrorism: Putting the Pieces Together* (Santa Monica, Calif.: RAND, 2009), xvii, xx, http://www.rand.org/pubs/monographs/MG849/.

9. Farah Stockman, "Knowing the Enemy, One Avatar at a Time," *Boston Globe*, May 30, 2010, http://www.boston.com/news/nation/washington/articles/2010/05/30/knowing_the_enemy_one_avatar_at_a_time/; Harry Goldstein, "Modeling Terrorists," *IEEE Spectrum*, September 2006, http://spectrum.ieee.org/computing/software/modeling-terrorists/.

10. Quoted in American Anthropological Association Commission on the Engagement of Anthropology with the U.S. Security and Intelligence Communities, *Final Report on the Army's Human Terrain System Proof of Concept Program*, October 14, 2009, 16. On the goals for human terrain data see also Sheila Miyoshi Jager, *On the Uses of Cultural Knowledge* (Strategic Studies Institute, U.S. Army War College, November 2007), and Nathan Finney, *Human Terrain Team Handbook* (Fort Leavenworth, Kans.: Human Terrain System, October 2008), 34.

11. Quoted in OSD Budget Item Justification, "Human, Social and Culture Behavior Modeling (HSCB) Applied Research," February 2007, http://www.dtic.mil/descriptivesum/Y2008/OSD/0602670D8Z.pdf.

12. Tim Hsia, "Rolling Stone Article's True Focus: Counterinsurgency," *New York Times*, June 23, 2010, http://atwar.blogs.nytimes.com/2010/06/23/rolling-stone-articles-true-focus-counterinsurgency-coin/ (accessed October 26, 2012).

13. Bacevich quoted in Hsia, "Rolling Stone Article's True Focus."

14. "Program History and Overview," Minerva Initiative, http://minerva.dtic.mil/overview.html (accessed June 9, 2012).

15. "Priority Research Topics," Minerva Initiative, http://minerva.dtic.mil/topics.html (accessed June 9, 2012).

16. "Finding Allies for the War of Words: Mapping the Diffusion and Influence of Counter-Radical Muslim Discourse," *Second Annual Minerva Conference: Minerva Research Summaries* (September 15–16, 2011), 36.

17. "The Evolution of Revolution," *Second Annual Minerva Conference*, 41.

18. "Minerva Chairs Program," Minerva Initiative, http://minerva.dtic.mil/chairs.html (accessed June 9, 2012).

19. Dana Priest and William M. Arkin, "Top Secret America: National Security Inc.," July 20, 2010, http://projects.washingtonpost.com/top-secret-america/articles/national-security-inc/ (accessed June 8, 2012).

20. Ibid., "Psychological Operations," http://projects.washingtonpost.com/top-secret-america/functions/psychological-ops/ (accessed June 10, 2012). On General Dynamics revenues see http://projects.washingtonpost.com/top-secret-america/companies/general-dynamics/.

21. On CACI's tie to PAMIS see Frank M. Tims, Robert C. Sorensen, and Frances C. Mushal, *New Indicators of Psychological Operations Effects* (McLean, Va.: General Research Corp., 1975); "Special Operations," in Priest and Arkin, "Top Secret America," http://projects.washingtonpost.com/top-secret-america/functions/special-ops/ (accessed June 10, 2012); Mike Musgrove, "Court Rejects Suit against CACI over Abu Ghraib Torture," *Washington Post*, September 12, 2009, http://www.washingtonpost.com/wp-dyn/content/article/2009/09/11/AR2009091103285.html.

22. Martha Minow, "Outsourcing Power: Privatizing Military Efforts and the Risks to Accountability, Professionalism, and Democracy," in Freeman and Minow, *Government by Contract*, 110.

23. On early, failed efforts to manage contracts see Hanrahan, *Government by Contract*, 92–93; Freeman and Minow, "Reframing the Outsourcing Debates," in Freeman and Minow, *Government by Contract*, 10.

24. Cf. Freeman and Minow, *Government by Contract*; Hanrahan, *Government by Contract*; and Richard L. Cooper, *Contract-Hire Personnel in the Department of Defense*, P-5864 (Santa Monica, Calif.: RAND, 1977).

25. Deborah Avant, "Mercenaries," *Foreign Policy* 143 (July–August 2004): 20–28; Freeman and Minow, "Reframing the Outsourcing Debates," 6; Singer, *Corporate Warriors*, 8.

26. Avant, "Mercenaries," 23. See also Freeman and Minow, "Reframing the Outsourcing Debates."

27. Christopher D. McKenna, *The World's Newest Profession: Management Consulting in the Twentieth Century* (Cambridge: Cambridge University Press, 2006), 81; and Warren Suss, quoted in Bernard Wysocki, "Private Practice: Is U.S. Government 'Outsourcing Its Brain'?" *Wall Street Journal*, March 30, 2007, p. A1.

28. Freeman and Minow, "Reframing the Outsourcing Debates"; Markusen, "Case against Privatizing National Security."

29. See, for example, Jay Stanley and Catherine Crump, *Protecting Privacy from Aerial Surveillance: Recommendations for Government Use of Drone Aircraft* (New York: American Civil Liberties Union, December 2011); and Shane Harris, *The Watchers: The Rise of America's Surveillance State* (New York: Penguin, 2011).

30. Sherry, *Shadow of War*, 312, 325.

31. Quoted in Lloyd C. Gardner and Marilyn B. Young, eds., *Iraq and the Lessons of Vietnam: Or, How Not to Learn from the Past* (New York: New Press, 2007), 10.

32. Quoted ibid., 4.

Bibliography

ARCHIVAL AND MANUSCRIPT COLLECTIONS

Anderson, Hurst R. Office of the President. Papers. American University Archives and Special Collections, Washington, D.C.

Army Staff. Records. Record Group 319. National Archives 2, College Park, Md.

Dungan, Ralph A. Papers. John F. Kennedy Library, Boston.

Mintz, Jeanne S. Papers. Library of Congress Manuscripts Division, Washington, D.C.

National Academy of Sciences Division of Behavioral Sciences. Records. National Academy of Sciences–National Research Council Archives, Washington, D.C.

Pool, Ithiel de Sola. Papers. MC 440. Massachusetts Institute of Technology, Institute Archives and Special Collections, Cambridge, Mass.

Smithsonian Institution Research Group in Psychology and the Social Sciences. Records. Record Unit 179. Smithsonian Institution Archives, Washington, D.C.

Special Operations Research Office. Papers. American University Archives and Special Collections, Washington, D.C.

Special Operations Research Office Personnel. Records. American University Archives and Special Collections, Washington, D.C.

State Department. General Records. Record Group 59. National Archives 2, College Park, Md.

Williams, George H. President. Papers. American University Archives and Special Collections, Washington, D.C.

PRINTED SOURCES

"Academic Research: Foster Defends DoD Support in Universities." *Science* 158, no. 3804 (1967): 1032–34.

Acheson, Dean. "The Eclipse of the State Department." *Foreign Affairs* 49 (1971): 593–606.

Adams, Richard N. "Ethics and the Social Anthropologist in Latin America." *American Behavioral Scientist* 10, no. 10 (1967): 16–22.

Aftergood, Stephen. "National Security Secrecy: How the Limits Change." *Social Research* 77 (2010): 839–52.

Almond, Gabriel A. "Remarks." *Background* 9 (1965): 173–76.

Almond, Gabriel A., and Sidney Verba. *The Civic Culture: Political Attitudes and Democracy in Five Nations.* Princeton, N.J.: Princeton University Press, 1963.

Altman, Irwin. "Mainstreams of Research in Small Groups." *Public Administration Review* 23 (1963): 203–8.

American Anthropological Association Commission on the Engagement of Anthropology with the U.S. Security and Intelligence Communities. *Final Report on the Army's Human Terrain System Proof of Concept Program.* October 14, 2009.

American Institutes for Research. *Human Values and the War of Ideas: A Set of Discussion Materials.* Kensington, Md.: AIR, 1971.

American Political Science Association, Research Committee. "Instruction and Research: War-Time Priorities in Research." *American Political Science Review* 37 (1943): 505–14.

Anderson, Hurst. *An Educational Journey: Trivia and More Important Things in the Life of a Teacher and College and University President.* Lakeside, Ohio: privately printed, 1977.

Anderson, Lisa. *Pursuing Truth, Exercising Power: Social Science and Public Policy in the Twenty-First Century.* New York: Columbia University Press, 2003.

Arens, W. "Urban Dynamics in Black Africa." *American Anthropologist* 75 (1973): 1828–29.

Avant, Deborah D. *The Market for Force: The Consequences of Privatizing Security.* Cambridge: Cambridge University Press, 2005.

Avant, Deborah D. "Mercenaries." *Foreign Policy*, no. 143 (2004): 20–28.

Azar, Edward E., Paul Jureidini, and R. D. McLaurin. "Protracted Social Conflict: Theory and Practice in the Middle East." *Journal of Palestine Studies* 8 (1978): 41–60.

Bacevich, Andrew J. *The Pentomic Era: The U.S. Army between Korea and Vietnam.* Washington, D.C.: National Defense University Press, 1986.

Balogh, Brian. "Reorganizing the Organizational Synthesis: Federal-Professional Relations in Modern America." *Studies in American Political Development* 5, no. 1 (1991): 119–72.

Bannister, Robert. *Sociology and Scientism: The American Quest for Objectivity, 1880–1940.* Chapel Hill: University of North Carolina Press, 1987.

Baumol, William J. "On the Financial Prospects for Higher Education: The Annual Report on the Economic Status of the Profession." *AAUP Bulletin* 54 (1968): 182–241.

Beals, Ralph. *The Politics of Social Research: An Inquiry into the Ethics and Responsibilities of Social Scientists.* Chicago: Aldine Press, 1969.

Beinin, Joel. "Media and Policy Analysis: The Washington Institute for Near East Policy." *Middle East Report*, no. 180 (1993): 10–15.

Bell, William Gardner, compiler. *Department of the Army Historical Summary: Fiscal Year 1972.* Washington, D.C.: Center of Military History, 1974.

Benda, Harry J. "Democracy in Indonesia." *Journal of Asian Studies* 23 (1964): 449–56.

———. Review of *Marxism in Southeast Asia: A Study of Four Countries*, Frank N. Trager, ed. *Far Eastern Survey* 29 (1960): 141–42.

Bender, Thomas. "Politics, Intellect, and the American University, 1945–1995." In *American Academic Culture in Transformation*, edited by Thomas Bender and Carl E. Schorske, 17–54. Princeton, N.J.: Princeton University Press, 1998.

Bernard, Jessie. Letter to the editor. *American Sociologist* 1, no. 1 (1965): 24–25.

Bernstein Committee. "Bernstein Committee Interim Report: Ethical Problems of Social Scientists." *PS* 1, no. 1 (1968): 5–16.

Birtle, Andrew J. *U.S. Counterinsurgency and Contingency Operations Doctrine, 1942–1976.* Washington, D.C.: Center of Military History, United States Army, 2006.

Bix, Amy Sue. "Backing into Sponsored Research: Physics and Engineering at Princeton University, 1945–1970." *History of Higher Education Annual* 13 (1993): 9–52.

Blackmer, Donald L. M. *The MIT Center for International Studies: The Founding Years, 1951–1969.* Cambridge, Mass.: MITCIS, 2002.

Blanksten, George I. Letter to the editor. *American Behavioral Scientist* 9, no. 2 (October 1965): NS-12.

Blumer, Herbert. "Threats from Agency-Determined Research." In *The Rise and Fall of Project Camelot*, edited by Irving L. Horowitz, 153–74. Cambridge, Mass.: MIT Press, 1967.

Boffey, Philip. "Defense Research: Pressure on Social Sciences." *Science* 164, no. 3883 (1969): 1037.

Boguslaw, Robert. "Ethics and the Social Scientist." In *The Rise and Fall of Project Camelot*, edited by Irving L. Horowitz, 107–27. Cambridge, Mass.: MIT Press, 1967.

———. *The New Utopians: A Study of System Design and Social Change*. Englewood Cliffs, N.J.: Prentice-Hall, 1965.

———. "Social Action and Social Change." In *Handbook on the Study of Social Problems*, edited by Erwin O. Smigel, 421–34. Chicago: Rand McNally, 1971.

———. *Systems Analysis and Social Planning: Human Problems of Post-Industrial Society*. New York: Irvington Publishers, 1982.

Borklund, C. W. *The Department of Defense*. New York: Praeger, 1968.

Bowers, Raymond V. "The Military Establishment." In *The Uses of Sociology*, edited by Paul F. Lazarsfeld, William H. Sewell, and Harold Wilensky, 234–74. New York: Basic Books, 1967.

Bowles, Chester. "Toward a New Diplomacy." *Foreign Affairs* 40 (1962): 244–51.

Brezina, Dennis W. "The Congressional Debate on the Social Sciences in 1968." Staff Discussion Paper 400, Program of Policy Studies in Science and Technology. Washington, D.C.: George Washington University, December 1968.

Brodie, Janet Farrell. "Learning Secrecy in the Early Cold War: The RAND Corporation." *Diplomatic History* 35 (2011): 643–70.

Cantril, Hadley. *The Human Dimension: Experiences in Policy Research*. New Brunswick, N.J.: Rutgers University Press, 1967.

Capozzola, Christopher. "Afterburn: Knowledge and Wartime." *Social Research* 77 (2010): 811–26.

Capshew, James H. *Psychologists on the March: Science, Practice, and Professional Identity in America, 1929–1969*. Cambridge: Cambridge University Press, 1999.

Carter, Luther J. "Project Themis: More Research Dollars for the Have-Nots." *Science* 155, no. 3762 (1967): 548.

———. "Social Sciences: Problems Examined by Senate Panel." *Science* 153, no. 3732 (1966): 154–56.

———. "Social Sciences: Where Do They Fit in the Politics of Science?" *Science* 154, no. 3748 (1966): 488–91.

Chomsky, Noam. *American Power and the New Mandarins*. New York: Pantheon, 1969.

Ciepley, David. *Liberalism in the Shadow of Totalitarianism*. Cambridge, Mass.: Harvard University Press, 2006.

Clinton, Yvette, Virginia Foran-Cain, Julia Voelker McQuaid, Catherine E. Norman, and William H. Sims. *Congressionally Directed Assessment of the Human Terrain System*. Alexandria, Va.: Center for Naval Analyses, November 2010.

Coburn, Judith. "University Contractors Cut Ties with CRESS, HumRRO, Army's Two Main Centers of Social, Behavioral Research." *Science* 164, no. 3883 (1969): 1039–41.

Cocke, Karl E., compiler. *Department of the Army Historical Summary: Fiscal Year 1974*. Washington, D.C.: Center of Military History, 1978.

———, compiler. *Department of the Army Historical Summary: Fiscal Year 1975*. Washington, D.C.: Center of Military History, 2000.

"Comment: Social Science Fiction." *Transaction* 5, no. 3 (1968): 7–20.

Condit, D. M. *A Counterinsurgency Bibliography*. Washington, D.C.: SORO, 1963.

———. *Modern Revolutionary Warfare: An Analytical Overview*. Kensington, Md.: AIR, 1973.

———. "The Relationship of Certain Strategic Characteristics to Military Outcome in Internal Conflict Situations." *Proceedings of the Fifteenth Annual Human Factors Research and Development Conference*, 117–23. Washington, D.C.: U.S. Army, 1969.

Cooper, Richard L. *Contract-Hire Personnel in the Department of Defense.* P-5864. Santa Monica, Calif.: RAND, 1977.

Cottrell, Leonard S., Jr. "Social Research and Psychological Warfare." *Sociometry* 23 (1960): 103–19.

Cozean, Jon, Suheila Haddad, Phillip P. Katz, R. D. McLaurin, and Charles H. Wagner. *The Arab Elite Worldview: A Report on a Study of Arab Perceptions of Regional Security Issues.* Washington, D.C.: AIR, July 1975.

CRESS. *Center for Research in Social Systems Work Program, Fiscal Year 1967.* Washington, D.C.: CRESS, August 1966.

Critchlow, Donald T. "Think Tanks, Antistatism, and Democracy: The Nonpartisan Ideal and Policy Research in the United States, 1913–1987." In *The State and Social Investigation in Britain and the United States,* edited by Michael J. Lacey and Mary O. Furner, 279–332. Cambridge: Woodrow Wilson Center Press and the Press Syndicate of the University of Cambridge, 1993.

Dahl, Robert A., Merle Fainsod, Harry Eckstein, Heinz Eulau, Austin Ranney, and Clinton Rossiter. "Report of the Executive Committee." *American Political Science Review* 61 (1967): 565–68.

Dame, Hartley. "The Causes and Effects of Military Intervention in Politics in Hispanic America: Argentina, a Case Study." MA thesis, American University, 1969.

Dame, Hartley, and Aubrey Lippincott. *Selected Aspects of the San Blas Cuna Indians.* Washington, D.C.: SORO, CINFAC, 1964.

Damms, Richard V. "James Killian, the Technological Capabilities Panel, and the Emergence of President Eisenhower's 'Scientific-Technological Elite.'" *Diplomatic History* 24 (2000): 57–78.

Davis, Paul K., and Kim Cragin, eds. *Social Science for Counterterrorism: Putting the Pieces Together.* Santa Monica, Calif.: RAND, 2009. http://www.rand.org/pubs/monographs/MG849/.

Davison, W. Phillips. "Foreign Policy." In *The Uses of Sociology,* edited by Paul F. Lazarsfeld, William H. Sewell, and Harold L. Wilensky, 391–417. New York: Basic Books, 1967.

De Grazia, Alfred. "Government and Science: An Editorial." *American Behavioral Scientist* 9, no. 1 (September 1965): 40.

Deitchman, Seymour. *The Best-Laid Schemes: A Tale of Social Research and Bureaucracy.* Cambridge, Mass.: MIT Press, 1976.

DeLong, Earl H. "Powers and Duties of the State Attorney-General in Criminal Prosecution." *Journal of Criminal Law and Criminology* 25 (1934): 358–400.

——. "Which Man for the Job?" *State Government* 8 (1935): 64–68.

——. "Who Are the Career Executives?" *Public Administration Review* 19 (1959): 108–13.

DeLong, Earl H., and Newman F. Baker. "The Prosecuting Attorney and Reform in Criminal Justice." *Journal of Criminal Law and Criminology* 26 (1936): 821–46.

Denney, George C., Jr. "State Department Procedures for Reviewing Government Sponsored Foreign Area Research." *Background* 10 (1966): 95–110.

Dennis, Michael A. "'Our First Line of Defense': Two University Labs in the Postwar American State." *Isis* 85 (1994): 427–55.

Dickinson, Laura A. *Outsourcing War and Peace.* New Haven, Conn.: Yale University Press, 2011.

Dickson, Paul. *Think Tanks.* New York: Atheneum, 1971.

"Distinguished Professional Contribution Award for 1976." *American Psychologist* 32 (1977): 72–79.

Dodds, Harold W. "The Dangers of Project Research." *Social Problems* 1 (1954): 90–93.

Eagle (American University). "AU, CRESS Begin Break," April 29, 1969.

——. "Extra No. 5," April 29, 1969.

——. "Quit Classified Research, Policy Unit Recommends," March 28, 1969.

——. "Reform Committee Diagnoses AU's Ills," October 4, 1968.

——. "Williams Calls for AU's 'New Era,'" October 18, 1968.

Eckstein, Harry. "Internal Wars." In *Proceedings of the Symposium "The U.S. Army's Limited-War Mission and Social Science Research,"* edited by William Lybrand, 250–62. Washington, D.C.: SORO, 1962.

——. *A Theory of Stable Democracy.* Center of International Studies Research Monograph 10. Princeton, N.J.: Woodrow Wilson School of Public and International Affairs, 1961.

Eder, Richard. "School Limits Tie to Army Project." *New York Times*, May 8, 1966.

Edmonson, Munro S., et al. Letter to the editor. *American Sociologist* 1 (1965–66): 207–8.

Edwards, Lyford P. *The Natural History of Revolution.* Chicago: University of Chicago Press, 1927.

Eisenberg, Terry, Robert H. Frosen, and Albert S. Glickman. *Project PACE: Police and Community Enterprise: A Program for Change in Police-Community Behaviors, Final Report.* Washington, D.C.: AIR, August 1971.

Eisenhower, Dwight D. "Farewell Address to the Nation." *Public Papers of the Presidents of the United States: Dwight D. Eisenhower, 1960–61,* 1038–39. Washington, D.C.: National Archives and Records Administration, 1961.

Ellman, Jesse, Reed Livergood, David Morrow, and Gregory Sanders. *Defense Contract Trends: U.S. Department of Defense Contract Spending and the Supporting Industrial Base.* Washington, D.C.: Center for Strategic and International Studies, May 2011.

Ellul, Jacques. *The Technological Society.* New York: Vintage Books, 1964.

Engerman, David C. "The Rise and Fall of Wartime Social Science: Harvard's Refugee Interview Project, 1950–1954." In *Cold War Social Science: Knowledge Production, Liberal Democracy, and Human Nature,* edited by Mark Solovey and Hamilton Cravens, 25–43. New York: Palgrave Macmillan, 2012.

Ernst, John. *Forging a Fateful Alliance: Michigan State University and the Vietnam War.* East Lansing: Michigan State University Press, 1998.

"External Research in the Department of State." *FAR Horizons* 3 (Summer 1972): 1–4, 7.

Farish, Matthew. *The Contours of America's Cold War.* Minneapolis: University of Minnesota Press, 2010.

Finney, Nathan. *Human Terrain Team Handbook.* Fort Leavenworth, Kans.: Human Terrain System, October 2008.

Flanagan, John C. "The American Institutes for Research." *American Psychologist* 39 (1984): 1272–76.

——. "The American Institute for Research: A New Type of Resource Organization." In *Planning for Progress: Proceedings of an A.I.R. Planning Conference,* edited by John C. Flanagan, 5–12. Pittsburgh: American Institute for Research, March 22, 1956.

——., ed. *Planning for Progress: Proceedings of an A.I.R. Planning Conference.* Pittsburgh: American Institute for Research, March 22, 1956.

Ford, Clellan. "Human Relations Area Files: 1945–1969." *Behavior Science Notes* 5 (1970): 1–27.

Ford, Thomas R. Review of *Systems Analysis and Social Planning,* by Robert Boguslaw. *Contemporary Sociology* 13 (1984): 65.

Forman, Paul. "Behind Quantum Electronics: National Security as a Basis for Physical Research in the United States, 1940–1960." *Historical Studies in the Physical Sciences* 18 (1988): 149–229.

Frances, Albert. "Structural and Anticipatory Dimensions of Violent Social Conflict." PhD diss., University of Pittsburgh, 1967.

Freeman, Jody, and Martha Minow, eds. *Government by Contract: Outsourcing and American Democracy*. Cambridge, Mass.: Harvard University Press, 2009.

Fremont-Smith, Eliot. "Peace—It Could Be Horrible." *New York Times*, November 20, 1967.

Friedberg, Aaron L. *In the Shadow of the Garrison State: America's Anti-Statism and Its Cold War Grand Strategy*. Princeton, N.J.: Princeton University Press, 2000.

Fulbright, J. William. "The War and Its Effects: The Military-Academic Industrial Complex." In *Super-State: Readings in the Military-Industrial Complex*, edited by Herbert I. Schiller and Joseph D. Phillips, 173–78. Urbana: University of Illinois Press, 1970.

Furner, Mary O. *Advocacy and Objectivity: A Crisis in the Professionalization of American Social Science, 1865–1905*. Lexington: University Press of Kentucky, 1975.

Gagne, John. "The New Intelligence Requirements: Introduction." *Background* 9 (1965): 171–72.

Galtung, Johan. "Scientific Colonialism." *Transition*, no. 30 (1967): 10–15.

Gardner Lloyd C., and Marilyn B. Young, eds. *Iraq and the Lessons of Vietnam: Or, How Not to Learn from the Past*. New York: New Press, 2007.

Gavin, James M. *War and Peace in the Space Age*. New York: Harper, 1958.

Geary, Daniel. *Radical Ambition: C. Wright Mills, the Left, and American Social Thought*. Berkeley: University of California Press, 2009.

Geiger, Roger L. *Research and Relevant Knowledge: American Research Universities since World War II*. New York: Oxford University Press, 1993.

Gendzier, Irene L. *Managing Political Change: Social Scientists and the Third World*. Boulder, Colo.: Westview Press, 1985.

George, Carole Shelbourne, Peter Lowry, Ritchie P. Lowry, and Susan Meeker-Lowry. *Tracking Responsible Investments: A Stock Average for Responsive Corporations*. Worcester, Vt.: Catalyst Press, 1983.

Germani, Gino. "In Memoriam: Rex D. Hopper, 1898–1966." *American Sociologist* 1 (1966): 259.

Geyer, David C., and David H. Herschler, eds. *Foreign Relations of the United States, 1964–1968*. Vol. 31, *South and Central America; Mexico*. Washington, D.C.: Government Printing Office, 2004.

Geyer, Michael. "The Militarization of Europe, 1914–1945." In *The Militarization of the Western World*, edited by John R. Gillis, 65–102. New Brunswick, N.J.: Rutgers University Press, 1989.

Ghamari-Tabrizi, Sharon. *The Worlds of Herman Kahn: The Intuitive Science of Thermonuclear War*. Cambridge, Mass.: Harvard University Press, 2005.

Gieryn, Thomas F. *Cultural Boundaries of Science: Credibility on the Line*. Chicago: University of Chicago Press, 1999.

Gilman, Nils. *Mandarins of the Future: Modernization Theory in Cold War America*. Baltimore: Johns Hopkins University Press, 2003.

Glock, Charles Y. "Applied Social Research: Some Conditions Affecting Its Utilization." In *Case Studies in Bringing Behavioral Science into Use*, edited by Charles Y. Glock, 1–19. Stanford, Calif.: Stanford University Institute for Communication Research, 1961.

Goldschmidt, Walter. "Anthropology and the Coming Crisis: An Autoethnographic Appraisal." *American Anthropologist* n.s. 79 (1977): 293–308.

Goldstein, Harry. "Modeling Terrorists." *IEEE Spectrum*, September 2006. http://spectrum.ieee.org/computing/software/modeling-terrorists/.

González, Roberto J. "'Human Terrain': Past, Present, and Future Applications." *Anthropology Today* 24, no. 1 (February 2008): 21–26.

Goode, William. Letter to the editor. *American Sociologist* 1 (1966): 255–57.

Gough, Kathleen. "World Revolution and the Science of Man." In *The Dissenting Academy*, edited by Theodore Roszak, 135–58. New York: Pantheon Books, 1968.

Gouldner, Alvin W. "Anti-Minotaur: The Myth of a Value-Free Sociology." *Social Problems* 9 (1962): 199–213.

"Government Guidelines for Foreign Area Research." *FAR Horizons* 1, no. 1 (January 1968): 1–6.

Greenberg, Daniel. "IDA: University-Sponsored Center Hit Hard by Assaults on Campus." *Science* 160, no. 3829 (1968): 744–48.

——. "Social Sciences: Expanded Role Urged for Defense Department." *Science* 158, no. 3803 (1967): 886–88.

——. "Social Science: Federal Agencies Agree to End Covert Support." *Science* 159, no. 3810 (1968): 64–66.

——. "Social Sciences: Harris Bill Evokes Limited Support." *Science* 155, no. 3764 (1967): 812–14.

Greene, T. N., ed. *The Guerrilla—and How to Fight Him: Selections from the Marine Corps Gazette.* New York: Frederick A. Praeger, 1962.

Gunnell, John G. *The Descent of Political Theory: The Genealogy of an American Vocation.* Chicago: University of Chicago Press, 1993.

Gurr, Ted. "A Causal Model of Civil Strife: A Comparative Analysis Using New Indices." *American Political Science Review* 62 (1968): 1104–24.

Guttman, Daniel, and Barry Willner. *The Shadow Government.* New York: Pantheon Books, 1976.

Hackman, Ray C. "Purity, Body, and Flavor: The Applied Scientist." *Scientific Monthly* 81 (1955): 213–14.

Hanna, William John, and Judith Lynne Hanna. *Urban Dynamics in Black Africa: An Interdisciplinary Approach.* Chicago: Aldine Atherton, 1971.

Hanrahan, John D. *Government by Contract.* New York: W. W. Norton, 1983.

Harris, Shane. *The Watchers: The Rise of America's Surveillance State.* New York: Penguin, 2011.

Harvard University. *The Behavioral Sciences at Harvard: Report by a Faculty Committee, June 1954.* Cambridge, Mass.: Harvard University Press, 1954.

Haskell, Thomas L. *The Emergence of Professional Social Science: The American Social Science Association and the Nineteenth-Century Crisis of Authority.* Urbana: University of Illinois Press, 1977.

——. *Objectivity Is Not Neutrality: Explanatory Schemes in History.* Baltimore: Johns Hopkins University Press, 1998.

Hauser, Philip M. "Are the Social Sciences Ready?" *American Sociological Review* 11 (1946): 379–84.

Hays, Margaret P., Christy Ann Hoffman, and Hartley Dame. *The Political Influence of University Students in Latin America.* Washington, D.C.: SORO, CINFAC, 1965.

Hazen, William, and Abraham R. Wagner. *Israeli Perceptions of American Security Policy: Current Trends and Future Alternatives.* Alexandria, Va.: Abbott Associates, October 1976.

Herman, Ellen. *The Romance of American Psychology: Political Culture in the Age of Experts*. Berkeley: University of California Press, 1995.

Hermes, Walter G. *Truce Tent and Fighting Front: The Last Two Years*. Washington, D.C.: Center of Military History, 1990.

Heymont, Col. Irving. "The U.S. Army and Foreign National Development." *Military Review* 51, no. 11 (November 1971): 17–23.

Hollinger, David A. "The Defense of Democracy and Robert K. Merton's Formulation of the Scientific Ethos." *Knowledge and Society* 4 (1983): 1–15.

———. "Science as a Weapon in *Kulturkämpfe* in the United States during and after World War II." *Isis* 86 (1995): 440–54.

Hopper, Rex D. "Cybernation, Marginality, and Revolution." In *The New Sociology: Essays in Social Science and Social Theory, in Honor of C. Wright Mills*, edited by Irving L. Horowitz, 313–30. New York: Oxford University Press, 1964.

———. "Indicators of Revolutionary Potential." Presentation to the Operations Research Symposium. Washington, D.C.: SORO, May 1964.

Horowitz, Irving L. "The Rise and Fall of Project Camelot." In *The Rise and Fall of Project Camelot*, edited by Irving L. Horowitz, 3–44. Cambridge, Mass.: MIT Press, 1967.

———, ed. *The Rise and Fall of Project Camelot*. Cambridge, Mass.: MIT Press, 1967.

———. "Social Science Objectivity and Value Neutrality: Historical Problems and Projections." *Diogenes* 39 (1962): 17–44.

———. "Social Science and Public Policy: An Examination of the Political Foundations of Modern Research." *International Studies Quarterly* 11 (1967): 32–62.

———. "Social Science Yogis and Military Commissars." *Transaction* 5, no. 6 (1968): 29–38.

Horowitz, Irving L., and Lee Rainwater. "Comment: Our CIA Problem and Theirs." *Transaction* 4, no. 7 (1967): 2.

Houk, John L., et al. *Psychological Operations: Laos; Project PROSYMS*. Washington, D.C.: SORO, 1959.

Humphrey, Robert L. *Scientific Ethic Dual Life Value: Theory and Ramifications*. San Diego: Grossmont Press, 1974.

Ingersoll, Jasper. "Howard Keva Kaufman (1922–2000)." *Journal of Asian Studies* 60 (2001): 247.

Institute for Defense Analyses. *Five Year Report: Activities of the Institute for Defense Analyses, FY 71–75*. Arlington, Va.: IDA, 1975.

Jacobs, Milton, Farhad Farzanegan, and Alexander Askenasy. "A Study of Key Communicators in Thailand." *Social Forces* 45 (1966): 192–99.

Jacobs, Milton, Charles E. Rice, and Lorand Szalay, assisted by James DeShields. *The Study of Communication in Thailand with an Emphasis on Word-of-Mouth Communication*. Washington, D.C.: SORO, July 1964.

"Jacobs, Norman." *American Men and Women of Science: Social and Behavioral Sciences*, 12th ed., edited by Jacques Cattell Press, 1117–18. New York: R. R. Bowker, 1973.

Jager, Sheila Miyoshi. *On the Uses of Cultural Knowledge*. Strategic Studies Institute, U.S. Army War College, November 2007.

Janka, Les. Review of *Beyond Camp David*, by Paul A. Jureidini and R. D. McLaurin. *Middle East Journal* 35 (1981): 642–43.

Jardini, David R. "Out of the Blue Yonder: The RAND Corporation's Diversification into Social Welfare Research, 1946–1968." PhD diss., Carnegie Mellon University, 1996.

Johnson, Dale L. "Ethics of the Nature, Procedures, and Funding of Research in Other Countries." *American Anthropologist* 68 (1966): 1016–17.

——. Letter to the editor. *American Sociologist* 1 (1966): 206–7.

Johnson, Harold K. "The Army's Role in Nation Building and Preserving Stability." *Army Information Digest* 20 (November 1965): 6–13.

Jureidini, Paul A. *Casebook on Insurgency and Revolutionary Warfare: 23 Summary Accounts*. Washington, D.C.: SORO, 1962.

Jureidini, Paul A., and William Hazen. *The Palestinian Movement in Politics*. Lexington, Mass.: Lexington Books, 1976.

Jureidini, Paul A., and John M. Lord. *An Ethnographic Summary of the Ethiopian Provinces of Harar and Sidamo*. Washington, D.C.: SORO, October 1964.

Jureidini, Paul A., and R. D. McLaurin. *Beyond Camp David: Emerging Alignments and Leaders in the Middle East*. Syracuse, N.Y.: Syracuse University Press, 1981.

Jureidini, Paul A., R. D. McLaurin, and James Price. *Military Operations in Selected Lebanese Built-Up Areas, 1975–1978*. Aberdeen Proving Ground, Md.: U.S. Army Human Engineering Laboratory, 1979.

Kaiser, David E. *American Tragedy: Kennedy, Johnson, and the Origins of the Vietnam War*. Cambridge, Mass.: Belknap Press of Harvard University Press, 2000.

Karcher, E. K. "Army Social Science Programs and Plans." In *Proceedings of the Symposium "The Limited-War Mission and Social Science Research,"* edited by William Lybrand, 344–59. Washington, D.C.: SORO, 1962.

Katz, Elihu, and Paul Lazarsfeld. *Personal Influence: The Part Played by People in the Flow of Mass Communications*. New York: Free Press, 1960.

Katz, Phillip, and R. D. McLaurin. *Psychological Operations in Urban Warfare: Lessons from the 1982 Middle East War*. Springfield, Va.: Abbott Associates, July 1987.

Katz, Phillip P., R. D. McLaurin, and Preston S. Abbott. "Persuasive Communications: A Critical Analysis of U.S. Psychological Operations in War and Peace." *Interdisciplinary Science Reviews* 4 (1979): 71–85.

Kaufman, Howard K. "Attitude Research: The Theoretical Basis and Some Problems of Application in Rural Thailand." In *Linguistics and Anthropology: In Honor of C. F. Voegelin*, edited by M. Dale Kinkade, Kenneth L. Hale, and Oswald Werner, 351–83. Lisse, Netherlands: Peter de Ridder Press, 1975.

——. *Socio-economic Factors in Farmer Response to Irrigation in Northeast Thailand*. Bangkok: U.S. Operating Mission, September 1971.

"Kaufman, Howard Keva." In *American Men and Women of Science: Social and Behavioral Sciences*, 12th ed., edited by Jacques Cattell Press, 1:1196. New York: R. R. Bowker, 1973.

Kecskemeti, Paul. *Strategic Surrender: The Politics of Victory and Defeat*. Stanford, Calif.: Stanford University Press, 1958.

Kelly, Orr. "DOD: Solving the Double-Barreled Dilemma." *Armed Forces Journal*, September 28, 1968, 8–11.

Kenworthy, E. W. "Pentagon Refuses to Release Secret Study on U.S. Hegemony." *New York Times*, February 16, 1968.

Kinard, Col. William H. "The New Dimensions of Special Warfare." In *Proceedings of the Symposium "The Limited-War Mission and Social Science Research,"* edited by William Lybrand, 56–63. Washington, D.C.: SORO, 1962.

Kipp, Jacob, Lester Grau, Karl Prinslow, and Captain Don Smith. "The Human Terrain System: A CORDS for the 21st Century." *Military Review* 86, no. 5 (2006): 8–15.

Klare, Michael T. "Bringing It Back: Planning for the City." In *Policing America*, edited by Anthony M. Platt and Lynn Cooper, 97–104. Englewood Cliffs, N.J.: Prentice-Hall, 1974.

———. *War without End: Planning for the Next Vietnams.* New York: Vintage Books, 1972.

Kleinman, Daniel Lee, and Mark Solovey. "Hot Science / Cold War: The National Science Foundation after World War II." *Radical History Review* 63 (1995): 110–39.

Knorr, Klaus. "Social Science Research Abroad: Problems and Remedies." *World Politics* 19 (1967): 465–85.

Kohn, Richard H. "The Danger of Militarization in an Endless 'War' on Terrorism." *Journal of Military History* 73 (2009): 177–208.

Kuklick, Bruce. *Blind Oracles: Intellectuals and War from Kennan to Kissinger.* Princeton, N.J.: Princeton University Press, 2006.

LaCharite, N.A., and E.W. Gude. "Project Revolt." *Army Information Digest* 20 (February 1965): 39–41.

Langor, Elinor. "Uprising on Morningside Heights: Background." *Science* 162, no. 3856 (1968): 879.

Lasswell, Harold D. "The Garrison State and Specialists on Violence." *American Journal of Sociology* 46 (1941): 455–68.

———. "The Policy Orientation." In *The Policy Sciences*, edited by Daniel Lerner and Harold D. Lasswell, 3–15. Stanford, Calif.: Stanford University Press, 1951.

Latham, Michael E. *Modernization as Ideology: American Social Science and "Nation Building" in the Kennedy Era.* Chapel Hill: University of North Carolina Press, 2000.

Lee, Manwoo, R.D. McLaurin, and Chung-in Moon. *Alliance under Tension: The Evolution of South Korean–U.S. Relations.* Boulder, Colo.: Westview Press, 1988.

Lemov, Rebecca M. *World as Laboratory: Experiments with Mice, Mazes, and Men.* New York: Hill & Wang, 2005.

Leonnig, Carol D. "Residents' Federal Lawsuits Blocked; Weapons Tested in Spring Valley." *Washington Post*, September 17, 2003.

Lerner, Daniel. *The Passing of Traditional Society: Modernizing the Middle East.* Glencoe, Ill.: Free Press, 1958.

———. "Social Science: Whence and Whither?" In *The Human Meaning of the Social Sciences*, edited by Daniel Lerner, 13–42. New York: Meridian Books, 1959.

Lerner, Daniel, and Harold D. Lasswell, eds. *The Policy Sciences.* Stanford, Calif.: Stanford University Press, 1951.

Leslie, Stuart W. *The Cold War and American Science: The Military-Industrial-Academic Complex at MIT and Stanford.* New York: Columbia University Press, 1993.

Levy, Avigdor. Review of *Beyond Camp David*, by Paul A. Jureidini and R.D. McLaurin. *Modern Judaism* 4 (1984): 343–46.

Light, Jennifer S. *From Warfare to Welfare: Defense Intellectuals and Urban Problems in Cold War America.* Baltimore: Johns Hopkins University Press, 2003.

Linebarger, Paul. *Psychological Warfare.* Washington, D.C.: Infantry Journal Press, 1948.

Lipset, Seymour Martin. *Political Man: The Social Bases of Politics.* Garden City, N.Y.: Anchor Books, 1960.

Lord, John M., Carl F. Rosenthal, and James M. Dodson. *Communist Theory and Practice in Subversive Insurgencies.* Washington, D.C.: SORO, 1965.

Lowen, Rebecca. *Creating the Cold War University: The Transformation of Stanford.* Berkeley: University of California Press, 1997.

Lowry, Ritchie P. "Changing Military Roles: Neglected Challenge to Rural Sociologists." *Rural Sociology* 30 (1965): 219–25.

——. Feature Review. *Sociological Quarterly* 19 (1978): 152–56.

——. *Good Money: A Guide to Profitable Social Investing in the '90s.* New York: W. W. Norton, 1991.

——. "To Arms: Changing Military Roles and the Military-Industrial Complex." *Social Problems* 18 (1970): 3–16.

——. "Toward a Sociology of Secrecy and Security Systems." *Social Problems* 19 (1972): 437–50.

Lutz, Catherine. *Homefront: A Military City and the American 20th Century.* Boston: Beacon Press, 2001.

Lybrand, William, ed. *Proceedings of the Symposium "The Limited-War Mission and Social Science Research."* Washington, D.C.: SORO, 1962.

Lyons, Gene M. *The Uneasy Partnership: Social Science and the Federal Government in the Twentieth Century.* New York: Russell Sage Foundation, 1969.

Lyons, Gene M., and Louis Morton. *Schools for Strategy: Education and Research in National Security Affairs.* New York: Praeger, 1965.

MacArthur, Donald M. "Current Emphasis on the Department of Defense's Social and Behavioral Sciences Program." *American Psychologist* 23 (1968): 104–7.

Markusen, Ann R. "The Case against Privatizing National Security." *Governance* 16 (2003): 471–501.

Marvel, William. "Remarks." *Background* 9 (1965): 177–83.

McClintock, Michael. *Instruments of Statecraft.* New York: Pantheon Books, 1992.

McEnaney, Laura. *Civil Defense Begins at Home: Militarization Meets Everyday Life in the Fifties.* Princeton, N.J.: Princeton University Press, 2000.

McFate, Montgomery. "The Military Utility of Understanding Adversarial Culture." *Joint Force Quarterly*, no. 38 (2005): 42–48.

McFate, Montgomery, and Andrea Jackson. "An Organizational Solution for the DoD's Cultural Needs." *Military Review* 85, no. 4 (1985): 18–21.

McKeachie, W. J., and Orville G. Brim Jr. "Lessons to Be Learned from Large Behavioral Research Organizations." *American Psychologist* 39 (1984): 1254–55.

McKenna, Christopher D. *The World's Newest Profession: Management Consulting in the Twentieth Century.* Cambridge: Cambridge University Press, 2006.

McLaurin, R. D. "From Professional to Political: The Redecline of the Lebanese Army." *Armed Forces and Society* 17 (1991): 545–68.

——. *The Middle East in Soviet Policy.* Lexington, Mass.: Lexington Books, 1975.

——. *Military Propaganda: Psychological Warfare and Operations.* New York: Praeger, 1982.

——. *The Political Role of Minority Groups in the Middle East.* New York: Praeger, 1979.

McLaurin, R. D., and Suhaila Haddad. *The Political Impact of U.S. Military Force in the Middle East.* Washington, D.C.: AIR, 1977.

McLaurin, R. D., and Mohammed Mughisuddin. *The Soviet Union and the Middle East: Final Report.* Washington, D.C.: AIR, October 1974.

McLaurin, R. D., Mohammed Mughisuddin, and Abraham R. Wagner. *Foreign Policymaking in the Middle East: Domestic Influences on Policy in Egypt, Iraq, Israel, and Syria.* New York: Praeger, 1977.

McLaurin, R. D., Don Peretz, and Lewis W. Snider. *Middle East Foreign Policy: Issues and Processes.* New York: Praeger, 1982.

McLaurin, R. D., and James R. Price. *Soviet Middle East Policy since the October War.* Alexandria, Va.: Abbott Associates, 1976.

McLaurin, R. D., Carl F. Rosenthal, Sarah A. Skillings, et al., eds. *The Art and Science of Psychological Operations: Case Studies in Military Application.* Washington, D.C.: Department of the Army, 1976.

McLaurin, R. D., and Lewis W. Snider. *Recent Military Operations on Urban Terrain.* Alexandria, Va.: Abbott Associates, July 1982.

"McLaurin, R. D." In *American Men and Women of Science: Social and Behavioral Sciences*, 13th ed., edited by Jacques Cattell Press, 806. New York: R. R. Bowker, 1978.

McPhail, Clark, David Schweingruber, and John McCarthy. "Policing Protest in the United States: 1960–1995." In *Policing Protest: The Control of Mass Movements in Western Democracies*, edited by Donatella della Porta and Herbert Reiter, 49–69. Minneapolis: University of Minnesota Press, 1998.

Melman, Seymour. *Pentagon Capitalism.* New York: McGraw-Hill, 1970.

Mendelsohn, Everett. "Robert K. Merton: The Celebration and Defense of Science." *Science in Context* 3 (1989): 269–89.

Miller, Clark A. "'An Effective Instrument of Peace': Scientific Cooperation as an Instrument of U.S. Foreign Policy, 1938–1950." In *Global Power Knowledge: Science and Technology in International Relations*, edited by John Krige and Kai-Henrik Barth, 133–60. Osiris 21. Chicago: University of Chicago Press, 2006.

Millikan, Max F. "Inquiry and Policy: The Relation of Knowledge to Action." In *The Human Meaning of the Social Sciences*, edited by Daniel Lerner, 158–80. New York: Meridian Books, 1959.

Mills, C. Wright. *The Power Elite.* New York: Oxford University Press, 1956.

——. *The Sociological Imagination.* New York: Oxford University Press, 1959.

Minow, Martha. "Outsourcing Power: Privatizing Military Efforts and the Risks to Accountability, Professionalism, and Democracy." In *Government by Contract: Outsourcing and American Democracy*, edited by Jody Freeman and Martha Minow, 110–27. Cambridge, Mass.: Harvard University Press, 2009.

Mintz, Jeanne S. *Indonesia: A Profile.* Princeton, N.J.: Van Nostrand, 1961.

——. *Mohammed, Marx, and Marhaen: The Roots of Indonesian Socialism.* London: Pall Mall Press, 1965.

Mollenhoff, Clark R. *The Pentagon.* New York: G. P. Putnam's Sons, 1967.

Molnar, Andrew R., William A. Lybrand, Lorna Hahn, James L. Kirkman, and Peter B. Riddleberger. *Undergrounds in Insurgent, Revolutionary, and Resistance Warfare.* Washington, D.C.: SORO, 1963.

Molnar, Andrew R., Jerry M. Tinker, and John D. Lenoir. *Human Factors Considerations of Undergrounds in Insurgencies.* Washington, D.C.: SORO, 1966.

Morrill, J. L. "Higher Education and the Federal Government." *Annals of the American Academy of Political and Social Science* 301 (1955): 41–45.

Morse, Wayne. "Dangers in Government Sponsorship of Research on Foreign Policy and Foreign Areas." *Background* 10 (1966): 123–30.

Musgrove, Mike. "Court Rejects Suit against CACI over Abu Ghraib Torture." *Washington Post*, September 12, 2009. http://www.washingtonpost.com/wp-dyn/content/article/2009/09/11/AR2009091103285.html.

Myers, Allen. "Scholars Join with US Government for Purposes of Counterinsurgency." *Student Mobilizer*, April 2, 1970.

National Academy of Sciences Advisory Committee on Government Programs in the Behavioral Sciences. *The Behavioral Sciences and the Federal Government.* Washington, D.C.: National Academy of Sciences, 1968.

Navasky, Victor. Introduction to *Report from Iron Mountain on the Possibility and Desirability of Peace*, by Leonard C. Lewin, v–xvi. New York: Free Press, 1996. Originally published in 1967.

Nelson, Bryce. "Military Funds: Senate Whets the Ax for ABM, Research, 'Think Tanks.'" *Science* 160, no. 3830 (1968): 860–64.

——. "Political Scientists: More Concern about Political Involvement, Ethics." *Science* 161 no. 3846 (1968): 1117–18.

Network of Concerned Anthropologists. *The Counter-Counterinsurgency Manual: Or, Notes on Demilitarizing American Society*. Chicago: Prickly Paradigm Press, 2009.

"News in Brief." *Science* 158, no. 3802 (1967): 749.

New York Times. "Burying Camelot." August 12, 1965.

——. "Colombian Scores U.S. over Survey." February 4, 1966.

——. "Indonesian Aide Going to Harvard." September 30, 1951.

——. "Ottawa Is Upset over a U.S. Study." March 3, 1966.

Niebuhr, Gustav. "Wilfred C. Smith Dies at 83; Scholar of Religious Pluralism." *New York Times*, February 11, 2000.

Nieburg, H. L. *In the Name of Science*. Chicago: Quadrangle Books, 1966.

O'Connor, Alice. "Financing the Counterrevolution." In *Rightward Bound: Making America Conservative in the 1970s*, edited by Bruce J. Schulman and Julian E. Zelizer, 148–68. Cambridge, Mass.: Harvard University Press, 2008.

——. *Social Science for What? Philanthropy and the Social Question in a World Turned Rightside Up*. New York: Russell Sage Foundation, 2007.

Okes, Imogene E. "Effective Communication by Americans with Thai." MA thesis, American University, 1960.

Oren, Ido. *Our Enemies and Us: America's Rivalries and the Making of Political Science*. Ithaca, N.Y.: Cornell University Press, 2003.

Orlans, Harold. *Contracting for Knowledge: Values and Limitations of Social Science Research*. San Francisco: Jossey-Bass, 1973.

——. "The Contract State—or Is it the Welfare State of the Professional Classes?" In *Government-Sponsored Nonprofits*, edited by Harold Orlans, 152–85. Washington, D.C.: National Academy of Public Administration, November 1978.

——. *The Non-Profit Research Institute: Its Origin, Operation, Problems, and Prospects*. New York: McGraw-Hill, 1972.

Osgood, Robert Endicott. *Limited War: The Challenge to American Strategy*. Chicago: University of Chicago Press, 1957.

Owens, Larry. "The Counterproductive Management of Science in the Second World War: Vannevar Bush and the Office of Scientific Research and Development." *Business History Review* 68 (1994): 515–76.

Pearson, Roger. "John C. Flanagan and the Development of Psychological Surveys: The U.S. Aviation Psychology Program." *Mankind Quarterly* 38 (1997): 85–97.

Pells, Richard H. *The Liberal Mind in a Conservative Age: American Intellectuals in the 1940s and 1950s*. New York: Harper & Row, 1985.

Pescheck, Joseph G. *Policy-Planning Organizations: Elite Agendas and America's Rightward Turn*. Philadelphia: Temple University Press, 1987.

Pettee, George Sawyer. *The Process of Revolution*. New York: Harper & Bros., 1938.

Platt, Anthony M., and Lynn Cooper, eds. *Policing America*. Englewood Cliffs, N.J.: Prentice-Hall, 1974.

Pool, Ithiel de Sola. "The Necessity for Social Scientists Doing Research for Government." *Background* 10 (1966): 111–22.

Pool, Ithiel de Sola, et al. *Social Science Research and National Security*. Washington, D.C.: Smithsonian Institution, 1963.

Porter, Theodore M. *Trust in Numbers: The Pursuit of Objectivity in Science and Public Life*. Princeton, N.J.: Princeton University Press, 1995.

Preston, Andrew. *The War Council: McGeorge Bundy, the NSC, and Vietnam*. Cambridge, Mass.: Harvard University Press, 2006.

Preston, Harley O. "Research Planning for AIR Programs: V. Operations and Systems Analysis," in *Planning for Progress: Proceedings of an A.I.R. Planning Conference*, edited by John C. Flanagan, 35–36. Pittsburgh: American Institute for Research, March 22, 1956.

Price, David H. *Threatening Anthropology: McCarthyism and the FBI's Surveillance of Activist Anthropologists*. Durham, N.C.: Duke University Press, 2004.

Priest, Dana, and William M. Arkin. "Top Secret America." *Washington Post*, July 20, 2010. http://projects.washingtonpost.com/top-secret-america/.

Proctor, Robert N. *Value-Free Science? Purity and Power in Modern Knowledge*. Cambridge, Mass.: Harvard University Press, 1991.

Proxmire, William. *Report from Wasteland*. New York: Praeger, 1970.

Purcell, Edward A., Jr. *The Crisis of Democratic Theory: Scientific Naturalism and the Problem of Value*. Lexington: University Press of Kentucky, 1973.

Pye, Lucien. "The Role of the Military in Political Development." In *Proceedings of the Symposium "The Limited-War Mission and Social Science Research,"* edited by William Lybrand, 159–69. Washington, D.C.: SORO, 1962.

Reissman, Leonard, and Kalman H. Silvert. "Ethics and the Third Culture." *American Behavioral Scientist* 10, no. 10 (1967): 1–2.

Reynolds, John R., and Joanne E. King. *Highlights in the History of the American University, 1889–1976*. Washington, D.C.: Hennage Creative Printers, 1976.

Ricci, David M. *The Tragedy of Political Science: Politics, Scholarship, and Democracy*. New Haven, Conn.: Yale University Press, 1984.

——. *The Transformation of American Politics: The New Washington and the Rise of Think Tanks*. New Haven, Conn.: Yale University Press, 1993.

Rich, Andrew. *Think Tanks, Public Policy, and the Politics of Expertise*. Cambridge: Cambridge University Press, 2004.

Riley, David P. "Should Communities Control Their Police?" In *Policing America*, edited by Anthony M. Platt and Lynn Cooper, 190–97. Englewood Cliffs, N.J.: Prentice-Hall, 1974.

Robin, Ron Theodore. *The Making of the Cold War Enemy: Culture and Politics in the Military-Industrial Complex*. Princeton, N.J.: Princeton University Press, 2001.

Rodgers, Daniel T. *Age of Fracture*. Cambridge, Mass.: Belknap Press of Harvard University Press, 2011.

Rohde, Joy. "Last Stand of the Psychocultural Cold Warriors: Military Contract Research in Vietnam." *Journal of the History of the Behavioral Sciences* 47 (2011): 232–50.

——. "The Social Scientists' War: Expertise in a Cold War Nation." PhD diss., University of Pennsylvania, 2007.

Roland, Alex. *The Military-Industrial Complex*. Washington, D.C.: American Historical Association, 2001.

Rosenthal, Carl F. "Communist Insurgency in Theory and Practice." MA thesis, University of Illinois at Urbana-Champaign, 1967.

——. *Economic, Social, and Political Factors in Counterinsurgency Intelligence Planning*. Washington, D.C.: CRESS, 1966.

———. *Phases of Civil Disturbances: Characteristics and Problems*. Kensington, Md.: AIR, June 1971.

———. *Social Conflict and Collective Violence in American Institutions of Higher Learning*. Vol. 1, *Dynamics of Student Protest*. Kensington, Md.: AIR, 1971.

Rosenthal, Carl F., and Curtis B. Brooks. *Effects of Military Assistance Programs on Developing Countries: A Bibliography*. Washington, D.C.: SORO, 1966.

Rosenthal, Carl F., James Dodson, and Elaine Murphy. "Some Theoretical Observations on the Assessment of Psychological Operations Effectiveness." Washington, D.C.: CRESS, 1967.

Ross, Dorothy. *The Origins of American Social Science*. Cambridge: Cambridge University Press, 1991.

Roszak, Theodore. "On Academic Delinquency." In *The Dissenting Academy*, edited by Theodore Roszak, 3–43. New York: Pantheon Books, 1968.

Sahlins, Marshall. "The Established Order: Do Not Fold, Spindle, or Mutilate." In *The Rise and Fall of Project Camelot*, edited by Irving L. Horowitz, 71–79. Cambridge, Mass.: MIT Press, 1967.

Sandler, Stanley. *Cease Resistance: It's Good for You! A History of U.S. Army Combat Psychological Operations*. Fort Bragg, N.C.: United States Army Special Operations Command, 1996.

Scheips, Paul J. *The Role of Federal Military Forces in Domestic Disorders, 1945–1992*. Washington, D.C.: Center of Military History, 2005.

Schwartz, Leonard E. "Social Science and the Furtherance of Peace Research." *American Behavioral Scientist* 9, no. 7 (1966): 24–28.

Science News. "Campuses and Conscience." May 4, 1968.

———. "Research Absorbs the Cuts." May 18, 1968.

Sherry, Michael S. *In the Shadow of War: The United States since the 1930s*. New Haven, Conn.: Yale University Press, 1995.

Silvert, Kalman H. "American Academic Ethics and Social Research Abroad: The Lesson of Project Camelot." *Background* 9 (1965): 215–36.

Singer, P. W. *Corporate Warriors: The Rise of the Privatized Military Industry*. Ithaca, N.Y.: Cornell University Press, 2003.

Smith, Bruce L. R. *The RAND Corporation: Case Study of a Nonprofit Advisory Corporation*. Cambridge, Mass.: Harvard University Press, 1966.

Smith, James Allen. *The Idea Brokers: Think Tanks and the Rise of the New Policy Elite*. New York: Free Press, 1991.

Smith, Mark C. *Social Science in the Crucible: The American Debate over Objectivity and Purpose, 1918–1941*. Durham, N.C.: Duke University Press, 1994.

Smith, Rogers M. "Still Blowing in the Wind: The American Quest for a Democratic, Scientific Political Science." In *American Academic Culture in Transformation*, edited by Thomas Bender and Carl E. Schorske, 271–305. Princeton, N.J.: Princeton University Press, 1998.

"Social Science Research Abroad: Problems and Remedies." *World Politics* 19 (1967): 482.

Solovey, Mark. "The Politics of Intellectual Identity and American Social Science, 1945–1970." PhD diss., University of Wisconsin–Madison, 1996.

———. "Project Camelot and the 1960s Epistemological Revolution: Rethinking the Politics–Patronage–Social Science Nexus." *Social Studies of Science* 31 (2001): 171–206.

———. "Senator Fred Harris's Effort to Create a National Social Science Foundation: Challenge to the U.S. National Science Establishment." *Isis* 103 (2012): 54–82.

Sorokin, Pitirim. *The Sociology of Revolution*. Philadelphia: J. B. Lippincott Co., 1925.

The Spook Who Sat by the Door. Directed by Ivan Dixon. Bokan / United Artists, 1973.

Stanley, Jay, ed. *Essays on the Garrison State*. New Brunswick, N.J.: Transaction Publishers, 1997.

Stanley, Jay, and Catherine Crump. *Protecting Privacy from Aerial Surveillance: Recommendations for Government Use of Drone Aircraft*. New York: American Civil Liberties Union, December 2011.

"State's External Research Program: End-of-the-Fiscal-Year Report." *FAR Horizons* 4, no. 4 (1971): 1–4, 7.

Stockman, Farah. "Knowing the Enemy, One Avatar at a Time." *Boston Globe*, May 30, 2010. http://www.boston.com/news/nation/washington/articles/2010/05/30/knowing_the_enemy_one_avatar_at_a_time/.

Stren, Richard. "Urban Dynamics in Black Africa." *American Political Science Review* 67 (1973): 1400–1401.

Sweet, L. E. Review of *Middle Eastern Subcultures*, by William E. Hazen. *Middle East Journal* 31 (1977): 501.

Swisher, Ralph B. *Military Civic Action*. 3 vols. Kensington, Md.: American Institutes for Research, June 1972.

Szalay, Lorand B. *Cultural Influences and Drug Abuse: Psychological Vulnerabilities of Puerto Ricans in the United States*. Chevy Chase, Md.: Institute of Comparative Social and Cultural Studies, 1991.

——. *The Hispanic American Cultural Frame of Reference: A Communication Guide for Use in Mental Health, Education, and Training*. Washington, D.C.: Institute of Comparative Social and Cultural Studies, 1978.

——. *Hispanic American Psychocultural Dispositions Relevant to Personnel Management*. Institute of Comparative Social and Cultural Studies, 1984.

——. *Iranian and American Perceptions and Cultural Frames of Reference: A Communication Lexicon for Cultural Understanding*. Washington, D.C.: Institute of Comparative Social and Cultural Studies, 1979.

——. *Regional and Demographic Variations in Public Perceptions Related to Emergency Preparedness*. Silver Spring, Md.: Institute of Comparative Social and Cultural Studies, 1986.

Szalay, Lorand B., and Jack E. Brent. "The Analysis of Cultural Meanings through Free Verbal Associations." *Journal of Social Psychology* 72 (1967): 161–87.

Szalay, Lorand B., and Jean A. Bryson. *Measurement of Ethnic-Racial and Cultural Perceptions and Attitudes through Word Associations*. Kensington, Md.: AIR, March 1976.

——. "Measurement of Psychocultural Distance: A Comparison of American Blacks and Whites." *Journal of Personality and Social Psychology* 26 (1973): 166–77.

——. *Subjective Culture and Communication: A Puerto Rican–U.S. Comparison*. Kensington, Md.: AIR, 1975.

Szalay, Lorand B., Jean A. Bryson, and Garmon West. *Ethnic-Racial Perceptions and Attitudes by Word and Picture Stimulated Associations*. Kensington, Md.: AIR, October 1974.

Szalay, Lorand B., Won T. Moon, and Jean A. Bryson. *Communication Lexicon on Three South Korean Audiences* (Domains: Family, Education, International Relations). Kensington, Md.: AIR, May 1973.

Szalay, Lorand B., with Robert Walker et al. *Persuasion Overseas (Republic of Vietnam Emphasis)*. Washington, D.C.: SORO, June 1965.

Szalay, Lorand B., et al. *Communication Lexicon on Three South Korean Audiences*. Kensington, Md.: AIR, May 1973.

Taylor, Maxwell D. *The Uncertain Trumpet*. New York: Harper, 1960.

Tims, Frank M., Robert C. Sorensen, and Frances C. Mushal. *New Indicators of Psychological Operations Effects*. McLean, Va.: General Research Corp., 1975.

Trager, Frank N., ed. *Marxism in Southeast Asia: A Study of Four Countries*. Stanford, Calif.: Stanford University Press, 1959.

Tullis, Tracy. "A Vietnam at Home: Policing the Ghettos in the Counterinsurgency Era." PhD diss., New York University, 1999.

U.S. Congress. House. Committee on Foreign Affairs. Subcommittee on International Organizations and Movements. *Behavioral Sciences and the National Security, Report No. 4, Together with Part IX of the Hearings on Winning the Cold War: The U.S. Ideological Offensive*, 89th Cong., 2nd sess., July–August 1965. Washington, D.C.: Government Printing Office, 1965.

——. House. Committee on Government Operations, Research and Technical Programs Subcommittee. *The Use of Social Research in Federal Domestic Programs: Federally Financed Social Research*. Washington, D.C.: Government Printing Office, 1967.

——. House. Committee on Internal Security. *Investigation of Students for a Democratic Society Part 4 (American University), Hearings*. 91st Cong., 2nd sess., July 24, 1969. Washington, D.C.: Government Printing Office.

——. House. Committee on Science and Astronautics. Subcommittee on Science, Research, and Development. *Technical Information for Congress*. Report prepared by Library of Congress Science Policy Research Division. Washington, D.C.: Government Printing Office, 1969, rev. 1971.

——. House. Select Committee to Investigate Foundations. *Final Report of the Select Committee to Investigate Foundations and Other Organizations*, 82nd Cong., 2nd sess. Washington, D.C.: Government Printing Office, 1953.

U.S. Congress. Office of Technology Assessment. *History of the Department of Defense Federally Funded Research and Development Centers*. Washington, D.C.: Government Printing Office, 1995.

U.S. Congress. Senate. Committee on Foreign Relations. *Defense Department Sponsored Foreign Affairs Research: Hearings before the Senate Committee on Foreign Relations*. 90th Cong., 2nd sess., Part 1, May 9, 1968, and Part 2, May 28, 1968. Washington, D.C.: Government Printing Office, 1968.

——. Senate. Committee on Government Operations. Subcommittee on Government Research. *Federal Support of International Social Science and Behavioral Research, Hearings*. 89th Cong., 2nd sess., June 27–28, July 19–20, 1966. Washington, D.C.: Government Printing Office, 1966.

——. Senate. Committee on Government Operations. Subcommittee on Government Research. *National Foundation for Social Sciences, Hearings on S. 836, a Bill to Provide for the Establishment of the National Foundation for the Social Sciences*. 90th Cong., 1st sess., 1967. Washington, D.C.: Government Printing Office, 1967.

——. Senate. Committee on Post Office and Civil Service. Subcommittee on Federal Manpower Policies. *Report on Manpower Utilization by the Federal Government through the Use of Private Contract Labor*. 83rd Cong., 1st sess., 1953. Washington, D.C.: Government Printing Office, 1953.

U.S. Department of the Army. Office of the Chief of Research and Development. *Report of the Eleventh Annual Human Factors Research and Development Conference*. Washington, D.C.: Department of the Army, 1965.

——. *Psychological Operations, FM 33–1*. Washington, D.C.: Department of the Army, August 1979.

U.S. Department of Defense. Office of the Secretary of Defense. *Second Annual Minerva Conference: Minerva Research Summaries.* 2011. http://minerva.dtic. mil/.

U.S. General Accounting Office. *Need for Improved Guidelines in Contracting for Research with Government-Sponsored Nonprofit Contractors, Report to the Congress.* Washington, D.C.: General Accounting Office, 1969.

Vallance, Theodore R. "Methodology in Propaganda Research." *Psychological Bulletin* 48 (1951): 32–61.

van den Berghe, Pierre L. Letter to the editor. *American Sociologist* 2 (1967): 99.

Wakin, Eric. *Anthropology Goes to War: Professional Ethics and Counterinsurgency in Thailand.* Madison: University of Wisconsin Center for Southeast Asian Studies, 1992.

Walsh, John. "Defense Research: Questions for Vietnam Dissenters." *Science* 161, no. 3847 (1968): 1225–26.

Wang, Jessica. "Merton's Shadow: Perspectives on Science and Democracy since 1940." *Historical Studies in the Physical and Biological Sciences* 30 (1999): 279–306.

Ward, John. "Spring Valley Sick Blame Chemicals in WWI Dumping: A Survey Finds a Disquieting Number of Serious Illnesses." *Washington Times*, November 14, 2004.

Westad, Odd Arne. *The Global Cold War: Third World Interventions and the Making of Our Times.* Cambridge: Cambridge University Press, 2005.

Wolfle, Dael. "Social Science Research and International Relations." *Science* 151, no. 3707 (1966): 155.

Wysocki, Bernard. "Private Practice: Is U.S. Government 'Outsourcing its Brain'?" *Wall Street Journal*, March 30, 2007.

Yans-McLaughlin, Virginia. "Science, Democracy, and Ethics: Mobilizing Culture and Personality for World War II." In *Malinowski, Rivers, Benedict and Others: Essays on Culture and Personality*, edited by George W. Stocking, 184–217. Madison: University of Wisconsin Press, 1986.

Young, Marilyn B. "The Age of Global Power." In *Rethinking American History in a Global Age*, edited by Thomas Bender, 274–94. Berkeley: University of California Press, 2002.

Index

Abbott, Preston, 119, 125
Abbott Associates, 125, 128–29, 149
Abt, Clark, 101
academic research
    anthropology, 20, 63, 83–85, 122, 130,
        143–46
    area studies, 4, 12, 14–17, 95, 130
    classified material access, 6, 15, 32, 101, 107,
        113
    conflict resolution, role in, 34
    disciplinary inflexibility, 22
    engineering, 12–13
    international learning, 26–27, 96
    military connections, 2, 5, 12–18, 21, 25–27,
        66–67, 80, 94–96, 107–8, 113–14, 120–21,
        132–33, 141–42, 149
    philosophy, 30, 45, 58, 99
    physical sciences, 5, 9, 12, 41
    political science, 22, 40, 43, 46, 49, 63, 85,
        146
    Project Camelot, role in, 65
    psychology, 11, 23, 32–33, 63, 107, 117
    scholarly publications, 27, 34, 57, 67, 77, 95,
        128, 133, 142, 155
    sociology, 20, 54–55, 57–58, 63, 84, 95
    Special Operations Research Office (SORO),
        role of, 4–5, 25–27, 31–32, 42, 67,
        93–94
    See also social science; *individual universities*
Adams, Richard N., 97
Advanced Research Projects Agency (ARPA),
    51, 106, 118, 124, 129, 144
Afghanistan, 1–2, 28, 150, 152, 154
Agency for International Development, 81
Allied Forces, 5, 11
Almond, Gabriel, 46–47, 65, 74, 76, 83–84
Altman, Irwin, 32
Alvarez, Luis, 10
American Anthropological Association (AAA),
    83–84, 143–46
American Anthropologist, 77, 95
American Enterprise Institute (AEI), 126–27
American Institutes for Research (AIR),
    117–22, 124–30, 133–36, 138–41, 149

American Management Systems, 147
American Mathematical Society, 132
American Political Science Association, 43,
    85, 146
American Political Science Review, 95
American Psychological Association, 107
American Psychologist, 107
American Sociologist, 77
American University, 4, 17–18, 21, 25–28, 31,
    42, 67, 93–94, 112–16, 119
Anderson, Hurst R., 18, 26–27, 112–13
Andrade, Ramiro, 93
anthropology, 20, 63, 83–85, 122, 130, 143–46
area studies, 4, 12, 14–17, 95, 130
Argentina, 65, 67
Arizona State University, 153
Arms Control and Disarmament Agency, 81
Army Research Office, 67, 86, 132
Art and Science of Psychological Operations,
    150
Asia Society, 49
Associative Group Analysis (AGA), 122–23
atomic bombs, 5, 9, 15
Autobiography of Malcolm X, The, 140
Avant, Deborah, 155

Bacevich, Andrew, 152
BAE Systems, 2
Bayton, James, 105
Beals, Ralph, 84, 86, 100–101, 145
Beard, Charles, 40, 55, 57
behavioral science. *See* social science
Benda, Harry J., 50
Bernard, Jessie, 68
Beyond Camp David, 130
Birtle, Andrew J., 10
Blumer, Herbert, 85–86
Boguslaw, Robert, 39–40, 54–60, 62–63, 68,
    98–100, 142, 146
Bolivia, 65
Booz Allen Hamilton, 2
Boston University, 142, 152
Bray, Charles, 9, 12, 14
Brayfield, Arthur, 79